GREAT PREACHING ON

SOUL WINNING

GREAT PREACHING ON

SOUL WINNING

COMPILED BY
CURTIS HUTSON

SWORD of the LORD
PUBLISHERS

P. O. BOX 1099, MURFREESBORO, TN 37133

Printed and Bound in the United States of America

Preface

What is the measure of a man's ministry?—his faithfulness? the geographical extent his ministry covers? the numbers of people to whom he is able to give the Gospel? the churches he establishes?

Can a man's ministry be measured? Yes, it can. A study reveals that Christians of outstanding success through the ages have been those who were the great soul winners, men with a strong, almost consuming passion for the lost.

See, first, the example of *Jesus*. Never was there such a compassionate winner of men! He saw people as sheep having no shepherd and "had compassion on them." He wept over Jerusalem. He sought the fallen woman to forgive her; the publican to make him an example.

O Saviour, teach us so to love sinners, to weep over them, to find pillows hard, food tasteless and life not worth living until we get them saved! Send us out with compassion and tears to win the lost!

Then we have *Paul*. How he wept over sinners! He so longed for the salvation of his countrymen that he said, "I could wish that myself were accursed from Christ for my brethren, my kinsmen according to the flesh." A stoning . . . a shipwreck . . . a Philippian jail at midnight could not quench Paul's tears for lost men.

John Knox, who cried out in his earnestness, "Give me Scotland or I die!" carried with him that zeal for souls to the close of his ministry. Often he would be supported by attendants in order to reach the pulpit; but when he arose to speak, his divine passion so filled his soul that one of his friends said, "So mighty was he in his yearning for souls that I thought he would break the pulpit into bits."

D. L. Moody may well have been the greatest evangelist of all time, in a 40-year period winning a million souls. He was sold out to soul winning. In public and in private, in sermons and in songs, in lip and in life, Moody sought to save souls. He determined that daily he would personally witness to at least one individual about his soul. And he did.

Let the soul-winning fervor and fire of Mr. Moody's mantle fall upon your ministry as you read herein "True Wisdom—Soul Winning"!

Joe Henry Hankins was called "the weeping prophet." That passion for lost souls that produced that tide of tears as he preached and pled for sinners to get right with God was a hallmark of Hankins' ministry. Is not the notable need of the ministry today preachers with the same passion? Catch it from "Visualize, Agonize, Evangelize."

Tom Malone began winning souls his first week in Bible college, and he has never lost the thirst for it, the thrill in it, nor the task of it since. Other heavy duties have not deterred Malone from the mainline ministry—soul winning. Let him challenge you through his message, "Two-by-Two Soul Winning."

Jack Hyles—I guess we can call him MR. SOUL WINNING since his name is synonymous with those words. How has his church grown to such tremendous size? By his stressing soul winning, going and bringing in hither the poor, the maimed, the halt and blind, going into the highways and hedges and compelling them to come in.

What a challenge is his "Four Calls for Soul Winning"!

Soul winning was the heartbeat of *John R. Rice*. In a Christmas letter, dictated a few days before his death, he bared his soul-winner's heart: "I still, from my armchair, preach in great revivals. I still vision hundreds walking the aisles to accept Christ. I still feel hot tears for the lost. . . . I want no Christmas without a burden for lost souls, a message for sinners, a heart to bring in the lost. May food be tasteless, music a discord, Christmas a farce if I forget the dying millions; if this fire in my bones does not still flame. Not till I die or not till Jesus comes will I ever be eased from this burden, these tears, this toil to save souls."

You will find that heartbeat in "The Sevenfold Sin of Not Winning Souls."

You hold in your hand the 16 best messages by 15 soul winners selected from the last 52 years of sermons in THE SWORD OF THE LORD, but every Christian holds in his hand the Gospel of pardon for whosoever will accept it. Tragically, so many die without that pardon because we fail to tell them the gospel story.

Back in 1890 A. B. Simpson wrote:

> **A hundred thousand souls a day**
> **Are passing one by one away**
>   **In Christless guilt and gloom;**
> **Without one ray of hope or light,**
> **With future dark as endless night,**
>   **They're passing to their doom.**

World population has increased greatly since then. The total now is over 5 billion; and to bring the poem up to date the words should be:

> **Three hundred thousand souls a day**
> **Are passing one by one away**
>   **In Christless guilt and gloom.**

This volume goes forth, hoping to inspire you to win others. Through the pen of these fishers of men may we find what we need to effectively touch our generation for Christ.

Curtis Hutson, Editor
THE SWORD OF THE LORD

Table of Contents

CURTIS HUTSON
1934–1995

ABOUT THE MAN:

In 1961 a mail carrier and pastor of a very small church attended a Sword of the Lord conference, got on fire, gave up his route and set out to build a great soul-winning work for God. Forrest Hills Baptist Church of Decatur, Georgia, grew from 40 people into a membership of 7,900. The last four years of his pastorate there, the Sunday school was recognized as the largest one in Georgia.

After pastoring for 21 years, Dr. Hutson—the great soul winner that he is—became so burdened for the whole nation that he entered full-time evangelism, holding great citywide-areawide-cooperative revivals in some of America's greatest churches. As many as 625 precious souls have trusted Christ in a single service. In one eight-day meeting, 1,502 salvation decisions were recorded.

As an evangelist, he is in great demand.

At the request of Dr. John R. Rice, Dr. Hutson became Associate Editor of THE SWORD OF THE LORD in 1978, serving in that capacity until the death of Dr. Rice before becoming Editor, President of Sword of the Lord Foundation, and Director of Sword of the Lord conferences.

All these ministries are literally changing the lives of thousands of preachers and laymen alike, as well as winning many more thousands to Christ.

Dr. Hutson is the author of many fine books and booklets.

I.

The Importance of Soul Winning

CURTIS HUTSON

Nearly two thousand years ago our Lord gave the Great Commission, "Go ye into all the world, and preach the gospel to every creature" (Mark 16:15). Yet today three billion of the world's population of five billion have never heard the Gospel.

Did the Lord assign us an impossible task? I do not think so. Dr. Bob Jones, Sr., used to say, "God puts omnipotence back of His commands, and you can do anything you ought to do."

The next question is, if God did not assign us an impossible task, then why have we failed? Why is it that over half the world's population has never yet heard the Gospel? The answer is simple: the Christian world as a whole has not taken the Great Commission seriously.

Dr. Lee Roberson was pastor of the Highland Park Baptist Church for more than forty years. During that forty-year period they baptized more than 60,000 converts—an average of more than 1500 a year. That's phenomenal! We don't know of any church that has such a forty-year record of winning souls and baptizing converts. Yet in this editor's presence Dr. Lee Roberson said, "I doubt that five percent of the members of Highland Park Baptist Church have ever led a soul to Christ."

Now think about it. Here was one of the greatest soul-winning churches in the world; and yet, according to Dr. Roberson's own estimate, ninety-five percent of the membership had never led a soul to Christ. Yet God's plan is for every Christian to lead others to the Saviour.

In John 15:16 Jesus said, "Ye have not chosen me, but I have chosen you, and ordained you, that ye should go and bring forth fruit, and that your fruit should remain." The fruit of a Christian is not love, joy, peace, longsuffering, etc. This is the fruit of the Spirit. The fruit of a Christian is other Christians.

Proverbs 11:30 says, "The fruit of the righteous is a tree of life; and he that winneth souls is wise." We have failed to evangelize the world because we have not followed God's ordained plan of one-on-one evangelism with every Christian actively involved in soul winning. John Wesley was certainly right when he said, "All at it and always at it." That is the Bible plan.

The Scripture says in Matthew 28:19, "Go ye [all of you] therefore, and teach all nations. . . . " Then verse 20 closes by saying, ". . . even unto the end of the world. . ." (always at it).

Why is it that every Christian is not involved in the most important business in the world—soul winning? The answer is simple: we just simply do not see the importance of it. We always find time, money and energy to do the things we feel are important. We signed the mortgage and agreed to pay hundreds of dollars every month for the next thirty years because we thought buying a house was important. In the middle of the night we rushed the baby to the hospital, not caring for our inconvenience or even considering the cost, because we felt the baby's health was important.

If somehow we could see the extreme importance of winning souls to Christ, I believe that we would go to any extreme short of violating the Scriptures in order to get sinners saved. I am convinced that we would make any sacrifice and suffer any inconvenience to keep one soul out of Hell. Getting people saved is the most important thing in the world.

Soul Winning Is Important Because of the Peril of Souls

Every person who has not trusted Jesus Christ as Saviour is already condemned. He is not going to die, go to a judgment, and there have God decide whether he is saved or lost. That is already determined. The Scripture plainly says in John 3:18, "He that believeth on him is not condemned: but he that believeth not is condemned *already*, because he hath not believed in the name of the only begotten Son of God." Here the Bible says, as plain as day, that the person who is not trusting Jesus Christ as Saviour is already condemned. He is already under sentence. All he is waiting for is for his heart to beat the last time, and he goes immediately into Hell, there to stay for an eternity.

The young child who has reached the age of accountability, though he may be moral and pure, is already condemned if he has not trusted Jesus Christ as Saviour. If his life were to be suddenly snatched away in an automobile accident, like the rich man in Luke 16, he would lift his eyes in Hell. What an awful, awful thought!

Hell is not the figment of someone's imagination; it is a real, literal, physical place, a place of eternal torment, a place of excruciating suffering, a place of annoying, nagging memory. In Hell men will remember the many times they had an opportunity to trust Jesus Christ as Saviour but chose to reject Him. After all, it takes just as much energy and will to say no to Christ as it does to say yes.

When I was a twelve-year-old boy in Atlanta, Georgia, the Winecoff Hotel caught fire. I remember going to the kitchen early that morning, and my mother was weeping. When I asked why she was crying, she pointed to a little plastic Emerson radio where she was listening to the screams and cries of those at the scene of the great tragedy. One hundred sixteen people lost their lives in that fire, many of whom leaped from the windows and were killed as their bodies crushed on the pavement below. Others fell into power wires and were electrocuted. Some fell into treetops. The fire department did their best, but they could not possibly catch in their safety nets all those who were leaping from the windows of that blazing inferno.

What would cause men and women to leap from those windows to an awful death? They were trying to get away from the fire. They could not stand the pain of the heat. They preferred anything to burning.

But wait a minute. The fires of Hell are as real as were the fires of the Winecoff Hotel. However, in Hell there are no windows to leap from. There is no way to get away from the fire. Hell is one solid flame. If a person leaps, he only leaps into the same flame he was trying to escape.

Oh, if somehow Christians could see the reality of Hell and realize that every person who dies without Jesus Christ goes there to be tormented day and night forever and ever, I believe we would spend the rest of our lives telling everyone we could about the Saviour and explaining very carefully how they could be saved. I am convinced that sermons on Hell are more important for Christians than for the unsaved. If somehow we could load all Christians on chartered buses, drive them into Hell and leave them there for five minutes and then bring them back to this world, they would spend the rest of their lives telling others about the Saviour, trying to keep men and women and boys and girls from going to that awful place of burning.

Soul winning is important because of the peril of souls. Every person you see is either believing on Christ, and therefore is not condemned, or else he is not believing on Christ and is condemned already, "because he hath not believed in the name of the only begotten Son of God." That is not my opinion; it is not someone's peculiar doctrine. It is the clear, unmistakable language of Scripture.

Soul Winning Is Important Because of the Price of Souls

A French doctor once claimed that he knew the weight of a human soul. According to the doctor, he made the determination by placing the body of terminal patients on very sensitive scales and noticed that, when the patient died, the scale dropped 21 grams. So he concluded that a soul weighs 21 grams.

Well, I don't know how much a soul weighs, but I have some idea what one soul is worth. Jesus said in Mark 8:36,37, "For what shall it profit a man, if he shall gain the whole world, and lose his own soul? Or what shall a man give in exchange for his soul?"

According to Jesus, one soul is worth the entire world. When I first heard that statement, I saw the world as the material universe. All the gold, silver, diamonds, precious stones, etc., all the real estate, all the buildings, all the automobiles, all the money in all the banks—to me this was the world. If that was all there was to the world, the value of a soul would be more than human tongue could explain.

However, the world consists of more than the material universe. First John 2:15, 16 says, "Love not the world, neither the things that are in the world. If any man love the world, the love of the Father is not in him. For all that is in the world, the lust of the flesh, and the lust of the eyes, and the pride of life, is not of the Father, but is of the world."

According to these two verses, the world consists of three things: first, the lust of the flesh. The lust of the flesh is a consuming desire to do. It is the cravings of the flesh. Imagine that one was able to fulfill every desire of his flesh, no matter what that desire was or when the desire occurred, and he was able to fulfill these desires from the time of birth until the time of his death. If that were possible, then he would only have acquired one-third of the world. "For all that is in the world, the lust of the flesh, and the lust of the eyes, and the pride of life, is not of the Father, but is of the world."

The lust of the eyes is a compelling urge to have. The eye sees something and wants it. That is the lust of the eye. Imagine that everything your eye ever saw and wanted, you could have, from the time you were born until the time you died. Anything you saw and wanted was yours. It is hard for the human mind to comprehend such a thing. But if you could have everything your eye ever saw and wanted, you would have received the second third of the world. However, you would not have the whole world, "For all that is in the world, the lust of the flesh, and the lust of the eyes, and the pride of life, is not of the Father, but is of the world."

The pride of life is a constant thrust to be. It is ambition. Now imagine that you realized every ambition of life from the time you were born until the time you died. Imagine that you were everything you ever wanted to be and would ever want to be, with no ambition unfulfilled. Then you would have gained the third third of the world.

I call the lust of the flesh the ultimate in fun, having all the fleshly, carnal fun that one can have, with nothing else to be enjoyed. I call the lust of the eyes the ultimate in fortune, owning all that one could own, with nothing else to own. And I call the pride of life the ultimate in fame, being all that one could be with nothing else to be. Now place all three of these together on one side—fun, fortune and fame. And then put one single soul on the other side, and ask Jesus which is the most valuable, and He would answer in Mark 8:36, 37, "For what shall it profit a man, if he shall gain the whole world, and lose his own soul? Or what shall a man give in exchange for his soul?"

To start from nothing in this world and earn a fortune of a billion dollars in a lifetime is quite an accomplishment. If a man could earn perhaps ten billion, he would become the richest man in the world and would be remembered in history for his great accomplishments. However, in God's sight he would accomplish far, far more if he had led only one soul to Christ because one soul is worth more than all the money in the entire world.

Oh, if somehow we could see the price of one soul, the value of one soul, I don't think we would let another day go by without telling someone about Jesus, without handing someone a gospel tract and praying that he would read it and trust Christ as Saviour! How I pray and how

I hope that everyone reading these lines will make a solemn resolution to do his best to lead at least one soul to Christ within the next thirty days. Christians who have money in savings accounts and in stocks and bonds ought to make sure they do not die and leave this money to be squandered on things of no importance.

Of course, it is only right to see that you have enough money to live the rest of your life. But I am sure that many Christians reading these lines will never spend all the money they have. The sad thing is, they will die; and when it is all said and done, much of the money will go back to the State because no Will was left; and relatives fighting over the estate will be obligated to pay the lawyer, in most cases, at least one-third of the estate. How sad that many Christians die with no preparations for how their worldly goods are to be used after their death!

Please, for the sake of souls that are dying, invest your money in some good soul-winning enterprise. Make out a Will and be sure that you leave your estate, or at least part of it, to some good soul-winning enterprise.

How I wish we had millions of dollars to put the Gospel in printed form and send it around the world! How I wish we could put the plan of salvation in every major newspaper in the country at least once a year, and better still, once a month, from now until Jesus came. It would take millions of dollars to do it. But if Christians would see that what the Lord has given to them and entrusted to them was left for the purpose of winning souls, it would surely help us to take a giant step in evangelizing the world.

Soul Winning Is Important Because of the Payment Jesus Made for Souls

The song writer correctly wrote,

> **But none of the ransomed ever knew**
> **How deep were the waters crossed;**
> **Nor how dark was the night that the Lord passed through**
> **Ere He found His sheep that was lost.**

No Christian can ever fully comprehend the indescribable sufferings of Jesus to pay our sin debt. I once said, "No one will ever know how much Jesus suffered except those who die and go to Hell and stay there forever." I reasoned that those in Hell were paying their sin debt and therefore would know how much Jesus suffered on the cross when He paid our sin debt, but I was wrong because those who die and go to Hell will be forever paying on the sin debt; but they will never get it paid.

John 3:36 warns, ". . . he that believeth not the Son shall not see life; but the wrath of God *abideth* on him." Notice the language of the text, ". . . the wrath of God *abideth* on him." When a soul has been in Hell for a million years, that verse will still be true: ". . . the wrath of God *abideth* on him." The individual in Hell will never get his sin debt paid; but on the cross in a few hours Jesus suffered enough to pay in full the sin debt of every person who has ever lived or ever will live.

Our Lord uttered seven things while hanging on the cross, and the sixth utterance was, "It is finished" (John 19:30). When Jesus said, "It is finished," He meant, "The sin debt is paid in full. It is complete."

So even those who die and go to Hell will never know how much Jesus suffered because they will never suffer enough to pay the debt; and Jesus suffered enough to pay it in full.

How could one individual suffer so much in such a short time? The only way I can explain it is to remind you that Jesus Christ was infinite, and we are finites; and no number of finites equals infinitude, no matter how large the number. If the sin debt was to be paid, either the finite must suffer infinitely, or the infinite must suffer finitely.

At the cross the Infinite suffered finitely. The sin debt is paid. No purchase in the world was ever so expensive as our redemption. No object in the world was ever so costly as a precious soul. But, thank God, the payment has been made, and made in full.

Soul Winning Is Important Because of the Products of Soul Winning

I am convinced that soul winning produces almost everything the average pastor wants in his church. I pastored the same church for more than twenty years, and I think I know what preachers want.

First, they want attendance. They want a large crowd. We do not know of any preacher who is totally satisfied with the size of his congregation. And if you know of some pastor who *is* satisfied, then he is no more good as the pastor of the church because we never grow beyond the place where we become satisfied and complacent. Soul winning produces increase in attendance. The Scripture says in II Corinthians 9:6, ". . . He which soweth sparingly shall reap also sparingly; and he which soweth bountifully shall reap also bountifully."

And the Scripture says in Matthew 6:26, "Behold the fowls of the air: for they sow not, neither do they reap, nor gather into barns. . . ." Notice what it says about the sparrows—no sowing, no reaping and no gathering into barns. And then notice the plain teaching of II Corinthians 9:6—sow sparingly, reap sparingly; sow bountifully, reap bountifully.

That is as simple as it can be, and it explains why some churches have no growth, others have little growth, while still others have much growth. You reap according to the way you sow. It is true in the individual life, and it is true in the church life.

Just last Sunday I spoke in my home church for a very special day called "No Room" Sunday. The people worked hard inviting friends and loved ones, and the church reported 2213 in attendance with 111 decisions for salvation, church membership or baptism. Now, the church does not have that many every Sunday. Neither do they have that many conversions or additions to the church. Why the good results? The answer is simple: they had sown bountifully. For weeks before the special day, people had invited friends and loved ones to attend the special services. Literally hundreds were signed up to attend on this special day. The results were great with a much larger than average attendance and over 100 decisions.

The truth of the matter is, if that same crowd worked that hard every week, they would have the same results every week. Now, I am not scolding them nor even implying that they could do that week after week. But if they could, they would get the same results week after week. The reaping, according to the Scripture, is always in proportion to the sowing.

Soul winning not only produces attendance and church growth, it also produces joy among members. Nearly every pastor I know wants a joyful, or happy, congregation. And nothing brings more joy to the people than soul winning. Psalm 126:6 promises, "He that goeth forth and weepeth, bearing precious seed, shall doubtless come again with rejoicing, bringing his sheaves with him." And verse 5 plainly says, "They that sow in tears shall reap in joy." This is the plain, unmistakable promise of Scripture: soul winners come back rejoicing.

There are five crowns that one could possibly receive at the judgment seat of Christ. One of those crowns is "the crown of rejoicing." This is the soul winner's crown. In I Thessalonians 2:19 Paul says, "For what is our hope, or joy, or crown of rejoicing? Are not even ye in the presence of our Lord Jesus Christ at his coming?"

It is difficult to find a sad face at a hospital nursery where the new babies are displayed. As a matter of fact, I do not think I have ever seen a sad face in front of that big glass window. And why are they happy? Why are they smiling? Because of the new babies.

The same is true in the local church when people are being saved in every service and converts are coming forward to make professions of faith and receive believer's baptism. There is joy among the members.

But soul winning not only produces increase in attendance and joy in the congregation, it also produces love among the members. John 15:16 says, "Ye have not chosen me, but I have chosen you, and ordained you, that ye should go and bring forth fruit, and that your fruit should remain. . . ." Then verse 17 adds, "These things I command you, that ye love one another." We are commanded to go and bring forth fruit so that we will love one another.

I have never known two Christians to go out soul winning together and come back fighting. Usually the quarrels come when a handful of members meet in a church building and discuss what color to paint the walls or on which side of the auditorium to put the piano, etc. Soul-winning churches are usually loving churches. After all, that is exactly what Jesus promised in John 15:16,17.

But soul winning not only produces increase in attendance, joy in the church and love among members, it also produces finances. The story is recorded in Matthew 17 of how Peter was instructed to catch a fish, take the money from its mouth and then pay his taxes. When Simon told the Lord that he had no money to pay his taxes, Jesus told him to cast a hook into the sea and, when he caught a fish, to open its mouth and take money out of its mouth and go pay his taxes.

Some may argue that such a thing never happened. But we who believe the Bible know that it happened exactly as the Lord said. Simon caught the fish; and when he opened its mouth, he found money with which to pay his taxes.

Later Simon was told in Luke 5:10, ". . . from henceforth thou shalt catch men."

The best way to raise money in the local church is to go fishing, fishing for souls. Some of the greatest financial miracles we have ever experienced came through those we had the opportunity to lead to Christ.

A man came to see me about getting married, and I explained to him that I could not perform the ceremony unless both he and his bride-to-be were Christians. He was not sure that he was saved, so I opened the Bible and in a few minutes led him to the Saviour. After the wedding and the honeymoon, they both joined the church.

One day he came to my office with a sizable gift for the church, saying that he and his new wife wanted to make a donation to the Lord's work.

If a man had a dairy and was milking 100 cows and wanted to have an increase in milk production, he would be wise to add more cows to the herd. The best way to see the offerings increase in the local church is to win more souls to Christ and have more members added to the congregation.

I recall leading one man to Christ whose tithe amounted to more than $1,000 a week; and another whose tithe amounted to more than $500 a week. Now, to be sure, our motive for winning souls should not be to have an increase in the offering. We ought to win souls to Christ simply because Jesus loved them and died for them. However, an increased offering is a result of soul winning and a by-product of a soul-winning church.

Soul winning not only produces increase in attendance, joy in the congregation, love among members and an increase in the offerings, it also produces clean members. I mean by that separated, dedicated Christians. John 15:2 says, "Every branch in me that beareth not fruit he taketh away: and every branch that beareth fruit, he purgeth it . . . ." We mentioned earlier that the fruit of a Christian is other Christians. The fruit-bearing Christian is a soul-winning Christian. Here the Scripture plainly promises that Jesus will purge every branch that bears fruit.

Usually the most separated Christians in the church are soul winners. Why? First of all, because Jesus promised to purge the fruit-bearing branch. And second, because it is difficult for a man to live worldly and still be an effective soul winner. Sooner or later someone will call attention to his worldly living and shame him for his inconsistent life. We have heard unbelievers say regarding certain Christians, "Why, he does things that I wouldn't do, and I'm not even a Christian!"

The man who is busy winning souls cannot have some pet sin in his life without having some sinner sooner or later call it to his attention.

Now, we are not suggesting that soul winning will solve every single problem in the local church. But if there is such a thing as a cure-all, it is soul winning. It solves more problems in the local church than anything I know of.

The Power of the Saviour

We have given four important reasons to win souls to Christ, any one of which should be sufficient to make every concerned Christian do his best to win souls, but we have left out the biggest and most important reason of all. In fact, it is the only reason Jesus gave; and it is found in the Great Commission in Matthew 28:18-20. Here we read, "All power is given unto me in heaven and in earth. Go ye therefore, and teach all nations, baptizing them in the name of the Father, and of the Son, and of the Holy Ghost." In verse 18, Jesus said, 'All authority is given unto Me in Heaven and in earth. I am the Chief Authority in Heaven and the Chief Authority on earth.' And then He adds, 'Go ye therefore. Because I am the Chief Authority, go into all the world and teach all nations.' Now the Lord could have said, 'Because men are lost and unless they trust Christ they will burn eternally in Hell, go ye therefore and teach all nations,' but He didn't. He could have said, 'One soul is worth more than the entire world, go ye therefore and teach all nations,' but He didn't. He could have said, 'Being saved is the most important thing that can happen to a man, go ye therefore . . . ,' but He didn't. He simply said, 'All authority is Mine in Heaven and in earth; go ye therefore and teach all nations, baptizing them in the name of the Father, and of the Son, and of the Holy Ghost.' The greatest reason to win souls is because the greatest Authority of all told us to do it.

I recently received a letter from our sheriff, asking me to appear before one of the judges here in Murfreesboro, in view of serving on jury duty. Now the sheriff has a certain amount of authority in Murfreesboro. His position gives him authority over me. And I responded to his letter for one reason—because of his authority. Now he is just a sheriff in a small town among thousands of other sheriffs across the country. He is not even a State Senator or Governor, but because of his authority I did what he said.

When one receives a notice from the IRS to appear at the tax office at a certain time to have his returns audited, he doesn't question it; he simply responds because of the authority of the one sending the letter.

But the greatest of all authorities is the Lord Jesus Christ. Some day

He will return, and the Bible says He will reign as King over kings and Lord over lords and that every knee will bow and every tongue will confess that Jesus Christ is Lord to the glory of God the Father. In view of that great authority, Jesus says to us, "Go ye therefore, and teach all nations, baptizing them in the name of the Father, and of the Son, and of the Holy Ghost."

Not to win souls is to disobey the greatest Authority of all and perhaps to be the greatest rebel that one could possibly be, rebelling against the One who has all authority in Heaven and in earth.

When I was a boy, sometimes when my father asked me to do something, I would ask, "Why must I do that?" And in plain, unmistakable language, he would say, "Because I said so!"

Every Christian ought to be busy at the most important task in the world—winning souls to Christ—because God Almighty Himself said so.

Conclusion

We have tried, but it is impossible to show the extreme importance of soul winning. My beloved predecessor, Dr. John R. Rice, had a sermon he entitled, "The Sevenfold Sin of Not Winning Souls"—the sin of disobedience to Christ, the sin of little love for Christ, the sin of not following Christ, the sin of not abiding in Christ, the sin of dishonesty in a sacred trust, the sin of the short-sighted fool, the sin of blood-guilt—the manslaughter of souls.

Not to win souls is a sin. Don't you see that nothing under Heaven is more important than the salvation of sinners? It is the one thing for which Jesus died.

We plead with every Christian reading these lines to make some definite commitment about soul winning. Wouldn't it be wonderful if hundreds of readers would make a holy vow to tell at least one person about the Saviour every day for the next thirty days, and then keep that vow? You could do it by handing someone a gospel tract each day and asking him to read it. And wouldn't it be wonderful if some preacher reading these lines would make a holy vow to lead at least one soul a week to Christ and to do his best to baptize at least one convert every week for the remainder of the year?

And what about our families? Don't you think it would be wise if each of us made a holy vow to witness to every member of our family this year, making sure that each one knew how to be saved? Many could set a goal to win 100 to Christ within the next year, or maybe 200. Some could even set a goal to try to lead at least one soul a day to Christ.

Please join me in making some definite commitment regarding this all-important matter of soul winning. And write and tell us about your goal. We will be happy to pray with you. Let's make this the most fruitful year ever in our individual lives and in the life of our churches.

May God bless each of us to win more souls this year than we have ever won in any other year in our entire life.

JOHN R. RICE
1895-1980

ABOUT THE MAN:

Preacher...evangelist...revivalist...editor...counselor to thousands...friend to millions—that was Dr. John R. Rice, whose accomplishments were nothing short of miraculous. Known as "America's Dean of Evangelists," Dr. Rice made a mighty impact upon the nation's religious life for some sixty years, in great citywide campaigns and in Sword of the Lord Conferences.

At age nine, after hearing a sermon on "The Prodigal Son," John went forward to claim Christ as Saviour. In 1916, with only $9.35 in his pocket, he rode off on his cowpony toward Decatur Baptist College. He was now on the road to becoming a world-renowned evangelist, although he was then totally unaware of God's will for his life.

There was many a twist and turn before Rice rode through the open door into full-time preaching—the army, marriage, graduate work, more seminary, assistant pastor, pastor—then FINALLY, where God planned to use him most—in full-time evangelism.

Dr. Rice and his ministry were always colorful (born in Cooke county, in Texas, December 11, 1895, and often called "Will Rogers of the Pulpit" because of their likeness and mannerisms)—and controversial. CONTROVERSIAL—and correctly so—because of his intense stand against modernism and infidelity and his fight for the Fundamentals.

Dr. Rice lived and died a man of convictions—intense convictions. But, like many other strong fighters for the Faith, Rice was also marked with a sincere spirit of compassion. Those who knew him best knew a man who loved them. In preaching, in prayer, and in personal life, Rice wept over sinners and with saints. But there is more...

Less than seventy-one hours before the dawning of 1981, one of the most prolific pens in all Christendom was stilled. Dr. John R. Rice left behind a legacy in writing of more than 200 titles, with a combined circulation of over 61 million copies. And through October of 1981, a total of 24,058 precious souls reported trusting Christ through his ministries, not counting those saved in his crusades nor in foreign countries where his literature has been translated.

And who but God knows the influence of THE SWORD OF THE LORD magazine which he started and edited for forty-six years!

And while "Twentieth Century's Mightiest Pen"—and man—has been stilled, thank God, the fruit remains! Though dead, he continues to speak.

II.

The Sevenfold Sin of Not Winning Souls

JOHN R. RICE

1. **The Sin of Disobedience to Christ**
2. **The Sin of Little Love for Christ**
3. **The Sin of Not Following Christ**
4. **The Sin of Not Abiding in Christ**
5. **The Sin of Dishonesty in a Sacred Trust**
6. **The Sin of the Shortsighted Fool**
7. **The Sin of Blood-Guilt — the Manslaughter of Souls!**

The winning of souls is the principal duty of every Christian and the thing nearest the heart of God. For this He sent His Son into the world to live a sinless life and die on the cross. Jesus said, "I came not to call the righteous, but sinners to repentance" (Luke 5:32). And Paul said in I Timothy 1:15, "This is a faithful saying, and worthy of all acceptation, that Christ Jesus came into the world TO SAVE SINNERS!" And even now, "joy shall be in heaven over one sinner that repenteth, more than over ninety and nine just persons, which need no repentance" (Luke 15:7).

Soul winning is the one thing that brings rejoicing in Heaven. So it should be the unceasing principal job of every Christian.

The preachers in the New Testament churches were set on winning souls. Every one did the work of an evangelist, covering the Roman Empire with millions of believers in the first century after Christ died!

The ministry of Jesus was largely one of personal soul winning. He won Nicodemus one night. He won the woman at the well of Sychar in Samaria. He won the woman taken in adultery. He won the sinner woman who wept over His feet at the home of Simon the Pharisee.

He won the Gadarene demoniac, Mary Magdalene, and the woman who stooped to touch the hem of His garment in a throng. He won Zacchaeus the publican and Levi, another of the same kind. It was His daily business.

Soul winning was the normal thing for individual Christians in Bible times. John the Baptist pointed Andrew and John to Jesus. Andrew won Peter. Jesus won Philip. Philip won Nathaniel. The woman at the well of Sychar, a new convert, won many in her own town the same day she was saved. The jailer at Philippi found Christ at midnight and before morning had his whole family saved and baptized! When persecution began at Jerusalem, scattering all except the preachers, then "they that were scattered abroad went every where preaching the word" (Acts 8:4).

The Bible makes it clear that soul winning is the duty of every Christian. One who does not win souls is guilty of a list of sins which block revival, deaden the churches, grieve the Spirit of God, cause Christians to miss the joy and manifestation of the Holy Spirit, and damn millions of souls!

Consider the seven terrible sins of every Christian who does not win souls.

I. THE SIN OF DISOBEDIENCE TO CHRIST

Christ's Great Commission as given in Matthew 28:18-20 is:

"All power is given unto me in heaven and in earth. Go ye therefore, and teach all nations, baptizing them in the name of the Father, and of the Son, and of the Holy Ghost: Teaching them to observe all things whatsoever I have commanded you: and, lo, I am with you alway, even unto the end of the world."

To these eleven disciples Jesus explained that all authority was His; therefore, He commanded them to go and make disciples in all nations, winning souls and getting them baptized.

The commission as given in Mark 16:15 is, "Go ye into all the world, and preach the gospel to every creature." To preach the Gospel to every creature in all nations, even to the end of the world, was obviously more than those eleven disciples could do. They were simply to begin this work, doing what they could, then others were to carry on.

That is exactly what these eleven disciples were commanded to teach others. After they made disciples (got people to trust Christ) and got them baptized, they were to continue "teaching *them* to observe all things whatsoever I have commanded *you*." They were to teach the new converts to set out to carry out the Great Commission *just exactly as the apostles were commanded to do it.*

So we see that every Christian has exactly the same command as the apostles had *to get people saved!* Every newborn soul is to be taught to observe all things whatsoever Jesus commanded the apostles to observe, as the plain words of the Great Commission say.

Every Christian is equally responsible for taking the Gospel to every creature.

In the last chapter of the Bible, in Revelation 22:16,17, Jesus Himself gives this command:

"I Jesus have sent mine angel to testify unto you these things in the churches. I am the root and offspring of David, and the bright and morning star. And the Spirit and the bride say, Come. And let him that heareth say, Come. And let him that is athirst come. And whosoever will, let him take the water of life freely."

Jesus said He had sent His angel to testify unto us in the churches, "And let him that heareth say, Come." Everyone who hears the Gospel is commanded to tell lost sinners to come!

If you are not a soul winner, then you are disobeying Jesus Christ, the One to whom all authority is given in Heaven and earth. Not carrying out His commands makes you a disobedient child of God, if child of God you are. However much money you give, however well you may teach the Bible, however separated you are, you are not right in your heart and are disobeying Christ if you are not a soul winner.

Remember that for disobedience and rebellion Saul lost his kingdom and he and his house were rejected by the Lord. God had the prophet Samuel say to Saul:

"Hath the Lord as great delight in burnt offerings and sacrifices, as in obeying the voice of the Lord? Behold, to obey is better than sacrifice, and to hearken than the fat of rams. For rebellion is as the sin of witchcraft, and stubbornness is as iniquity and idolatry. Because thou hast rejected the word of the Lord, he hath also rejected thee from being king."—I Sam. 15:22,23.

No sacrifice you can make will be pleasing to God as long as you disobey Him. Rebellion is as the sin of witchcraft, stubbornness is as iniquity and idolatry. The sin of not winning souls is a sin of direct disobedience to the main command of Jesus Christ, disobedience of the last command Jesus gave His people before going away, disobedience in the one thing nearest His heart.

Oh, wicked we are when we do not win souls!

II. THE SIN OF LACK OF LOVE FOR CHRIST

Those who do not win souls are disobedient Christians, but that is not all. That disobedience proves lack of love for Christ.

In John 14:15, Jesus said to the same apostles to whom He first gave the Great Commission, "If ye love me, keep my commandments." Then the same night He was betrayed, Jesus continued: "If a man love me, he will keep my words" (vs. 23). Then in the next verse He said, "He that loveth me not keepeth not my sayings: and the word which ye hear is not mine, but the Father's which sent me."

There it is, as clear as it can be, that if you love Christ you will obey Him and will keep His words—the words of the Father as well as of the Son. Disobedience is an evidence of lack of love.

All of us can well be ashamed that we do not love our Saviour better. But those who love Him most are the best soul winners. Those who love the Saviour less win fewer souls and work less at winning souls. Those who do not win any souls to Christ at all may love Him, but, oh, so poorly! That statement is backed up by the words of Jesus Himself: "If a man love me, he will keep my words," and again, "He that loveth me not keepeth not my sayings."

In Dallas, Texas I was called at about 3:00 in the early morning to the bedside of a dying saint. "Daddy Hickman," with cancer of the liver, was about to go to meet his Saviour. He called his grown sons to his bedside, took their hands and asked them a solemn question, one after another: "Son, are you going to meet me in Heaven? You can't tell me a lie on my deathbed, and I must know!"

One by one the boys promised they would take Christ as Saviour then and there, or declared that they had done so already and would live for Him. They made other holy promises. And I remember how moved one young couple, related to the family, was when he called them, placed their hands together and solemnly urged them to be done with their quarrelling and have peace and a happy home.

How solemn are the parting words of a loved one! How earnestly we take to heart the last command of a dying father! But how much more earnestly should we take to heart the last command of Jesus Christ—to go and preach the Gospel to sinners, to make disciples, to win souls.

Many a young man has, all his life, avoided the gambling table or alcoholic drinks because of his promise to a dear mother on her death-bed, a promise he felt he must keep. A late king of England read the Bible every day because he promised his mother, Queen Victoria, that he would. Loving her so much, he could not ignore that sacred request.

And those who love Jesus Christ cannot ignore His plain command, the last entreaty of His heart, to go after lost sinners for whom He died and for whom His heart yearns even yet, with inexpressible longing and love!

If you, then, do not win souls, your love for Christ has grown cold. Perhaps once you loved sinners, prayed for them, warned them, pled with them; but now you, like the church at Ephesus, have lost your first love.

Evangelists sometimes become "Bible teachers" because their love for Christ has grown cold. And Christians everywhere content themselves with the mere outward forms of worship and giving and praying and reading and doing "church work" when they ought to be winning souls. Oh, the trouble is, they are guilty of the sin of little love for Christ. For "if a man love me he will keep my words," Jesus said.

Do you love Christ? If so, then you will win souls. If you make small effort to win souls, then your love is small. If you make none, how can you say you love Him at all?

III. THE SIN OF NOT FOLLOWING CHRIST

In Matthew 4:19 Jesus said, "Follow me, and I will make you fishers of men." In Mark 1:17 He said, "Come ye after me, and I will make you to become fishers of men." These promises were made to the apostles, but He has given us the same commission, command and promise.

Following Jesus, being a disciple or learner of His ways, is often mentioned in His teaching in the Gospels. In Luke 9:23 He said, "If any man will come after me, let him deny himself, and take up his cross daily, and follow me." And to the rich young ruler who thought he had kept the law from his youth, Jesus said, "If thou wilt be perfect, go and sell that thou hast, and give to the poor, and thou shalt have treasure in heaven: AND COME AND FOLLOW ME" (Matt. 19:21).

We are to have the mind of Christ (Phil. 2:5). And I Peter 2:21 tells us, "For even hereunto were ye called: because Christ also suffered for us, leaving us an example, that ye should follow his steps." In John 12:26 Jesus said, "If any man serve me, let him follow me." And in John 14:12 we are promised that one who believes in Christ, "the works that I do shall he do also."

Every Christian is to follow Christ. And if you are not winning souls, you are not following Christ, for He admonishes us in Matthew 4:19, "Follow me, and I will make you fishers of men."

As a boy preacher I went with a dear old pastor one summer and led singing in five or six short country revival campaigns. When I started out to preach I used some of the same texts, illustrations and ideas he used. Later I went with an evangelist to sing in one or two campaigns, learning all I could from him. I used his methods and some of his sermon material. I was later assistant pastor to a godly man, a fine preacher, and to this day I acknowledge his help in many of my sermons. I followed these men, and so learned to do the work as they did it.

One of the best ways to be an evangelist is to go with an evangelist. But the very best way to be a soul winner is to follow the Master Soul Winner and get His passion, His burden for dying sinners, and be led by His Holy Spirit in winning them. No one really follows Jesus unless he becomes a soul winner. Jesus makes every true disciple, every learner, everyone who follows in His steps, into a soul winner.

If you, then, are not a soul winner, you are not following Jesus. What a sin!

IV. NOT TO WIN SOULS MEANS NOT ABIDING IN CHRIST

In John 15:1-8 the Lord Jesus gave a precious teaching about fruit bearing. Christ Himself is the true vine, and we are His branches. "Every branch in me that beareth not fruit he taketh away: and every branch that beareth fruit, he purgeth it, that it may bring forth more fruit."

The idea is that every Christian should be in such close touch with Christ that, as the sap comes from the vine into the branch with life-giving, fruit-bearing power, so the Holy Spirit may flow from Christ through us, making us fruit-bearing Christians, soul winners.

Again He said:

"Abide in me, and I in you. As the branch cannot bear fruit of itself, except it abide in the vine; no more can ye, except ye abide in me. I am the vine, ye are the branches: He that abideth in me, and I in him, the same bringeth forth much fruit: for without me ye can do nothing."—John 15:4,5.

There is no way to win souls except to abide in Christ, be in touch with Him, know His will, feel His heartbeat, be wholly committed to His will and work! But everyone who abides in Christ brings forth fruit, yea, much fruit! "He that abideth in me, and I in him, the same bringeth forth *much* fruit." Verse 8 says, "Herein is my Father glorified, that ye bear much fruit; so shall ye be my disciples."

Remember that the Lord Jesus wants souls saved. That is what He died for. That is why we preach the Gospel. That is what the Great Commission means. That is the work of the churches. That is what preachers are called to do and what every Christian is commanded to do. Christ "came to seek and to save that which was lost." Christ Jesus "came into the world to save sinners."

If I abide in Christ, my aim, my purpose, my burden, my business, my work, will be that same precious work. And my fruit will be that same precious fruit. Every Christian is called to be a soul winner. Precious souls are the fruit we should bear. And the fruit of a Christian is another Christian.

If you are not a soul winner, then the Bible makes it clear that you do not abide in Christ, that your heart is not at one with His heart. Whatever your activity, your reputation, however sanctimonious you feel and however much of a Pharisee you are, *you do not abide in Christ if you do not win souls!* What a sin for a Christian not to abide in Him with surrendered heart and perfect union, and so help in His blessed and main business of winning souls!

V. NOT TO WIN SOULS IS DISHONESTY IN A SACRED TRUST

In Matthew 25:14-30, in the parable of the talents, the Saviour illustrated His own coming and kingdom in the future by the story of a man who had gone into a far country and left his affairs in the hands of his own servants. To one he had given five talents, to another two, to another one. You remember that the first two men doubled the money left with them by trading; the third hid his talent in the earth, accusing his lord of reaping where he had not sown. But his master answered the servant, "Thou wicked and slothful servant.... Thou oughtest therefore to have put my money to the exchangers, and then at my coming I should have received mine own with usury."

In the similar parable of the pounds in Luke 19:11-27, Jesus told how a lord went away to receive for himself a kingdom. First, he gave his ten pounds to ten servants, saying, "Occupy till I come." When he returned—as Jesus will do one day—he called to them for an accounting. Again one man had laid up his pound in a napkin and had no increase, and Jesus called him, "Thou wicked servant"!

The idea in each case is that Jesus has given us His affairs to care for, and as honest stewards of that committed to our care, we must bring fruit; we must win souls.

Everyone who has received the Gospel and all the blessings of salvation and has not passed them on is dishonest—a servant who has robbed his master of the proper increase he has a right to expect for his investment. Those whose pounds multiplied were to rule with their lord when he returned. How guilty was the wicked man who cheated and had no increase to bring! So every Christian who does not win souls is a dishonest servant who will face Christ with shame.

Sometimes we hear of the frightful scandal of a man who, having been made executor of a Will, has stolen the funds he handled. Some man before his death appointed a friend to administer his estate and to see that his widow and children were properly cared for. But the unfaithful administrator has been known to use the money for his own ends, or to waste it in speculation. Sometimes the widow lives in poverty, and the children, instead of being provided for as the father intended, must leave school. The administrator who wastes the estate committed to his hand, or who uses it for his own selfish gain, is a crook, a thief, a dishonest man.

And that is exactly the kind of person a Christian is who takes salvation and all other blessings that God gives him and then, instead of passing them on to others as he has been commanded to do, makes his Christian life only a matter of his own safety, comfort and blessing, and never wins the souls for whom Christ died!

How wicked, how dishonest is that Christian who is an unfaithful steward of the Gospel!

But the sin of the Christian who does not win souls is also dishonesty toward *men*. Paul said:

"I am debtor both to the Greeks, and to the Barbarians; both to the wise, and to the unwise. So, as much as in me is, I am ready to preach the gospel to you that are at Rome also."—Rom. 1:14,15.

Paul was a man, one of a race of men. Paul could not wash his hands of his fellow men. Every man owes something to the race. Every child receives from mother and father more than he can ever repay. If he pays his debt at all it must be to the rest of the world. It is only a murderer like Cain who asks, "Am I my brother's keeper?"

We owe a debt to every dying sinner! We are crooked, dishonest, unfaithful to a trust, if we do not share with others the precious Gospel.

Dr. H. A. Ironside was in Dallas in 1943. In a letter to me he enclosed a circular announcing his engagements in a number of black churches with striking names. Across the top of the circular Dr. Ironside simply wrote, *"Trying to pay my debt to my black brethren."*

Every Christian owes a debt to sinners. He has received that which is not his alone. If he selfishly takes for himself of all the blessings of God and does not lead others to know Jesus and have peace, forgiveness and a home in Heaven; if he does not keep others out of the torments of Hell, he is a dishonest man, an unfaithful steward, a wicked sinner against both God and man!

VI. NOT TO WIN SOULS IS THE SIN OF A SHORTSIGHTED FOOL

These are strong words, but consider the words of the Scripture and see if they are not true. Proverbs 11:30 says, "The fruit of the righteous is a tree of life; and he that winneth souls is wise." Christians should bear fruit as a tree of life, and every wise Christian wins souls.

The same thing is taught in Daniel 12:2,3:

"And many of them that sleep in the dust of the earth shall awake, some to everlasting life, and some to shame and everlasting contempt. And they that be wise shall shine as the brightness of the firmament; and they that turn many to righteousness as the stars for ever and ever."

Oh, how bright will be the shining of soul winners in Heaven! They that turn many to righteousness shall shine "as the stars for ever an ever."

Here we see that the true wisdom takes the long look. A Christian with any spiritual wisdom can see it is not best to center his endeavors on things that pass away with life. To make money, friends, to enjoy pleasures of life—to be much concerned about these passing pleasures and this passing wealth is not good sense, nor is it spiritual wisdom. When "them that sleep in the dust of the earth shall awake," when Christians come before Christ to receive their awards, when God's bonfire burns up the wood, hay and stubble of wasted lives, then every Christian who did not win souls will find that he has played the consummate fool!

Psalm 53:1 says, "The fool hath said in his heart, There is no God." No Christian can be that kind of a fool. Jesus said to the two disciples on the way to Emmaus, "O fools, and slow of heart to believe all that the prophets have spoken." These were Christians but guilty of a folly kin to that of the atheist. And the Christian who never wins souls is a fool, too, and for a very similar reason.

The man who denies God and eternity is a fool. The man who does not believe the Bible is also a fool. And so the man who lives as if this world were the only world, as if it were better to make money than to win souls, as if it were more important to fill his belly, clothe his back, live in a fine home, drive a nice car and make a name for himself, than to lay up treasures and meet in Heaven a host of those he has won to Christ—that man is a fool!

Oh, the shortsighted folly of those who neglect eternal things for temporal things! Oh, the sin of those who do not accept the value that Christ put upon a soul! How wicked is the sin of us foolish Christians who do not win souls and thus who miss the chance to shine and rejoice forever with the Saviour by bringing sinners to love and trust Him!

VII. NOT TO WIN SOULS IS THE SIN OF BLOOD-GUILT, OF SOUL-MANSLAUGHTER

In Ezekiel 3:17-19, the word of the Lord came to Ezekiel, saying:

"Son of man, I have made thee a watchman unto the house of Israel: therefore hear the word at my mouth, and give them warning from me. When I say unto the wicked, Thou shalt surely die; and thou givest him not warning, nor speakest to warn the wicked from his wicked way, to save his life; the same wicked man shall die in his iniquity; but HIS BLOOD WILL I REQUIRE AT THINE HAND. Yet if thou warn the

wicked, and he turn not from his wickedness, nor from his wicked way, he shall die in his iniquity; BUT THOU HAST DELIVERED THY SOUL."

If Ezekiel did not warn the Israelites about their iniquity, and if they died in their sins, then God required their blood at the hand of Ezekiel! What a staggering thought, that God says to a man about sinners, "His blood will I require at thine hand"! But if Ezekiel warned the wicked, even if the wicked did not turn, then God said, "Thou hast delivered thy soul."

That strange commission was given to Ezekiel for the nation Israel. But surely it implies that God still holds people to account for the souls of those they do not warn! Surely we are guilty of the blood of every soul who goes to Hell if we had a chance to warn them, to weep over them, to woo them tenderly, win them and get them to come to Christ, but did not!

Paul had this in mind when he came to Miletus, the little port of the great city Ephesus, and had the elders of Ephesus meet him there. Solemnly facing these preachers, Paul told them that after his three years' ministry in Ephesus they would see his face no more, then, "Wherefore I take you to record this day, that I am pure from the blood of all men. For I have not shunned to declare unto you all the counsel of God" (Acts 20:26,27). He said again, "Therefore watch, and remember, that by the space of three years I ceased not to warn every one night and day with tears" (vs. 31).

Paul could solemnly say, 'After three years in Ephesus I am not to blame if anyone here goes to Hell. I have no blood on my hands! I have gone night and day with tears, publicly and from house to house, carrying the whole counsel of God. So I am not to blame if anybody goes to Hell!'

O Christian, is there blood on your hands? Are you guilty of the death of immortal souls for whom Christ died because you did not warn them?

When a boat overturned in a Chinese river, a missionary to China tells how he urged some nearby Chinese fishermen to bring their boat quickly and help him rescue a man who was struggling. The fishermen said it was none of their business. "How much?" they asked, insisting on a price of fifty dollars before they would rescue the drowning man. The missionary gave them all the money he had—about forty dollars— and at last persuaded them to try to rescue the drowning man. But when he was brought out of the water, life had already fled. The callous hearts of the fishermen took no responsibility for their drowning countryman. But they were guilty of murder as certain as there is a God in Heaven who holds men to account!

But are you much different, Christian, when you let people near you go to Hell and never warn, never weep, never see that they hear the Gospel?

In Roosevelt, Oklahoma I promised to see a dying woman who was distressed about her soul. But I waited until the second day, and she died before I saw her.

In Dallas, Texas an old man past eighty heard me on the radio and wrote, "I am dying with cancer, and I am not ready to die. Brother Rice, please come and pray with me and help me to get ready to die." But having so many burdens each day I postponed it. Finally, after two weeks, I sent a young preacher to visit the old man and help him prepare to meet God. When no one answered the doorbell a neighbor came to tell him that the old man had died and the family were then at his funeral!

I have hopes that in their extremity these two may have turned to the Lord and trusted Him. I say I have some hopes but no certainty. And oh, what will I say to the Lord Jesus if He asks me to give an account for the souls of these two who sent for me and I did not go!

The sin of not winning souls is the blood-guilty, the terrible sin of soul-manslaughter. I beg you in Jesus' name, consider how guilty you must be in God's sight if you do not put your heart's strength and love into the one precious business of soul winning!

Christian, if you do not win souls, you are not right with God. You may be saved, but you are not a good disciple. You may be born again into God's family, but you are a poor, disobedient, willful child. If you are God's child, then you are a disobedient one. If you are God's servant, then you are an unfaithful one. If you follow the Saviour at all, you follow afar off.

Consider again this sevenfold sin of failing to win souls. It is the sin of disobedience, of lack of love, of failing to follow Christ, of not abiding in Christ, the sin of dishonesty in a sacred trust, a sin of shortsighted folly, missing eternal rewards, and a sin of blood-guilt for which we must give an account!

May God convict all His people of the sin of not winning souls dying all around us.

JACK HYLES
1926-

ABOUT THE MAN:

If we could say but one thing about Dr. Hyles, I guess we would call him MR. SOUL WINNING.

Born in Italy, Texas, he began preaching at age nineteen. He pastored several churches in that state, most notably the Miller Road Baptist Church in Garland that was no doubt the fastest-growing church in the world for many years. In seven years it grew to the astounding number of 4,000 members.

Then on to the formal downtown First Baptist Church in the Calumet area of Hammond, Indiana. There, after fighting for separation in the church, he won victory after victory. Now that church is the largest Sunday school in the world. Attendance of over 25,000 is common on a Sunday.

Hammond Baptist Schools, Hyles-Anderson College, Hyles-Anderson Publications, and many other gospel projects have come forth from his fantastic ministry.

His best friend, the late Dr. John R. Rice, said about this giant: *"Jack Hyles is a tornado of zeal. He is pungent in speech, devastating in sarcasm. You will laugh and cry — and repent! Preachers who are not dead will preach differently after hearing him. Thousands point to a message from Jack Hyles as the time of a transformed life. He is simply beyond description, with a unique anointing from God."*

Dr. Hyles is the author of many books, including *Hyles Church Manual, Hyles Sunday School Manual, Kisses of Calvary,* and a great series of *How to . . .* books. He also has a large cassette ministry.

Place Dr. Jack Hyles among the giants of this generation!

III.

Four Calls for Soul Winning

JACK HYLES

(Preached at National Sword of the Lord Conference at Indianapolis, 1974)

Standing in judgment, the Apostle Paul declared, "I was not disobedient unto the heavenly vision."

When told not to preach anymore in His name in the book of Acts, Peter and John replied, "We cannot but speak the things which we have seen and heard."

The writer of Hebrews said, "Wherefore seeing we also are compassed about with so great a cloud of witnesses...."

In chapter 16 of Acts, the story is told about the Apostle Paul and his second missionary journey, when he heard the voice from Macedonia saying, "Come over into Macedonia, and help us."

Then in chapter 16 of Luke is the story of the rich man who, when he had been refused the privilege of being delivered from the fires of torment, suggested to Abraham that he send Lazarus to tell his five brothers how to be saved lest they too 'come to this awful place of torment.'

Now we will tie these passages together.

Fifteen years ago this month I became pastor of the First Baptist Church of Hammond, Indiana. I guess there never was a fellow who went from the South to the North with any more apprehension or fear than did I. You see, I was born and reared in the "Holy Land"—between Dallas and Fort Worth. And the Lord called me to go to Chicago! I did not want to go. It took the Lord seven months to talk me into coming to this Chicago area.

There were several reasons for my reluctance. The first reason was, I didn't want any Yankee to be in Heaven! To be quite frank with you, there was another place to which I had assigned all Yankees, and it wasn't purgatory! You see, the Yankees shot my great-granddaddy in the back in the Civil War. You say, "Why in the back?" Because he was running!

> I said, "Let me walk in the fields";
> He said, "Nay, walk in the town";
> I said, "There are no flowers there";
> He said, "No flowers, but a crown."

> I said, "But the sky is black,
> There is nothing but noise and din."
> But He wept as He led me back;
> "There is more," He said, "there is sin."

> I said, "But the air is thick,
> And fogs are veiling the sun."
> He answered, "Yet hearts are sick,
> And souls in the dark undone."

> I said, "I shall miss the light,
> And friends will miss me, they say."
> He answered me, "Choose tonight
> If I am to miss you, or they."

> I pleaded for time to be given;
> He said, "Is it hard to decide?
> It will not seem hard in Heaven
> To have followed the steps of your Guide."

> I cast one look at the field,
> Then set my face to the town;
> He said, "My child, do you yield?
> Will you leave the flowers for the crown?"

> Then into His hand went mine,
> And into my heart came He,
> And I walk in a light divine
> The path I had feared to see!

And so fifteen years ago this month I became pastor of the First Baptist Church at Hammond, Indiana. Shortly after—maybe two months—one of the wealthier members of the church came to me and said, "Pastor, could I have a conference with you, please?"

He called me off to the side and he said something like this:

> Pastor, I am one of the most influential members of this church. I have been a member for years. I want to tell you something, Pastor. Ever since you have been here, I have been nervous. Look at me! I am trembling right now! Before you came we used to have

revival meetings once or twice a year. We would hire an evangelist to come in and preach evangelistic sermons. We would get a song leader, and we would get people saved. But, now for these months since you have become pastor, it is like that every Sunday. Every Sunday morning it is soul winning. Every Sunday night it is soul winning. Monday it is soul winning. Tuesday it is soul winning. Wednesday it is soul winning. Thursday it is soul winning. Friday it is soul winning. Saturday it is soul winning.

Pastor, look at me. I am a nervous wreck. Our people were calm and tranquil before you came, but you have made half of this church nervous wrecks.

Pastor, do you know that last Sunday morning we sang fifty-three stanzas of "Just as I am, without one plea, But that Thy blood was shed for me"? We sang the song ten times all the way through during the invitation, and three stanzas over that.

Pastor, do you know that last Sunday morning my neighbor across the street who goes to the Lutheran church went to Sunday school, stayed for church, came home, changed clothes, ate lunch, read the paper, watched part of the ball game, took a nap and woke up just as I was getting home from our Sunday morning service?

Pastor, why, why, why can't you be like the other preachers in town? Why is it the pressure has got to be on every Sunday morning and every Sunday night? And even when we are not in church, somebody is trying to go out and get somebody so they can bring them down the aisle the next time we have a service.

Pastor, I stood on one foot, then I stood on the other foot. I thought you would never get through with the invitation! Why, why can't you be like the other preachers?

I said, "Come next Sunday night, and I will give you my answer."

The next Sunday I told my people this man's story, not calling his name. I just said, "A man has come to me representing others who are nervous, and they have asked me why this pressure is on all the time, why Sunday morning, Sunday night, Monday, Tuesday, Wednesday, Thursday, Friday, Saturday and starting the next Sunday morning again, the pressure is on—all the time. 'It is soul winning, soul winning, soul winning; evangelism, evangelism, evangelism,' he complained."

Tonight I will tell you why, as I told them why. There are four reasons.

I. A CALL FROM WITHIN

In the first place, there is a call from within. Something inside me says it has got to be that way. There is a call from within. Something inside of me speaks like the apostle spoke when he said, "I cannot be disobedient to the heavenly vision." Maybe it is sort of like the woman at Sychar's well who went back into the city and said, "Hey! Come see a man who told me all things I ever did." Or maybe it is like Peter and John who said, "Sir, we cannot but speak the things which we have seen and heard."

That is exactly what I am praying for God to burn in the bosom of every preacher who has been here this week. It is not, "What kind of a church will I have?" but, "What kind of church I *must* have." It is not, "What kind of a church will I choose?" but I trust that God will set a burning in the soul of every preacher who is here this week so that he will have to have an old-fashioned, soul-winning church when he goes back home. A call from within.

It has not always been that way. This call from within started when I was an older teenager. Anyone who has heard me preach knows this is true. I was an introvert when I was a boy. I was still sucking my thumb when I was fourteen. On my 17th birthday I weighed 93 pounds dripping wet and full of bananas. I could not pass public speaking. I was called "Jackie boy." Nobody took me seriously. When God called me to preach, the angels wept and Heaven's flag was flown at half-mast for three days!

One day when I was an older teenager, the chairman of our deacon board, Jesse Cobb, met me after the service on a Sunday morning in the back of the auditorium. Jesse was the best lay soul winner I think I ever met. He said, "Jack, will you do something with me this afternoon?"

"What, Jesse?"

"Will you go soul winning with me this afternoon?"

"Jesse, you know better than that! You know I am a timid introvert. I would not know what to say if I went out soul winning. Jesse, I couldn't do it."

"Jack, I will make you a deal. All you will have to do is to just go with me. I will do the talking. All you will have to do is listen."

Well, since I had a Ph.D. in listening, I said, "Now, let us get this straight. You talk, I listen."

He said, "Well, you may have to say hello."

I said, "I think I can do that."

So that afternoon for the first time in my life, I went soul winning.

Jesse Cobb and I knocked on a door. A big high school football player, tackle on the Adamson High School football team named Kenneth Florence, came to the door. Kenneth looked down at Jesse and at me. Jesse looked up to Kenneth and said, "Kenneth Florence?"

"Yes, sir."

"My name is Jesse Cobb."

"How do you do, sir?"

"And this is Jack Hyles."

I generated all the extraversion at my disposal and I said, "Hello."

"Kenneth, Jack here wants to say a few words to you."

Stuttering, I said, "Kenneth, will you go to church tonight?"

Jesse said Kenneth said, "Yes, I will."

And I said, "You will?"

Kenneth said, "Yes, I will."

I said, "I will come back and get you at seven o'clock tonight."

At seven o'clock that night I went by to get Kenneth Florence. For the first time in my life I knew that God had given me a soul I had to win. I didn't know one single Scripture of the Roman Road. I had never taken a soul-winning course. I had no idea in this world what to do.

The sermon was finished. I put my arm around Kenneth's big, broad shoulders and said, "Kenneth, would. . . would. . . wouldn't you like to be saved?"

He said, "Yes, I would."

I said, "I can't tell you how, but if you will come with me, the preacher can. Follow me."

We went down this aisle. The pastor met me. I said, "Pastor, Kenneth wants to be saved." I then turned and walked away. I got about two rows back, and the pastor said, "Hold it, Jack. Kenneth, Jack here wants to kneel and show you how to be saved." No, Jack didn't!

But I knelt and put my arms around Kenneth's big, broad shoulders and said, "Kenneth, I do not know how to tell you how to be saved. John 3:16 says something like this: Jesus died for you because God loved you and gave Himself for you. Now, I believe that if you would be willing to ask God to forgive you and trust Him as your Saviour, God would save you tonight."

Thank God, somebody had already told Kenneth how to be saved. So Kenneth Florence bowed his head, and on his knees he began to pray something like this: "Father, thank you that this fellow is interested in me. I know I am a sinner. I know Jesus died for me, and I know that You, God, can save me, and I do now trust You as my Saviour."

I said, "Kenneth, if you meant that, put your hand in mine."

Kenneth put his hand in mine. While he was praying, something turned loose inside my soul! I tell you, the fireworks of Heaven began to ignite! The lightning flashed, the thunder rolled, the sparklers began to sparkle as I realized that here was something I could do. I couldn't make the football team, but I could point a person to Heaven. I couldn't make the senior play, but I could point a person to Heaven. I couldn't get a date, but I could point a person to Heaven. I couldn't make the basketball team (I did make the team, but because my legs were so skinny, people laughed at me, and I would not go on the floor); but I could point a person to Heaven.

I got off my knees and said, "Dear God, this is something a little introvert can do. This is something 'Jackie boy' can do."

There is not a man or woman or a boy or a girl in this house tonight who can't point someone to Jesus Christ. You may not be able to be a Congressman like our brother here, but you can be a soul winner. You may not be able to be the editor of THE SWORD OF THE LORD like John Rice, but you can be a soul winner. Perhaps you could not pastor the largest Sunday school in the world, but you could be a soul winner.

I am saying, there was a call in my breast, a call from within! I am praying that God tonight will give you that call, burning in your soul, and you will leave this place determined to be a soul winner.

> Pastor, could I have a conference with you, please? I represent quite a few people in this church who are nervous. Look at my hands. I am nervous. I have been nervous ever since you came. You see, Pastor, before you came, we had revival meetings twice a year, sometimes once or twice a year. We hired a singer, we hired a preacher, and we had evangelistic services. But ever since you have come, Pastor, it has been soul winning on Sunday morning, soul winning on Sunday night, soul winning on Monday, soul winning on Tuesday, soul winning on Wednesday night, soul winning on Thursday, soul winning on Friday, soul winning on Saturday.
>
> Why, Pastor, last Sunday morning we sang fifty-three stanzas of "Just as I Am, Without One Plea." Do you know that my Lutheran neighbor across the street went to Sunday school, stayed for church, came home, changed his clothes, ate lunch, read the paper, watched a part of the ball game, took a nap and woke up

about the time I came home from our services Sunday morning? Why can't you be like other preachers?

And I gave my people a second reason why I can't be normal. Vance Havner has always said, "About all the Christians are so sub-normal that if anybody gets normal, everybody thinks he is abnormal."

II. A CALL FROM WITHOUT

Not only is there a call from within, but there is a call from without. "Come over into Macedonia, and help us." How can you drive down the streets of Indianapolis without hearing people calling you to be a soul winner?

Listen, there are tens of thousands of people in this city and in mine who have never one time heard the Gospel of Jesus Christ. Walk down the streets of Indianapolis and ask, "What do you have to do to go to Heaven?" Most will answer, "Well, I live a pretty good life," or, "I have been confirmed."

(Let me make a parenthesis. It does not matter how many times you have been baptized, confirmed, sprinkled or dipped or how many times you have turned over a new leaf or how many good deeds you have done, if you are not born again, you will never go to Heaven as long as this world lives or eternity lasts.)

There is a call from without. I believe this Book. I believe that everybody without Christ is lost. I believe that lost men go to Hell when they die. I believe that men who go to Hell burn forever and ever and ever and ever in the fires of torment. Because of that, there is a constant call from without.

That call began in me when I was a young preacher. I had preached for a year without having anybody saved. I will not go into the experience that took place and what caused this to happen, but God changed my life and filled me with the Holy Spirit. The next Sunday night when I came back to my country pulpit, three people got saved all at one time. I had never had anybody saved before. But we had three saved that night—three, three! Hallelujah! Three! I never thought I would see three people saved at one time.

Now, where I grew up in Texas, we used to shake hands with all the converts. When these three people got saved, a deacon made a motion that they be accepted after baptism, a second was made to the motion, and we voted them in the church, shook their hands and dismissed the service.

I was standing at the altar, saying, "Hallelujah! Praise the Lord!" You see, I have a Baptist head but a Pentecostal heart and the Jehovah's Witnesses' feet. And my Pentecostal heart got happy. I was saying, "Praise the Lord! Amen! Three people came and got saved!"

All of a sudden—wham! A great big fellow hit me from the rear. He was a trainman for the T. & P. Railway Company. He draped all over me and said, "Reverend, this is a wonderful service! My daughter Barbara is back in the corner leaning up against the wall. I believe if you would go talk to her, you could get her to be saved."

I went and told Barbara how to be saved, and she got saved. I went out on the front porch, called the folks back in, and we voted Barbara into the church. We came by to shake Barbara's hand, and then we dismissed the service. Praise the Lord! We had four people saved that night!

I was standing beside Barbara, and I was clapping my hands and saying, "Praise the Lord! Amen! Hallelujah!" when all of a sudden—wham! The same fellow hit me from the rear. Crying, he said, "Reverend, my married daughter, Dorothy Hall, is back there in that corner. I believe you would get her saved if you would go back there and talk to her."

I went back and told Dorothy how to be saved, and she got saved! I went out on the porch. "Hey! Come on back in! Come back in!" We voted Dorothy into the church, and we came by to shake her hand and then dismissed the service. Hallelujah! Praise the Lord! Five people got saved at one time in one service! I never thought I would see that!

I was saying, "Amen! Praise the Lord!" when all of a sudden—wham! The same fellow draped himself all over me and said, "Reverend, Dorothy's husband, Sam Hall, is on the front porch. He just throwed down his cigarette. Do you reckon that means anything?"

I went out on the front porch and said, "Sam, did you throw your cigarette down?"

"Yes, I did."

"Why?"

"I am about to die! I have got to get saved!" I told Sam Hall how to be saved on the front porch of that church. "Hey! Come on back here! Come on back in." We voted Sam into the church and came by to shake his hand and then dismissed the service.

You will not believe this, but it is true! I was standing at the altar beside Sam, praising the Lord that six people had been saved, when all of a sudden—wham! That same fellow draped himself all over me, and here is what he said: "Reverend, I think I will get saved myself before I go home!"

I knelt at the altar and told that man how to be saved. (He, today, is a lay preacher.) And he got saved. I went out on the front porch. "HEY! Come on back in." Some of them came back in, and we voted him into the church, came by to shake his hand and then again dismissed the service.

At 11:15 that night I went on over to the parsonage. I got on my face before God and I said, "O God, this is what I have been wanting all these years! O God, I am going to die! I am not going to be a powerless preacher. I am not going to be just a 'Reverend.' I am not going to have just a worship service on Sunday morning. We are going to have the kind of service where the Holy Ghost comes and the power of God comes and people get saved! I am not going to be just a powerless preacher!"

And blessed be God, through these years, I wish I could tell you how God has answered that prayer.

Becky, married to a preacher, is almost twenty-three. David is twenty. Linda is seventeen, and Cindy is almost fifteen. Not one of my children who lives at our house has ever been to church on Sunday without seeing somebody saved. Until she left our house, only two Sundays since Becky was born did she ever go to church without seeing her daddy baptize sometime on Sunday.

My preacher brothers, you do not have to have a powerless ministry! There is something better than these dry halls and dead services and worship services and sevenfold Amens and Gloria Patrias and Amen, Amen, Amen! There is an old-fashioned, Holy Ghost kind of Christianity.

Talk about our need in America! If we have America saved, it will be saved because God raises up a generation of old-fashioned, Hell-fire-and-damnation, Bible-preaching, soul-winning, Christ-honoring, God-fearing, sin-hating, sin-fighting preachers who dare to preach it like it is!

This man said to me, "Pastor, why, why?"

I said, "Because there is a call from within and there is a call from without."

Pastor, could I talk with you for a few minutes, please? We like you here. We think you are honest. We think you are a fine man.

But I represent a nervous group of people. You see, Pastor, before you came we used to have revival—the evangelist, the singer and all the trimmings. But ever since you have come—soul winning Sunday morning, soul winning Sunday night, soul winning Monday, Tuesday, Wednesday, Thursday, Friday and Saturday. Pastor, you have got a church of nervous people.

Do you know what we did last Sunday after the sermon? We sang fifty-three stanzas of "Just as I Am, Without One Plea." And that is not all, Pastor. My neighbor across the street is a Lutheran. He went to Sunday school, he stayed for church, came home, changed clothes, read the paper, watched part of the ball game, took a nap and woke up about the time I was coming home from our church service Sunday morning. Now, why can't you be like other preachers? Why? Why can't you?

III. A CALL FROM ABOVE

I said to my people, There is a third reason why. As long as I pastor the First Baptist Church of Hammond, Indiana, it will not be a formal kind of a ritualistic church. It will not be a dead kind of a dry service. It will be a place where we can weep over every erring one, lift up the fallen, tell them of Jesus, the power to save. We are going to have old-fashioned Christianity because there is a call from above. From above.

Jesus my Saviour is in Heaven, and He told me to go and preach the Gospel to every creature. But that is not all. The Bible says that there is a cloud of witnesses watching over us, watching all we do. Those clouds of witnesses tell us to go.

I have two little sisters in Heaven whose faces I have never seen. Each died at the age of seven. They are buried side by side in the little grave in Italy, Texas, not far from my father's grave. For these almost thirty years that I have been preaching, though I have never seen them, they have seen me. I think they look down at me tonight and say, "Jack, tell them to go soul winning. Tell them to go soul winning."

There is a call from above. Oh, the great host of people I have sent to Heaven through these years! They want us to go soul winning. You may not be for soul winning, but those in Heaven are for soul winning. The Bible says there is more joy in the presence of the angels over one sinner that repenteth, than of ninety and nine just persons that need no repentance. And all across this nation tonight, churches have deacons, committee members, board members, finance committee members who are trying to water down and soften the Hell-fire-and-brimstone, soul-winning pastors and to vote them out.

As I stand before God, I would rather be a great sinner than to be a man who tries to water down old-fashioned, soul-winning, New Testament Christianity. There is a call from above. God wants us to go soul winning!

I believe we need some help in politics. But that won't save America. I think we ought to make it against the law for communists to be allowed to speak on campuses and spread their filth of revolution to our boys and girls whom we have sent to college. But after it is all said and done, we will clean the colleges up when we will clean the pulpit up. As long as we have people who are afraid in the pulpit, we will have people intimidating us in the pew. As long as we have polar bears in the pulpit, we will have ice cubes in the pews. We have to have some men of God who have a call from above who say, "We are going to spend our lives trying to reach the souls of men."

When I was a kid preacher pastoring a growing church in Garland, Texas, there came to our services one Sunday morning a little man. He said he was seventy-two. He had a squeaky voice, his hair was white, he had stooped shoulders. In his broken voice he said, "Young man, could you tell me where the pastor is?"

"I am the pastor."

"You? I thought it would be an older man."

I said, "I am Brother Hyles."

"Brother Hyles, my name is James W. Moore. I am a Baptist preacher. The reason I talk like this is because when I preached, I really preached. I didn't pussyfoot nor compromise; I let 'er rip! I have preached my voice out for over fifty years. Now I am sick, and I have had to quit preaching. They sent me here to Garland, Texas, and I am just wondering if you would let me come to your church. I would not cause trouble. I would be for you every time you preach."

"Sure, you can come. You are welcome."

I bought him an old-fashioned platform rocker and put it next to the wall in the altar. And old Brother Moore would sit over there and rock and clap his hands while I preached. He had a Pentecostal heart, too! He would say, "Hallelujah! Amen! Praise the Lord!" He knew Billy Sunday personally. He had also known Mel Trotter, Paul Radar and other great preachers in an intimate, personal relationship.

I would preach on Sunday mornings, then go stand at the front door. Then I baptized only on Sunday nights. Old Brother Moore would come out. He always had just a stubble beard, about a quarter of an inch long. He would say, "That was a good sermon, Paul."

"Paul? My name is Jack."

"Oh, I thought you were Paul Radar there for awhile, the way you was preaching."

Then I would say, "Boy, you sure know good preaching when you hear it!" Then I would hug him, and we would laugh, and I would kiss him on the cheek.

Next Sunday morning he would come out and say, "That was a good sermon there, Billy."

"Billy? I am Jack."

"Oh, I thought you was Billy Sunday there this morning."

"Thank you! Thank you!"

And every Monday morning old Brother Moore would come by my office at nine o'clock. He would pace the floor. "Brother Jack, I just came by this morning to tell you about a stupid mistake I made when I was a kid preacher."

Strangely enough it was always the same mistake I had made the day before! But he never told me it was *my* mistake. It was always *his*. I would say, "You are coming through loud and clear, Brother Moore."

"Now I am not being critical. I just wanted to tell you how stupid I used to be."

I would say, "Yeah, and how stupid I was yesterday."

"Oh, no, no, no, no." I would kiss his cheek and hug him, and he would go his way.

Several months passed. He did not come to sit in his seat. It was empty. I missed his "Amen! Hallelujah." This corner was strangely quiet.

After a hard Sunday and near midnight, the telephone rang. A female voice said, "Is this Reverend Hyles?"

"This is Brother Hyles."

"An old man down here is dying. He has white hair, stooped shoulders. There is no identification on him, no one that he can call. No one knows who he is. All he keeps saying is, "Call Brother Jack. Call Brother Jack." Somebody here knew that you liked to be called "Brother" instead of Reverend, and your first name is Jack. We thought you might know who this man is."

"Of course I know him."

I walked into Room 11 of the little hospital, and there was Brother

Moore. I was a young preacher, so I wore a black suit, black shoes, black tie and carried a black Bible.

I walked in to say, "May the Lord comfort you in the valley of the shadow of death." I had never seen many folks die before. But when I walked in, Brother Moore looked up at me, and the nurse said, "He is dying, so be careful what you say."

When he saw me he said, "Come in, Brother Jack. Ha! Ha! Ha! I am just about to take a trip. Ha! Ha! Ha! I have been looking forward to it all these years. Ha! Ha! Ha! Guess what, Brother Jack! Any minute now, I am going to see Abraham and Isaac and Jacob and John the Baptist and Paul and Peter and JESUS! Is there anything you want me to tell them for you?"

To save my life, I could not think of anything except, "Tell them, 'Hi' "!

He said, "Brother Jack. . . ." Then he began to breathe heavily as if it were his last breath. He took the oxygen mask off his face, laid it down on the bed beside him, reached out and asked for my hand. As I put both of my hands in his right hand, he covered my hands with his left. I could not feel a pulse, and his hands were cold. He looked up at me as if he had planned it this way and he said, "Brother Jack! Keep preaching it!" He placed his right hand over his heart and made a cross with his left. His chin sunk against his breast. His eyes were opened in death.

I heard the rustling of the wings of angels. And one angel came and said, "Reverend, would you step out in the hall, please? We have a job to do."

I stepped out in the hall and heard the rustling of angels' wings as they took the spirit of that great giant of God and laid it in the presence of the One whom he had preached for over half a century and the One whom, bless God, we will see any day now!

I went back in the room and prayed, "O God, I pray that, as long as I have breath to breathe, You will help me keep preaching it!"

Oh, tonight, while I am preaching to you, I believe up there, in a pure gold platform rocker, a little old fellow with white hair, straight shoulders and a face as smooth as the face of his Saviour is saying, "Amen! Amen! Hallelujah!"

"Why, Preacher, why?" I will tell you why! Heaven wants our churches to be soul-winning churches.

Pastor, could I have a talk with you, please? I represent a

nervous committee of our church. Pastor, why can't you be like other preachers? Why can't our services be more ritualistic and dignified on Sunday morning? Why, Pastor, ever since you have been here, it has been revival meetings Sunday morning, Sunday night, Monday, Tuesday, Wednesday, Thursday, Friday, Saturday.

Do you know we sang fifty-three stanzas of "Just as I Am, Without One Plea" last Sunday morning, and my Lutheran neighbor across the street went to Sunday school, stayed for church, came home, changed his clothes, ate lunch, read the paper, watched part of the ball game, took a nap and woke up about the time I was getting home from my morning service? Why can't you be like other preachers?

IV. A CALL FROM BENEATH

I told my people the next Sunday night, "The fourth reason I cannot is that there is a call from beneath." A call from within! A call from without! A call from above! And a call from beneath!

You recall the story of Dives, the rich man who died and went to Hell. He lifted up his eyes and said, "Father Abraham, send Lazarus that he may dip his finger in water, and cool my tongue; for I am tormented in this flame." Abraham told him there is a great gulf between them, and it was impossible. He said, "Then tell Lazarus to go back and tell my five brothers not to come here where I am!"

You may not be interested in soul winning, but in Hell they are! There is a call from beneath tonight.

And now may I get very serious for a few minutes and enter into the little white sanctuary where I don't like to go but where I must take you in the closing moments of this message?

My father was an alcoholic. He is buried tonight in a drunkard's grave in Italy, Texas. My father heard me preach two sermons, one on Sunday morning and one on Sunday night, New Year's Day, 1949.

New Year's Eve I got burdened for my dad. So I got in my car in Marshall, Texas, and drove 150 miles to Dallas to the Hunt Saloon where my dad was a bartender and a drunk. I took my big Scofield Bible inside that bar, that tavern. My dad was sitting at the bar drinking beer. He was a big man, weighing 235 pounds, and the strongest man I ever knew.

I said, "Dad, this is Saturday night, New Year's Eve, 1949. I am going to take you back today to Marshall, Texas, to hear me preach tomorrow."

My dad cursed me. "I'm not going to go and hear any preacher preach."

"Dad, you weigh 235 pounds, and I weigh a little over half that. But we are going to have a brawl here in this bar, or you are going to go with me to Marshall, Texas."

He realized that I meant business. I gave him enough coffee to sober him up a bit; then we got in the car and I took him to Marshall, Texas. On New Year's Eve, 1949, my father went on our watch night service with us. We got on buses and rode around town and sang songs and had a wonderful time. We came back to church and prayed the old year out and the new year in.

Sunday was on New Year's Day that year. I stood to preach, and my dad sat on the fourth row from the front. The invitation time came, and he clawed the pew in conviction. I pleaded for him to come, but he would not.

That afternoon we went for a walk out in the pasture. I put my arms around his shoulder and said, "Dad, I want to see you be a Christian more than I want anything in all the world. Dad, will you not be saved?"

My dad opened the joybells of Heaven when he said, "Son, I am going to get saved. I am going to go back to Dallas and sell out. I am going to move to Marshall. I am going to buy me a little fruit stand or a small grocery store and set up a little business here. I am going to get saved in the spring and let you baptize me."

I said, "Dad, that is wonderful! That is good enough for me."

I wish I could relive that afternoon. I wish I had a chance to try again. I thought he had plenty of time. He was only 62. I clapped my hands. The last word my dad said when he got out of the car on Washington Street in Dallas, Texas, was, "Son, I am going to let you baptize me in the spring."

Every time I baptized that winter, I heard him say, "Son, I am going to let you baptize me in the spring."

On May 13, 1950, about ten o'clock in the morning, my telephone rang. The operator said, "Reverend Jack Hyles?"

"This is Brother Hyles."

"Go ahead, sir."

A man's voice said, "My name is Smith. Reverend Hyles, I worked with your dad. We hung dry wall together. He was up on a sawhorse this morning hanging dry wall on the ceiling, and he just a few minutes ago dropped dead with a heart attack."

I didn't say anything. I just put the phone down.

"Son, I am going to let you baptize me in the spring."

I got in my car and drove back to Dallas, Texas, to the O'Neil Funeral Home.

My dad was buried in Italy, Texas.

Several months passed. One Sunday night past midnight there came a knock on the door of my study. I went to the door, and my only sister was at the door weeping. "Earlyne, is it Mother?"

"No, Jack. Would you tell me how to be saved?"

"Sure I will." And I told my only sister how to be saved, and she was saved in my study about one o'clock in the morning.

After she got saved I said, "Earlyne, why tonight? You could have been saved anytime through these years. Why did you choose tonight, and why did you come so late at night to get saved?"

She said, "Jack, you know that I was daddy's pet."

"That is right."

"Daddy did not care much for you, Jack, but he loved me very much."

"That is right, Sister."

"Jack, when dad died, I thought I would die too. I couldn't sleep at night. I lost weight. I cried almost every waking hour. I had a dream shortly after he died. I dreamed that I was taken into a big building, about like this, by a heavenly creature up to the second floor of that building. I was taken to a corner. There I saw a casket. I looked in. That corpse had a look of peace on its face. There was a casket next to that. In that casket was a corpse. That corpse had a look of peace on its face. And the next and the next and the next. The entire wall was lined with caskets, and in each was a corpse. And on each face a look of peace. The same thing across that wall and across this wall."

She said, "Jack, we got to the last casket, and the heavenly creature said, 'You can't look in that one.'"

"I said, 'I must. I have looked at all of them.' The creature said, 'No, you can't look in that one.'"

She said, "Jack, I saw two hands raise themselves above the casket. They were daddy's hands. Jack, daddy was saying, 'Sister! Sister! Sister!'

"I broke away from the creature and went over and looked in daddy's face. Jack, his face was writhing in pain, and daddy was saying, 'Sister! Sister! I—I—I—ju—j—bu—bu—I—I—Sister, Sister!' I said, 'Daddy, what is it? Tell me! Tell me!' He said, 'Sister, Sister, I—I—I—eh—B—je—je—be—, Sister, Sister!'"

She said, "Jack, the creature took me then, but I knew what daddy was saying. When I heard you preach tonight on the rich man in Hell who said to go tell my five brothers not to come here, I knew that daddy was telling me not to come to Hell where he was."

And now for these twenty-four and a half years, the thing that has motivated my life and my ministry has been the fact that somewhere in the torments of the unprepared, my daddy says, "Jack, tell them *all* not to come here. Tell them *all!* Tell them *all!* Tell them *all!* Tell them *all!*"

> Pastor, could I talk with you, please? I represent a bunch of nervous people. Why can't you be like other preachers?

I will tell you why. I will tell you why.

"K—K—K—enneth, w—w—wouldn't you like to be saved?"

"I think I'll get saved myself before I go home."

"Brother Jack, ke—ke—eep preaching it!"

"Sister, Sister! I—I—eh—eh—b—b—bje—je, oh, Sister!"

That is why!

Would you bow your heads for prayer, please?

R. A. TORREY
1856-1928

ABOUT THE MAN:

Torrey grew up in a wealthy home, attended Yale University and Divinity School, and studied abroad. During his early student days at Yale, young Torrey became an agnostic and a heavy drinker. But even during the days of his "wild life," he was strangely aware of a conviction that someday he was to preach the Gospel. At the end of his senior year in college, he was saved.

While at Yale Divinity School, he came under the influence of D. L. Moody. Little did Moody know the mighty forces he was setting in motion in stirring young R. A. Torrey to service!

After Moody died, Torrey took on the world-girdling revival campaigns in Australia, New Zealand, England and America.

Like many another giant for God, Torrey shone best, furthest and brightest as a personal soul winner. This one man led 100,000 to Christ in a revival that circled the globe!

Dr. Torrey's education was obtained in the best schools and universities of higher learning. Fearless, quick, imaginative and scholarly, he was a tough opponent to meet in debate. He was recognized as a great scholar, yet his ministry was marked by simplicity.

It was because of his outstanding scholastic ability and evangelistic fervor that Moody handpicked Torrey to become superintendent of his infant Moody Bible Institute. In 1912, Torrey became dean of BIOLA, where he served until 1924, pastoring the Church of the Open Door in Los Angeles from 1915-1924.

Torrey's books have probably reached more people indirectly and helped more people to understand the Bible and to have power to win souls, than the writings of any other man since the Apostle Paul, with the possible exceptions of Spurgeon and Rice. Torrey was a great Bible teacher, but most of all he was filled with the Holy Spirit.

He greatly influenced the life of Dr. John R. Rice.

IV.

Why Every Christian Should Make Soul Winning His Life's Business

By R. A. TORREY

Our Lord said to Simon and his brother Andrew, "Follow me, and I will make you fishers of men" (Matt. 4:19).

These words set forth two great thoughts: first, that if one would be a follower of Jesus, he must be a fisher of men; second, that all that is really essential as a condition of success in being a fisher of men is that one be a true follower of Jesus.

We are concerned here with the first thought: our Lord Jesus distinctly tells us that if we follow Him, He will make us fishers of men. If, then, we are not fishers of men, we are not following Jesus.

The Greek word translated "fishers" is a peculiar word; it indicates a man with whom fishing is his business—a *fisherman*—not merely one who fishes occasionally as a pastime or sport.

The clear teaching, then, is that every follower of Jesus should make fishing for men and winning others to the Lord THE BUSINESS OF LIFE. Many make fishing for men an *incident* of life. Their *business* is something else—following a profession, carrying on some mercantile pursuit, making money, or something of that sort—and if incidentally it comes their way to lead someone to the Saviour, they do it. But the thought of the Saviour's words is that fishing for men is not to be an incident of life but the business of life, that for which we live and which we are constantly carrying on.

This does not mean that every Christian should enter the ministry or go as a foreign missionary; many can win more souls while following some secular occupation than they ever could in the ministry; but it does mean that whatever our secular occupation or business or profession may be, in that occupation or business or profession and through that occupation or business or profession, we should make fishing for men—soul winning—the real business of life.

SIX REASONS WHY EVERY CHRISTIAN SHOULD MAKE SOUL WINNING HIS LIFE'S BUSINESS

1. This Is the Work Our Lord Has Commanded Us to Do

Before He left this world, our Lord Jesus gave His standing marching orders for the church for all coming time:

"And Jesus came to them and spake unto them, saying, All authority hath been given unto me in heaven and on earth. Go ye therefore, and make disciples of all the nations, baptizing them into the name of the Father and of the Son and of the Holy Spirit."—Matt. 28:18,19 (A.S.V.).

This commandment was not given merely to the apostles, but to the rank and file of the church. It is evident from the Acts of the Apostles that the early church so understood it; for we read in Acts 8:4, "Therefore they that were scattered abroad went every where preaching the word." And the context in verse 1 tells us explicitly that those were the rank and file of the church.

So any Christian who is not leading others to be disciples of Christ is disobeying his Commanding Officer.

It is serious in warfare to disobey one's commanding officer, but it is especially serious in the Christian warfare. Our Lord says in John 15:14, "Ye are my friends, *if* ye do whatsoever I command you." So not to do what He commands means we are not His friends. Any professed Christian who is not leading others definitely to Christ is not a friend of Jesus.

2. It Was the Business of Life With Our Lord Himself

What is it to be a Christian? Some will reply, "To be a follower of Jesus." Very well, but what is it to be a follower of Jesus? Again they will reply, "To have the same purpose in life that the Lord Jesus had."

Very well, but what was our Lord's purpose in life? He has told us in the most explicit terms what His purpose in life was in Luke 19:10, "For the Son of man is come *to seek and to save that which was lost.*"

It was for this purpose He came into this world. It was for this purpose He left Heaven with all its glory and came down to earth with all its shame. It was for this purpose He gave up the praises of the angels and the archangel, cherubim and seraphim, and came down into this world to be despised and rejected of men, to be mocked, to be spit upon, to be scourged, to be blindfolded, to be crucified. It was for this purpose He came; it was for this purpose He prayed; it was for this purpose He labored; it was for this purpose He suffered; it was for this purpose He died. The seeking and saving of the lost was the all-absorbing ambition, the all-consuming passion of His life. Is this your ambition? Is this the all-consuming passion of your life? the all-controlling purpose of your life? If not, what right have you to call yourself a follower of Jesus? If He had one all-controlling purpose in life and you have an entirely different controlling purpose in life, what right have you to style yourself a follower of Jesus?

3. This Is the Work in Which We Enjoy the Unspeakable Blessing of the Personal Fellowship of Christ Himself

Our Lord says in the passage before referred to:

"All authority hath been given unto me in heaven and on earth. Go ye therefore, and make disciples of all the nations, baptizing them into the name of the Father and of the Son and of the Holy Spirit: teaching them to observe all things whatsoever I commanded you: and lo, I am with you always, even unto the end of the world."

Here we see clearly that the promise of our Lord to be with us always is conditioned upon our making disciples. Those who are not are constantly trying to appropriate this promise to themselves, which they have no right to do.

I once heard a prominent Christian say that he was glad there was one promise in the New Testament that had no condition—"Lo, I am with you alway." But the condition is plainly stated in the context. For our Lord to be with us in personal fellowship, we must make disciples as far as our line will reach, striving intelligently and persistently to bring others to be disciples of the Lord. Then, and then only, may we count upon His being with us. Our Lord says that if we will go His way, He will go ours; that, if we will go out with Him in fellowship in His work of saving souls, He will go out with us in personal fellowship.

No one who is not making disciples has any right to this precious promise of our Lord. The personal, conscious companionship of our Lord is dependent upon our having fellowship with Him in His work of saving souls.

4. In That Work Alone We Enjoy the Fullness of the Holy Spirit's Presence and Power

The Holy Spirit is given to the individual believer for the definite purpose of witnessing for Christ. The Lord says, "Ye shall receive power, after that the Holy Ghost is come upon you: and ye shall be witnesses unto me both in Jerusalem, and in all Judaea, and in Samaria, and unto the uttermost part of the earth" (Acts 1:8).

God does not give us the Holy Spirit merely that we may be happy, or even that we may be personally holy; He gives to us His Holy Spirit for the specific purpose that we may be fitted for witnessing. How perfectly futile for any to pray for the fullness of the Holy Spirit if they are not willing to be used as witnesses!

This explains why so many people who are reading books upon the fullness of the Holy Spirit, going to conventions for the deepening of the "Spiritual Life," praying in secret or in large gatherings that they may be filled with the Holy Spirit, are obtaining nothing. They are seeking the blessing along another line from God's will. They are seeking a blessing that terminates in themselves. They are either seeking the happiness which others who have been filled with the Holy Spirit bear witness to, or else they are seeking personal victory over sin.

Undoubtedly when one is filled with the Holy Spirit he will have a deeper joy than he ever had before. The secret of obtaining victory over sin is being filled with the Holy Spirit; but should one seek the Holy Spirit merely for these purposes, he will not receive Him.

Unless we are willing to be used in bringing others to Christ, no amount of reading devotional books or going to conventions or wrestling in prayer, will bring us the blessing that we seek. If we are to be filled with the Holy Spirit, we must seek that fullness along the line of God's will and plan. What that line is, is made perfectly clear in the passage quoted above. No Christian can enjoy the fullness of the Holy Spirit's power and presence, and the joy and victory that go with that fullness, until he definitely puts himself into God's hands to be used of Him in winning others to Christ.

5. The Work That Produces the Most Beneficent Results

This is made perfectly clear in James 5:20, "He who converteth a sinner from the error of his way shall save a soul from death." These words are very familiar to us all, but few have stopped to weigh their tremendous significance.

Three words here need especial emphasis—"save" and "soul" and "death."

Look first of all at the word "soul." I wish it were within my power to make every reader see the value of a single soul as God sees it. How can I do it? There is nothing with which we can compare its value. Gold is nothing, precious stones are nothing in comparison with a human soul.

During the World's Fair at Chicago in 1893 there was a place in the Tiffany exhibit in the Manufacturer's Building that always drew a crowd. I went there time and time again during the World's Fair but was never able to get right at the place. If I wished to see what the crowd was looking at, I had to stand on tiptoe and look over the heads of the people.

And what was the crowd looking at? Nothing but a cone of purple velvet revolving upon an axis, and toward the apex of the cone, a large diamond of fabulous worth.

It was well worth looking at, but as the years have passed and I have thought of the great crowds, the tens of thousands who went to look at that one stone, the thought has come to me again and again: *"One human soul"*—not merely the soul of some great and gifted man or woman, but the soul of the most ordinary man or woman, the soul of the ragged, illiterate urchin on the street, the soul of the bloated, bleary-eyed drunkard, or of the outcast woman lost to shame and womanhood, a vile, despicable thing scarcely deserving the name of woman—is of infinitely more value in God's sight than ten thousand diamonds like that! And when you and I sit down beside another man or woman or boy or girl, and with our open Bible lead such to a definite acceptance of Christ, we have saved a *soul!*

I had two friends in New York City who were in the same business and both had prospered in it. The first came to New York practically penniless, and by dint of rare business sagacity and unusual industry, accumulated a fortune of first a million dollars, then to that he added a second million, then to that a third million, and then to that a fourth million. Then one evening, as he was crossing one of the lower avenues of New York going to his beautiful home on Fifth Avenue, he was run down by a tramcar and taken home to die, leaving four millions of dollars. Yes, *he left it all;* he took not a penny of it with him.

I remember how the next day the New York and the Brooklyn papers (for he had begun life in Brooklyn) came out with encomium upon this man and his business ability, telling how he had come to New York practically penniless and had accumulated a fortune of four million dollars.

The other man had also prospered. I do not know just how much he accumulated—I think about half-a-million dollars. Then God came into his life. He had a little daughter, four years of age, the idol of his heart. This beloved child was taken from his home by death. He was a professing Christian, a member of St. George's Episcopal Church in New York, but leading an ordinary, formal sort of Christian life.

A few days after the burial of his child, while riding home from his business on the elevated train, he got to thinking of his little girl. He held his newspaper before his face to hide his tears from the strangers in the railway carriage.

Then this thought came to him, *Your daughter is dead! What are you doing for other men's daughters?* He had to reply, *I am doing nothing.* Then he added, *But I will.*

The next year he put $10,000 into the rescue of fallen girls in New York City. The next year he put $11,000 into the work. The next year he put himself into the work.

He turned his back upon his business. Oftentimes he would spend no more than two hours a week there, but sometimes it was eighteen or twenty hours a day down among the outcasts trying to win them to the Saviour. Finally, he turned his back upon his business altogether, capitalized it, and gave his whole time and strength going up and down America and other lands pleading with the lost to accept Christ. He was used to the salvation of thousands.

A while ago out here on our Pacific coast, upwards of seventy-five years of age, he was called Home.

Now in the light of eternity, in the light of that great judgment day when we all are to meet our Lord and give account of the deeds done in the body, which of these two men made the best use of his time, of his talents, his opportunities—the man who used all to accumulate a fortune of four million dollars, then left it all, or the man who used his time, his talents, his opportunities, his money, all that he had and was, to win thousands of souls to meet him in a never-ending eternity?

"Death" is one of the darkest words in our language. Some try to paint death in fair colors, but there is nothing fair in death. Death is a hideous thing, an appalling thing, an enemy. Thank God, for the Christian it is a conquered enemy, for "our Saviour Jesus Christ, who hath abolished death, and hath brought life and immortality to light through the gospel" (II Tim. 1:10); nonetheless, death itself is an enemy.

But that terrible word "death" gets the full significance of its dark meaning only when it is put side by side with another word—"soul."

The death of the body is sad, but the death of the soul is appalling. Remember that death, when applied to the soul, does not mean mere nonexistence any more than life means mere existence.

Life means right existence, holy existence, Godlike existence, the kind of being that was revealed in our Lord Jesus Christ (I John 1:2). It means the exaltation, the ennoblement, the glorification, the deification of existence. Death means just the opposite: wrong existence (I Tim. 5:6), debased existence, Devillike existence, the shame, the ignominy, the despair, the agony, the utter ruin of existence.

And when with our open Bible we sit down beside another and lead that one to a definite acceptance of Jesus Christ, we have saved a soul from *death*.

Some years ago two brothers were digging a well in Sauk Centre, Minnesota, in the old-fashioned way—one was down in the hole pitching the sand into a bucket; the other was at the top winding the full buckets up with a windlass. Suddenly they struck quicksand, and the sand commenced to silt in and around the man in the hole. The sand silted in all around him. But there was a plank in the hole and he got underneath that, where there was space enough left to breathe, though buried out of sight.

His brother, hearing his voice, sent for help. All the men of the township gathered together to dig the man out. But as they dug, the sand kept silting in. Night came on; torches and lanterns were brought. Far into the night in relays all the men of the township worked to dig out their imperiled fellowman. Before daylight, they succeeded in uncovering him and dragging him to the surface.

All the men of a township working all night to save one man—was it worthwhile? "Yes," you say, "well worthwhile."

But did you ever work all night to save one soul in peril of eternal death? And when you could not succeed in saving him alone, did you get someone to help you? And when the two could not succeed, did you get a third? And when the three could not succeed, did you get a fourth?

Oh, if we were as dead in earnest in saving the everlasting souls of our fellowmen as we are in saving their poor, perishable, transient, physical lives, it would not be long before there would be such a revival as this old world never saw!

Now look at the word "save." That is one of the great words, the grand words, the stupendous words, the glorious words!

When we were holding our meetings in Liverpool, a clergyman, who seemed on the whole in sympathy with our meetings, came out with a little criticism in one of the Liverpool papers, saying that he wished Dr. Torrey would not use the word "save" so much, that he did not like it.

But I do like it. It is a great, strong and meaningful Bible word. Mind you, it does not mean merely to save from, but to save to; not merely to save from Hell, though that would be enough to command our best endeavor, but to save to Heaven (a real Heaven), to save to holiness, to save to true manhood and true womanhood, to save to knowledge of God and communion with God and likeness to God; to save men and women to become heirs of God and joint-heirs with Jesus Christ, heirs of all God is and all God has.

Suppose a notice were given that on a certain day in the Royal Albert Hall in London, Dr. Torrey of America was to deliver at five o'clock in the morning an address to business and professional men upon a method which he had discovered whereby common ordinary stones picked out of the street or lane or road could be transformed into genuine diamonds of the very first water. And suppose the men of England really knew I had discovered such a process, that I was to tell it on this one occasion only, and that whoever put it in practice must put it into practice before the nightfall of that day. Would there be any men present in the Royal Albert Hall at that early hour in the morning?

The men of London and of England would camp around the Royal Albert Hall the night before; all the railways running into London would run special trains to the city bearing men to that meeting. Within a few minutes after the doors were open, the Royal Albert Hall would be packed with men from the body to the great dome.

As soon as I had described the process, the men would not wait for the close, but would hurry out into the streets and alleys of London, and out into the country roads surrounding the city, and get down on their knees hunting for stones. Then if someone should come along and see some leading banker of London on his knees in the dirt and should ask him, "What are you looking for?" he would hardly stop to answer, in his eagerness to find stones to transform into diamonds before the sunset of that day.

Well, I can tell you that very thing. I can tell you how to go out into the streets and alleys of London, or any other city, how to go out into the byways and lanes of the country, stoop down into the mud and mire of sin and pick up the common, ordinary rude stones of lost souls, and by the glorious art of the soul winner, transform them into diamonds worthy of a place in the Saviour's eternal diadem. Is it worthwhile? Is there anything else in all the world that really is worthwhile?

6. The Work That Brings the Most Abundant Reward

A verse in the book of Daniel should sink into the heart of every young Christian—yes, and of every older Christian, too—Daniel 12:3: "And they that be wise shall shine as the brightness of the firmament, and they that turn many to righteousness as the stars for ever and ever."

Many wish to shine down here in business, in politics, or in society. It is not worthwhile. The brightest star in any galaxy of any earthly glory soon fades.

The brightest star in our business firmament here in America a few years ago went out one day, and not a single newspaper, as far as I could find in the length and breadth of America, did him reverence. The brightest star in our American political firmament of a few presidential campaigns ago, a star that shone with absolutely unrivaled splendor, so that men began to couple this man's name with the two greatest names in American history—the names of Lincoln and of Washington—was popped out one day by the crack of the revolver of a half-crazy anarchist at the Buffalo Pan-American Exposition. Today that man is almost forgotten; few think or speak of McKinley today.

A few years ago it was all Roosevelt; then it was all Taft; now it is all Wilson; and in a very few years we shall have practically forgotten that there ever was a Roosevelt or a Taft or a Wilson.

Take the woman who, a few years ago, was the unquestioned queen of society, a woman who dazzled all with her beauty and bewitched them with the charm of her manner, until great statesmen were willing to lie down and let her walk over them. Where is she today? Dead, forgotten! Another has taken her place. That fair face is now a grinning skull, that shapely form an ungainly skeleton.

It does not pay to shine down here. But they that shine up yonder shall shine as the stars *forever and ever*. We could not, most of us, shine down here if we wished to; but we can all shine up there by turning many to righteousness, by winning others to Christ.

For these six reasons, then, every one of us should make soul winning, not a mere incident, but the very business of our lives.

First, because this is the work our Lord commanded us to do.

Second, because it was the business of life with our Lord Jesus Himself.

Third, because it is the work in which we enjoy the unspeakable blessing of the personal fellowship of Jesus Christ Himself.

Fourth, because it is the work in which alone we can enjoy the fullness of the Holy Spirit's presence and power.

Fifth, because it is the work that produces the most beneficent results.

And sixth, because it is the work that brings the most abundant reward.

Will you make it the business of your life? Bearing it in mind each day, shaping your business and your social engagements and your personal habits and everything else with this in view—the bringing as many definite persons as possible to a definite acceptance of the Lord Jesus Christ?

I never think of our responsibility for being soul winners without thinking of an incident that occurred many years ago in Evanston, Illinois. There Northwestern University is located. Years ago, before it had attained to the dignity of a university, two strong, husky farmer boys came to the college to study—Ed and Will Spencer. Ed was a famous swimmer. Early one morning word came to the college that north of Evanston, between Evanston and Winnetka, there was a wreck a little way off the shore of Lake Michigan. Ed, with the other students and people of the town, hurried northward along the shore toward the wreck. As he ran along a low bluff, He saw a man clinging to the wreckage trying to make the shore. He threw off his superfluous garments and sprang into the lake and swam out, caught hold of the man and the wreckage and made toward shore. He was struck in the head by the wreckage, and the blood from the wound filled his eyes so he could not see, but he succeeded in bringing the man to shore.

Going on a little further, he saw another man clinging to wreckage trying to make the shore. This time he took the precaution to tie a rope around his waist and throw the end to the fellow-students on the shore, and sprang into the lake and swam out, grasped the drowning man, gave the signal, and was pulled ashore. Again and again he sprang into the lake and swam out to rescue some who were drowning, until he had succeeded in bringing a fifth, a sixth, a seventh, an eighth, a ninth and a tenth safe to shore.

By now he was completely exhausted. His companions had made a fire of logs upon the shore, for the morning was cold and raw. He walked over to the fire, so weak that he could hardly stand and stood trying to get a little warmth into his shivering body.

After standing there a few moments he turned, looked out over the lake again and saw another man trying to make the shore. He cried to his companions, "Boys, I am going in again." "No, no, Ed," they cried; "your strength is all gone. You cannot save him. You will only be throwing your own life away. It will be suicide." "I will try, anyway," he cried.

Again he sprang into the lake and swam out and grasped a drowning man and was pulled to shore. And again and again and again and again, until he had brought an eleventh, a twelfth, a thirteenth, a fourteenth and a fifteenth safe to shore.

Then his strength seemed entirely gone. He tottered across the beach to the fire and stood beside it so pale and haggard and emaciated that it seemed as if the hand of death was already upon him. After standing by the fire a few moments he turned and looked out over the lake. In the distance he saw a spar drifting toward a point. To drift around meant certain death. Looking again and seeing a man's head above the spar, he cried, "There is a man trying to save his life!" He looked again and saw a woman's head beside the man's. "Boys," he cried, "there is a man trying to save his wife. I'll help him." "No, no!" they cried; "your strength is all gone. It will be suicide. You cannot help him." "I'll try," he cried.

He sprang again into Lake Michigan and swam out to the spar. Summoning all his fast-dying strength, he put his hands upon it and brought it around the right side of the point to safety.

Then they pulled him in through the breakers; tender hands lifted him from the shore, carried him to his room in the college, and laid him upon his bed apparently unconscious. A fire was built in the grate, and his brother sat in front of the grate to watch developments.

He had been sitting there awhile, looking into the fire and thinking of his brother's bravery, when suddenly he heard a footfall behind him and felt a touch upon his shoulder. Looking up, he saw his brother looking down wistfully into his eyes. "Will," he said, "did I do my best?"

"Why, Ed," Will replied, "you saved seventeen."

He said, "I know it; I know it; but I was afraid I did not do my very best. Will, do you think that I did my very best?"

His brother took him back to bed. During the night he tossed in a semi-delirium. His thought was not about the seventeen whom he had saved, but on the many who went down that day to an early grave. For in spite of his bravery and that of others, many perished that day.

His brother Will, as he sat by the bed, held his hand and tried to calm him. He said, "Ed, you saved seventeen."

"I know it; I know it," he cried, "but, oh, if I could only have saved just one more!"

We all stand beside a stormy sea today—the sea of life. There are wrecks everywhere. Young men, young women, older men, older women, are going down, not to a watery grave but to a hopeless eternity. They are going down all over England. They are going down all over America. They are going down in China and Japan and India. Oh, let us jump in again and again and again and rescue the perishing! And when at last every ounce of strength is gone and we sink utterly exhausted on the shore, let us cry in the earnestness of our desire to save the perishing, "Oh, if I could only have saved just one more!"

> Never a day nears its sunset,
>   Never the sea turneth tide;
> But lamps are gone out in the darkness,
>   Poor sinners for whom Christ died.
>
> Never a day brings its blessings,
>   But bids us with arms stretched wide,
> Persuade them away from their peril,
>   Those sinners for whom Christ died.
>
> Say, are you straitened in spirit?
>   Say, does one passion abide?
> Say, are you spending your heart's blood
>   For sinners for whom Christ died?

ROBERT REYNOLDS JONES, SR.
1883-1968

ABOUT THE MAN:

Called the greatest evangelist of all time by Billy Sunday, Robert Reynolds Jones, better known as Dr. Bob Jones, Sr., was born October 30, 1883, in Shipperville, Alabama, the eleventh of twelve children. He was converted at age 11, a Sunday school superintendent at 12 and ordained at 15 by a Methodist church.

"Dr. Bob" was a Christ-exalting, sin-condemning preacher who preached in the cotton fields, in country churches and in brush arbors. Later he held huge campaigns in American cities large and small, and preached around the world.

Billy Sunday once said of him: "He has the wit of Sam Jones, the homely philosophy of George Stuart, the eloquence of Sam Small, and the spiritual fervency of Dwight L. Moody."

He saw crowds up to 10,000 in his meetings, with many thousands finding Christ in one single campaign.

But Dr. Bob was more than an evangelist. He was also an educator—a pioneer in the field of Christian education, founding Bob Jones University over 60 years ago.

Behind every man's ministry is a philosophy. Dr. Bob's was spelled out in the sentence sermons to his "preacher boys" in BJU chapels. Who has not heard or read some of these: "Duties never conflict!" "It is a sin to do less than your best." "The greatest ability is dependability." "The test of your character is what it takes to stop you." "It is never right to do wrong in order to get a chance to do right."

"DO RIGHT!" That was the philosophy that motivated his ministry, saturated his sermons, and spearheaded his school.

His voice was silenced by death January 16, 1968, but his influence will forever live on and Christians will be challenged to "DO RIGHT IF THE STARS FALL!"

V.

Not Speculation but Soul Winning

BOB JONES, SR.

"When they therefore were come together, they asked of him, saying, Lord, wilt thou at this time restore again the kingdom to Israel? And he said unto them, It is not for you to know the times or the seasons, which the Father hath put in his own power. But ye shall receive power, after that the Holy Ghost is come upon you: and ye shall be witnesses unto me both in Jerusalem, and in all Judaea, and in Samaria, and unto the uttermost part of the earth."—Acts 1:6-8.

Three questions people are prone to ask God: "What are You going to do?" "How are You going to do it?" "When are You going to do it?" Under certain circumstances all these questions are legitimate.

The apostles on this occasion did not ask our Lord and Saviour Jesus Christ what He was going to do but when He was going to do it. The Old Testament prophets taught very definitely that someday the kingdom would be restored to Israel, but when it is to be restored was never revealed in God's Word. We read in verse 29 of chapter 29 of Deuteronomy, "The secret things belong unto the Lord our God: but those things which are revealed belong unto us and to our children for ever...." What for? "...that we may do all the words of this law."

AN OVEREMPHASIS ON PROPHECY
MAY BE HARMFUL

There is a kind of speculation—a morbid speculation—about what God is going to do that is not conducive to the right kind of spiritual living. Such speculation is a positive hindrance to spiritual growth. I have observed certain people whose lives have been blighted spiritually by morbid discussions of prophecy. These are more interested in the Antichrist than they are in the Christ. They are greatly interested in locating the "north country," concerned about the final federation of the Roman Empire and more concerned about a great many things that do not primarily belong in their realm—things not even addressed to the Christian church.

The Bible is God's Book. It reveals His will. But there are in it things He has said to the Jews, the Gentiles, the church, to the individual, to nations and to heads of nations. In studying the Bible we should keep those facts in mind.

We find out what God is going to do by searching the Scriptures, for "all scripture is given by inspiration of God, and is profitable." I want to know all I can about the Bible and what God's Word says about what God's plans are for the Jews, the Gentiles and the church of God. But we should be very careful how we ask God questions.

How is God going to do it? What is His method? He doesn't always tell us. A man said to me one time, "Since the dust of the dead is scattered over the face of the earth, how is God going to raise the dead?" I wouldn't ask that question. God didn't tell us how He is going to gather the dust of the dead. I would say that He will do it by His own power. He said we will be like Jesus Christ one day, and I take it for granted that I shall have a body like He had. God said He was going to raise the dead. He even tells us our bodies will put on incorruption. That should satisfy us.

God does tell us how He is going to do some things. For instance, He tells us how He is going to save people—and that is, by grace. He said, "It pleased God by the foolishness of preaching to save them that believe." That is His method of saving men, and He states that method clearly and definitely in the Bible. But He has not told us how He is going to do many things.

The question of "when" in the Bible is a very interesting one. The apostles asked Jesus, "Wilt thou at this time restore again the kingdom to Israel?" They kept wondering about that. But now He is this side of the tomb. He has been to the cross. He has laid down His life. One of these disciples had tried to keep Him from even going to the cross. When Peter said, "You must not go," Jesus called him "Satan": "Get behind me, Satan."

Now He is the risen Son of God. In answer to the disciples' question, He said, "It is not for you to know the times or the seasons, which the Father hath put in His own power. But there is something you can do: be witnesses unto Me."

NO BIBLE TEACHING IS GOOD UNLESS PRACTICAL

You will find, in studying the Word of God, that all revelations about what God is going to do, how He is going to do it, and when He is going to do it are given for our good.

Take, for instance, the passage where Jesus said there were going to be wars and rumors of wars, earthquakes in divers places, famines, pestilences and trouble. (That is not all He said, but that is about all some people mention.) He went on to say, "When these things begin to come to pass, then look up."

We don't hear many preachers preaching on the "looking up." People talk about the earthquake being a sign of His coming. A thunderbolt bursts and they say, "The Lord is coming!" The lightning flashes and they say, "The Lord is coming!" A famine comes in some part of the earth—"The Lord is coming!" There is an earthquake somewhere—"The Lord is coming!"

God has said to His people, "You are going to have earthquakes, famines, pestilences, trouble and sorrow; but when these things come, look up." Look up when you are in trouble, for redemption is coming. All He said about what was going to happen, He said so they would look up and find comfort.

When you talk about the calamities, curses and judgments that are coming on the earth, don't forget the practical emphasis. Don't look at the earthquake; look up! Don't look at the famine; look up! Don't look at the pestilence; look up! It is all right to listen to the exploding shells and feel the tremble of the earth if you look up. But when you get to looking down and around, you had better look out for you are about to get into trouble!

Paul in writing to Timothy said:

"In the last days perilous times shall come. . . men shall be lovers of their own selves, covetous, boasters, proud, blasphemers, disobedient to parents, unthankful, unholy, Without natural affection, trucebreakers, false accusers, incontinent, fierce, despisers of those that are good, Traitors, heady, highminded, lovers of pleasures more than lovers of God; Having a form of godliness, but denying the power thereof."

Certain Bible teachers go up and down this country saying, "We are living in the close of the age. Darkness is settling. Look at the way children disobey parents. Look at juvenile crime. Look at the dictator and his strut. There is a form of godliness but no power!"

All of that is in the Scripture, and all of it is true; but Paul wasn't writing to Timothy just to tell Timothy to look at all these things. What did he say? I will venture the assertion that you never heard a sermon preached from it: "From such turn away." That is the practical aspect. He is saying, "When this time of awful sorrow and trouble comes on the earth, when children disobey parents, when dictators walk across the continents, when men are heady and high-minded, turn away from those who, under these conditions, 'have a form of godliness but deny the power thereof.'

Concerning the Lord's coming, Paul writes to the Thessalonians:

"I would not have you to be ignorant, brethren, concerning them which are asleep, that ye sorrow not, even as others which have no hope. For if we believe that Jesus died and rose again, even so them also which sleep in Jesus will God bring with him. For this we say unto you by the word of the Lord, that we which are alive and remain unto the coming of the Lord shall not prevent them which are asleep. For the Lord himself shall descend from heaven with a shout, with the voice of the archangel, and with the trump of God: and the dead in Christ shall rise first: Then we which are alive and remain shall be caught up together with them in the clouds, to meet the Lord in the air: and so shall we ever be with the Lord."

Why does he write about these things? The answer is in the next verse: "Wherefore comfort one another with these words." He is saying, "I don't want you to cry: I want to comfort you. I want to bind up your broken heart. I want to comfort you in your sorrow."

If He had said it would not happen for two thousand years, some would have said, "Oh, it will be two thousand years before I see my loved ones again!" Jesus Himself didn't say a word about when it would happen. Paul said, "You are going to see your loved ones again when Jesus comes, and that may be any moment."

There is always a practical emphasis in connection with prophecy, but morbid teachers of prophecy never mention the practical. They create a morbid prying into the Word that is wrong. If God gives the answer in His Word, it is all right to ask, "How?" "Why?" "When?"

MARCHING ORDERS—A GREAT TASK

The apostles asked Jesus, "Are You going at this time to restore the kingdom to Israel?" He answered, "I am going to give you orders. I have something for you to do." With all due respect to those marvelous men who had been with Jesus for three years, wouldn't it have been a little nicer if they had said, "Now, Lord, we have been with You three years. We don't understand everything. We used to wonder about Your miracles and parables. We didn't clearly understand how You were to die. But since You have been raised from the dead, we have begun to see things. What would You have us do? Is there anything we can do for You?" Wouldn't you have thought they would have saluted Him and said, "We are waiting for orders"?

They didn't. They only asked, "When will Jerusalem be the capital of the world? When are we going to get out from under the Roman yoke?" It seems they should have been willing to have left everything in His hands.

If you believe God loves you enough to give His Son to die for you, you can leave your destiny and the future of the universe in His hands. Do not fret and fume. There is only one concern for you and me; and that is, "What does Jesus Christ want us to do?" We have the right to ask and should ask this question, "What is Thy will for my life?" Jesus said to the apostles, "I have a job for you. You are to be witnesses unto Me."

We talk lightly about witnessing. Jesus assigned those men the hardest task any men on earth ever had assigned to them. The job cost most of them their lives. The task which He set before them was a task of blood. It had dungeons, prisons, lashes and hatred connected with it.

Witnessing is never easy. Real witnessing is the hardest job any Christian ever had to do.

The task was so difficult, so hard, that He said, "You are not even ready to start out." They had been with Him three years. They were in His presence then. He was this side of the tomb. A royal stairway was being dropped from the sky to the mountain where they were. Angels were getting ready to roll the royal carpet down the stairway. He was just about to go to Heaven when He said, "I have given you a job you can't do. I am not asking you to stand up now. Do not get on the witness stand here. Sit down for awhile. Go to Jerusalem and sit down there. And remain seated until you get the power to do the job. It is going to cost something. You do not know what you are up against. And you are not fit to do it. You cannot do it. Sit there and wait until I get up to Heaven and have a little talk with My Father. We will fix it so you can do it."

God help all of us to realize we are living in the midst of a chaotic, sin-cursed, Hell-bound world; and the hardest job on earth is to witness for Jesus Christ. Let us quit talking lightly about this business.

BEGIN AT HOME

Notice what they were to do. They were to stand up and tell the world, "This Jesus whom you crucified rose from the dead, and we know it from personal experience." They were to tell it first in Jerusalem. Can you see one of those long-bearded, long-robed Pharisees getting provoked when someone witnessed for Christ? Those old Pharisees had said to the mob, "Ask for His blood!" Cry, "Crucify Him!" Yell, "Crucify Him!" Say it! Go on and say it!

To witness for Jesus Christ meant to condemn the Jews. It meant the condemnation of the religious leaders of that day. It meant the condemnation of the wisdom of the scribes. It meant the condemnation of pagan Rome. It meant the condemnation of the human race. The apostles had no little job. Don't talk lightly about what they were to do.

The Lord was very definite about where they were to go: "Begin at home, at Jerusalem." Some of them argued, "But this is the headquarters of religion. It wouldn't be so bad out in some little outlying province."

I imagine the first person Peter thought of was that little maid to whom he had spoken when he cursed and swore he had never known Jesus. I can imagine Peter thought, *She will think I am crazy.*

I have often wondered if that maid wasn't present on the day of Pentecost. Perhaps she was sticking her head through a window while Peter was preaching. If it were not so tragic, I would laugh every time I read it. Peter was saying, "You have taken and with wicked hands have crucified and slain the Son of God!" I can imagine that little maid's saying, "And where were you, Peter? You didn't drive any nails through His hands, but you were out there swearing to a girl that you never knew Him."

I can imagine that while Peter was preaching on that great occasion, some other person besides the maid who had heard him deny the Lord that night, also said, "Where were you? You are jumping on us, but where were you? You were either crooked or a liar then, or you are crooked or a liar now. Something is wrong."

The apostles were to begin at Jerusalem—at home.

Sometimes the hardest place on earth to witness for Jesus Christ, especially if we haven't lived right, is at home. Dad knows us. Mother knows us. Brother knows us. Sister knows us.

Peter hadn't lived right. Listen! He hadn't lived right after he had been with Jesus Christ. He hadn't lived right after he had heard the Sermon on the Mount. He hadn't lived right after Christ had said, "Upon this rock I will build my church."

It is not easy to stand up at home where you lose your temper, where you are selfish and mean, where you talk impudently to mother and dad, and then stick your Testament under your arm and go off to Sunday school. It isn't an easy business to witness there.

And it isn't so easy to witness to your roommate when you are not living right. She heard you gripe one day. What you said once speaks so loudly that your roommate hasn't heard anything you have said since.

Witnessing isn't easy.

Jesus said, "Witness in Jerusalem." I imagine they said, "Jesus, we can't do it." He said, "I will fix you so you can. I will fix you, Peter, so you can stand up on the Day of Pentecost and shake your fist in the face of the mob. I will give you enough boldness to hunt up that little maid and tell her how wicked you are. I will give you enough power to face the forces of Hell and all the guns mounted upon Hell's battlements."

The Lord Jesus Christ can give you the power to witness to sister, brother, mother, dad and the roommate, too.

A witness must have integrity. When a man takes the stand in a courtroom, the court wants to know whether what he says can be depended upon. It is not easy to be a witness, especially where you live and where you are known; but Jesus says the place to begin is at home, right where you live. By your words and your life, by the way you act, the way you live at home and at work, you are to tell people about Jesus.

YOUR OWN NEIGHBORHOOD BEFORE
CHINA OR AFRICA

The next step was "in all Judaea." That is your neighborhood, we shall say. Don't you go back to your home community or your church and say, "I am a student at Bob Jones College, and I have volunteered for the mission field," if there is a next-door neighbor to whom you have never witnessed! The command to witness in Jerusalem and in all Judaea is as definite as the command to go "unto the uttermost part of the earth."

Young people sometimes talk about being missionaries when what they really want is a trip, the romance of being a missionary, then a furlough to come home. **Nobody is a missionary at heart who doesn't begin at home and then take in the neighborhood about him.**

Mr. Smith has a daughter who isn't a Christian. Mr. Williams has a son who is a sinner. Mr. Jones across the street has a niece who is lost, yet you say, "I am going to China."

If you are going to China, you had better spend a few days in your own neighborhood getting ready for China. I am not trying to keep you from China, but don't pass up your unconverted next-door neighbor on your way to the port from which you are to sail for the foreign mission field.

I have heard people talk about the hardships of missionaries; but it would be easier for some of you to go to China or Africa than it would be to go back home to a person before whom you have not lived right and tell that one you have found Jesus Christ, tell him that you have been saved, tell him that you are sorry for your past life and that you want him to come to Jesus Christ. You might not be as comfortable physically in Africa, but I am not talking now about comfort.

I tell you, it is an easier thing for me to preach to ten thousand people on an occasion than it is to speak to one man about his soul. I have driven myself many a time, in the midst of great evangelistic campaigns, to speak to one person about his soul because that is the hardest thing I have ever had to do. I have done that type work for forty-five years under the whip and lash of my own will.

WE MUST GO TO ALL WHOM CHRIST LOVES

Jesus Christ doesn't call you to "flowery beds of ease." He didn't tell the apostles that was what He was calling them to; so don't you look for it. Jesus said, "Ye shall be witnesses unto me both in Jerusalem, and in all Judaea, and in Samaria...."

I can imagine the apostles said, "Wait a minute! Hold on there! We Jews and those Samaritans don't get along. We don't even go through that country if we can keep from it. We just can't witness to the

Samaritans. We were reared with prejudice against them. There is a vast difference—our traditions clash."

I think Jesus gently told them, "You can't now, but you can when I get through with you. You sit down and wait until My Father and I transact some business up in Heaven; then you can."

I had a letter asking if I would serve on an interracial child evangelism committee to reach the black children of the South. I was reared in the South. My wife was brought up in a county where there were ten blacks to one white. Mrs. Bob Jones, Jr., was brought up in a county where there were probably sixteen or twenty blacks to one white. There was then a social problem in this country. But let me tell you, a white man who is not interested in the soul of a black man has never sat down and waited for the outpouring of the Holy Spirit. A white man who isn't interested in the soul of a yellow man, a black man or any other kind of man anywhere in the world, is not a good witness for the Lord Jesus Christ.

Some people adjust their glasses and say, "I am called to a certain class." Paul was an apostle to the Gentiles, but he didn't confine himself to the Gentiles. Rather he said, "I am all things to all men that by all means I might win some of them. When I am with a Jew, I say, 'I am a Jew. My Saviour was a Jew.' When I am with a Gentile, I say, 'Jesus died for the Gentiles.' He had not Jewish prejudices—not my Lord! He wasn't bound by racial traditions as I was before I was converted. He wasn't a Pharisee with a narrow racial and religious outlook. He came from Heaven's noonday down to the midnight of this earth. He put His arms around the whole race of mankind and locked His nail-pierced hands on the other side and hugged everybody. That is the One I represent!"

THE SAME GOSPEL TO ALL THE WORLD

Let's start at Jerusalem—at home. Don't go to China until you talk to dad. I don't mean you are to stay at home and talk to dad, but you are to witness first at home. Then when you get on the boat and start, witness on the boat. His order was, "As ye go, preach"—not, "Wait until you get there to preach." If you are going off to hold a meeting, do a little preaching on the road.

". . . and unto the uttermost part of the earth." What is to be our message to the Japanese? We are not to jump on them for saying their emperor came down out of Heaven. We are to tell them where our Lord came from. We are to tell them He went to the cross and to the tomb, and that He rose again. We are to tell the Chinese the same thing. We are not to go to India and talk about the "Christ of the Indian Road." Our Christ is not the Christ of the Indian Road. He is the Christ of the Heavenly road! Oh, this thing of adulterating the testimony, sugar-coating it, fixing it up, mixing a little paganism with it, squeezing in a little human philosophy, offering some human ethics!

Jesus didn't say, "I am a way," but "I am *the* way"! The Bible doesn't say that this salvation is in His name and some other person's name. It says, "There is none other name under heaven given among men, whereby we must be saved."

Don't adulterate it! If those apostles, those early witnesses, could stand in the midst of the paganism, the heathenism, the sin and the philosophy of their day, with a Colosseum in Rome and with a dungeon in every town, you and I can stand in our day. But we can't do it without the anointing from on High.

Let us spend more time witnessing and less time on morbid speculation. We want you to know the teachings of the Scriptures. We have a prophetic hour at our annual Bible conference. We want you to know the cross-current of the thoughts and interpretations of the Word of God in our day. But our job is to witness.

Let me put myself on record. I, personally, believe that the shadows of the eveningtime are falling on the Gentile dispensation. I am not a great authority. My opinion doesn't have a great deal of value, but that is my personal feeling about the matter. The day has been long; the evening may be a little long, too. And whether the evening is long or short, I know my job. My time is short any way I look at it. Remember, our business as a Christian, our one obligation, our vocation in the time allotted us is to be a faithful witness of the Lord Jesus Christ by our life and our word of testimony. If some of the interpretations of prophecy with which we do not agree are right, we will still be right if we are true witnesses for the Lord Jesus Christ. We will be in a better fix when Jesus comes than those who do not do that, even if it turned out that we were not right about what we teach concerning prophecy.

Put the emphasis where God puts it. Let us start out today to do the job He has given us to do—witnessing for Him and winning souls to Him.

Prayer: Our Heavenly Father, all of us this morning have failed. There isn't a one of us who can sincerely look into Thy face without a feeling of guilt. We have failed Thee. We haven't been true witnesses. We have been interested in a great many things—sometimes to gratify our own curiosity, sometimes to merely satisfy our longing for knowledge, sometimes just to stimulate our imaginations—and forgotten our main business.

Help Bob Jones College to remember its main business. However high may be our scholastic standards, may people when they think of Bob Jones College, think first of Jesus. When they think of our ministry, may they think first of Jesus. When they think of us in our homes, may they be reminded of Jesus. Help us to the limit of our ability, supported by God's power, to go as far into the world toward the uttermost part of the earth as it is possible for us to go. None of us can go into all the world; but each one of us can start at home and go as far as he can. Some of us can and ought to go overseas. But help us to start today at Bob Jones College. And as we go, help us to preach by the way we live and by everything we do and say. Make us faithful to Thee. We pray in Jesus' name. Amen.

W. B. RILEY
1861-1947

ABOUT THE MAN:

Dr. W. B. Riley was for 45 years pastor of First Baptist Church, Minneapolis, and pastor emeritus three years. His ministry there built this church to the largest membership in the Northern Baptist Convention.

But all over America Dr. Riley moved and swayed audiences. Thousands were won to Christ in great campaigns.

Riley's ministry was one of preaching the Gospel as well as fighting foes of the Gospel. He sometimes prefaced what he wrote with: *"As one who has given his life to the defense and propagation of fundamentalism."*

William Jennings Bryan once called him *"the greatest Christian statesman in the American pulpit."*

The teaching of evolution was a hot issue in his day, so his debates became another phase of his ministry. Bryan had died in 1925, so the mantle for fighting evolution passed to Riley.

One can well compare Dr. Riley with Charles Spurgeon in the largeness of his work: 1. Like that prince of preachers in London, the Minneapolis pastor-evangelist-crusader carried on for several decades an effective ministry; his church grew about as large as Spurgeon's. 2. Like Spurgeon, he turned out many books, including a 40-volume sermon-commentary. 3. Even as Spurgeon, he was a prophet to a whole nation of moral decline and infidelity in the church. 4. As Spurgeon withdrew from the Baptist Union, so Riley withdrew from the Northern Baptist Convention. 5. Like Spurgeon, he founded a growing training college and seminary. 6. Like Spurgeon, he was an editor, editing *The Christian Fundamentalist* and *The Northwestern Pilot*.

Truly, in the days of his strength, Dr. Riley was one of America's greatest preachers.

VI.

Six Essentials in Soul Winning

W. B. RILEY

"He that winneth souls is wise."—Prov. 11:30.

It is clear that one of the most efficient ways of impressing any duty is to lend assistance to its sane discharge. Such is the purpose of this chapter.

Henry W. Longfellow, when yet in his youth, writing his father regarding the choice of a profession, remarked, "I am not sure as yet for what my talents fit me, but I am determined to be eminent in something."

To what extent that determination affected Longfellow's success in life, who can tell? Perhaps none will deny that such an ambition was wholesome for the boy, and both stimulated and directed his energies. Worldly people may have ambitions in many directions; the true Christian's ambitions should find expression in a single course, "He that winneth souls is wise."

The grand old Dr. Sharp of Charles Street Church, Boston, once said, "I would rather have one young man come to my grave and affirm, 'The man who sleeps there arrested me in the course of sin and led me to Christ,' than to have the most magnificent obelisk that ever marked the place of mortal remains."

It was an ambition worthy a Christian! Many consecrated Christians enjoy it and ask often, "How can we succeed in soul winning?"

The answers to this question would not necessarily be the same. No man has given a full and final answer to this question. Our largest hope looks only to helpful suggestions. But if experience, observation and Scripture can league themselves in teaching certain lessons, we believe that those to be mentioned in this chapter are established as worthy of the name of fundamentals.

Get God's Concept of the Soul's Worth

The Scripture voices it, "What shall it profit a man, if he shall gain the whole world, and lose his own soul?" The perishable world is not, in the mind of God, comparable in value to the immortal soul. Christ would never have died to redeem the silver and gold, the cattle upon a thousand hills, the precious stones of land and sea. But no evangelistic Christian doubts that Christ would have been willing to die to redeem a single man; such is God's estimate of a soul.

J. Wilbur Chapman related how some Abyssinians took prisoner a British subject by the name of Campbell. They carried him to the fortress of Magdala and consigned him to a dungeon without showing cause for the deed. It took six months for Great Britain to discover this. Then when she demanded an instantaneous release, King Theodore haughtily refused.

In less than ten days, ten thousand British soldiers were on shipboard sailing down the coast to a point where they disembarked. They then marched seven hundred miles under a burning sun up the mountain heights and unto the very dungeon where the prisoner was hid. There they gave battle. The gates were torn down, the prisoner was lifted upon their shoulders and borne down the mountainside, and thence to the ship.

It cost the British government $25 million to release that man. Such was the value they put upon the life and liberty of one English subject!

But God puts a greater price upon the life and liberty of a single soul. That is why He summoned all Heaven to its redemption and appointed His Son chief Captain and Leader to effect its liberty.

When we get God's conception of the soul's worth, no sacrifice will seem too great to make in the effort to save it; when we get God's conception of a soul's worth, no obstacle will seem insurmountable; when we get God's conception of a soul's worth, we will sacrifice, as did Christ, to reclaim it from sin, believing with Solomon, "He that winneth souls is wise."

Let Us Consecrate Ourselves to Soul Winning

Everyone knows the meaning of consecration—"Set apart as sacred; dedicated to sacredness, and hence separated from common use."

Lyman Abbott illustrates by the two cups made at the command of the king by a jeweler. They came of a common piece of silver and were of exact size and weight. One was put into the hand of the cupbearer to do service to man; one was sent to the temple to do service to God. The latter was consecrated.

Consecration is one of the secrets of successful soul winning. Dr. A. C. Dixon once remarked, "As one walks down the corridor of the Astor House, New York, on his way to the restaurant, he sees a man standing at the door who never looks at your face. His business is to black shoes. He is consecrated to it."

Consecration is more needed in soul winning than intelligence or extensive education. The world's greatest intellectual lights have not always been the world's greatest religious lights, and its most highly educated men are not always its most effective Christians. We have splendid genius in the church. We have more than our share of intellectuality. We think that statistics will prove without question that, as a class, Christian men are the world's best educated. But all of these things, if their possessors be without consecration, count for naught in soul winning.

We have known a boy, of medium ability, at work with his schoolmates, to win more souls between the day of his conversion at seven years of age and the time we parted company from him at twelve, than the average president of a Christian college has to his credit.

Henry Ward Beecher, the Shakespeare of the American pulpit, was led to Christ by a man as black as midnight, whose genius consisted of one thing and one thing only—he knew God and sought the salvation of his fellows.

Many have read *The Last Pages of an Officer's Diary* and recall how that army officer who had but thirty days to live, set about finding someone to show him the way of salvation.

In four or five pulpits, representing as many denominations, he heard men who were eloquent enough, but who gave his soul no assistance in its search after life.

When all but a few days of the thirty had passed and he was growing desperate in his darkness, he rose after a restless night, dressed himself, started for the street and stumbled over the old sexton who, in the early morning, sat upon the doorstep, in Bible study. Seeing that the sexton's Bible was marked and thumbworn, he clutched for it, but the old man held it with a covetousness such as some men show only for silver and gold. When, however, he learned the purpose of the officer, he invited him to a seat at his side, and in ten minutes had shown him the way of salvation and brought him to the point where he could say with Paul, "To live is Christ, and to die is gain" (Phil. 1:21).

Better be a sexton of any church at a small salary, knowing how to point men to the Lamb of God that taketh away the sins of the world, than the most eloquent preacher that ever graced any pulpit without that same knowledge.

Surrender to the Spirit's Counsel

"Yield ye yourselves unto him." He leads the yielded one, and His leadership insures success. It may take one by strange ways, and other men may question one's sanity at times; but, after all, the Spirit-led man is the only sane man.

It was a strange thing for Philip to leave the work in Samaria and go toward the south into a desert way; but it was Spirit-directed, and hence sane. No man plays the fool who follows the leadings of the Holy Spirit, even though that take him against what he would commonly regard his better judgment.

Dr. Wayland Hoyt related an experience in illustration of this point.

When he was pastor in Brooklyn, he was engaged in special meetings. Among those who evinced some interest was a gentleman for whom he had often prayed. He noticed his attendance one week night and thought he ought to speak to him about his soul, but through fear refrained.

Another night when he had returned to his home late, finding himself too nervous to sleep, he was reading in his study. As he read, something seemed to whisper in his ear, *Go and see that man tonight.* But the preacher mentally replied, *It is after twelve o'clock, and he is asleep and everyone in bed.* He read on. But the impression remained and grew. He argued, *It is snowing, and I am tired!* and finally, *I have been working hard all day, and I don't want to go!* But all excuses to the contrary, the Spirit persisted, and at last he yielded and went.

As he touched the man's doorbell, he thought, *What a fool I am to be ringing a man's bell at one o'clock in the morning. He will think I am insane.* But instantly the door opened, and the man stood there fully clothed and said, "Come in; and God bless you. You are the man I have been waiting for all night. Wife and children and the servants are all asleep, but I could not sleep; I felt that I must find Jesus tonight." And the great preacher testified, "It was no trouble to show that man the way, for the Spirit who had guided me had also gone before me."

Is it not a mistake to suppose that only sample saints can enjoy the guidance of the Spirit of God; that only a few of the world's great souls have been selected as the subjects of His special favor?

Many of us are fathers and know the joy of giving good gifts to our children. Let us never forget that God has more pleasure in giving the Holy Spirit to them that ask Him. Let us never refuse when He says, "Go"; for His guidance means good success!

Employ the Sword of the Spirit

It is the divinely appointed instrument of salvation. The man who uses it works under the promise:

"For as the rain cometh down, and the snow from heaven, and returneth not thither, but watereth the earth, and maketh it bring forth and bud, that it may give seed to the sower, and bread to the eater: So shall my word be that goeth forth out of my mouth: it shall not return unto me void, but it shall accomplish that which I please, and it shall prosper in the thing whereto I sent it."—Isa. 55:10,11.

It might be good for us to remember that the promise is to the *preached Word* rather than to the person preaching. Paul declared, "I am not ashamed of the gospel of Christ: for it is the power of God unto salvation to every one that believeth."

"The power of God unto salvation"! Truly it is at once a divinely appointed and potent instrument. "For the word of God is quick, and powerful, and sharper than any twoedged sword, piercing even to the dividing asunder of soul and spirit, and of the joints and marrow, and is a discerner of the thoughts and intents of the heart." Let us use it!

In preaching the Word, claim the promise, "It shall not return unto me void."

A friend who was somewhat in sympathy with higher criticism once asked this question of the writer:

You know E_____, his manner of life, his mental capacity; and you also know Pastor M_____, one of the most beautiful characters in this country, possessed also of one of the most brilliant intellects.

To my knowledge when Pastor M_____ was yet a young man, he prayed God to make him a winner of souls. On Saturdays he would go into his pulpit with his face in the dust and beg that next day he might see men turn to God in great numbers. But nothing came of it. He never was a soul winner; he is not a soul winner now. But E_____, both in his work in his own church while he was yet a pastor, and afterward in various cities about the country as an evangelist, saw thousands of people profess a faith in Christ as the result of his preaching.

Now, he is not a man of any such mental ability, nor of any such high moral character as my friend, Dr. M_____, the pastor mentioned. How explain why God made one a winner of souls, and refused that privilege to the other?

The answer was instant, and, as we believe, correct:

We admit all you say concerning these men, but there is one thing you forget. The pastor you mention is also my friend, and I ardently admire him for his moral character and his great brain; but never have I heard him so much as make mention of the blood of Jesus Christ. The heart of the Gospel has been left out of his preaching, and his sermons have been brilliant philosophical discussions, destitute often of even a quotation from the Word after he had parted company with his text. Our friend E_____ makes much of the blood, and adds Scripture to Scripture in his discussion. Let us remember that God's promise is to the preaching of the Word and not to eloquent utterance!

Whenever a man reaches the point where he feels it is as profitable to take a text from Shakespeare as from Paul, he must expect a fruitless ministry. Whenever a personal worker has nothing better than human arguments or even an exceptional experience to rehearse before a man under conviction, he need not look to see the man come to Christ. It is the Word of God that wins from sin to the Saviour; and without it, success in soul winning is unknown. By way of illustration, a personal experience:

It was on a Christmas evening at the Union Mission in Minneapolis. Many of the men present in that downtown mission were drunk; some were so boisterous that they had to be ejected to save the service from confusion.

When the sermon was finished, an opportunity was given for prayer. About a dozen men came forward, among them one who looked far worse than any of his unfortunate fellows. Drink had clothed him in rags, bloated his face and dulled his mind.

Once at his side, we called his attention to the promise in John 6:37, "All that the Father giveth me shall come to me: and him that cometh to me I will in no wise cast out." We emphasized it by reading it three or four times. Then we urged him to read it, which he did. We requested a second reading, a third, a fourth, a fifth, until evidently the meaning of the promise was clearly apprehended.

Then after prayer, we parted company. Eight days went by, and in a Sunday afternoon meeting for men only, where several came out for Christ, this man of the mission meeting was among them. He was sober, clean, clear-eyed; so marvelously improved in appearance that we failed to recognize him at first.

When he had made himself known, we involuntarily remarked, "Mr. Carroll, you look like another man." To which he replied, "By the grace of God, I am another man. I trusted that promise of John 6:37, and He has kept it. I have been sober ever since that night, with no desire even to use tobacco. I have been able daily to make an honest living, and now I have a new lease on life, or rather, a lease on a new life!" Up to the day when he sickened and died, he was a most faithful Christian.

Employ the sword of the Spirit! Mr. Spurgeon's maxim had occasion. It was often addressed to his students: "Have your own Bible, and turn to the passages showing the way of salvation. The most successful soul winner I know takes men captive by the sword of the Spirit."

Is not that what Paul meant when he wrote to Timothy, "Study to shew thyself approved unto God, a workman that needeth not to be ashamed, rightly dividing the word of truth"?

In This, the Divinest Work, Be Direct

Here Christ is our example. No indirectness with Him! To the fisherman He said, "Follow me"; to the publican, "Come after me"; to Nicodemus, "Ye must be born again"; to the woman at Sychar, "If thou knewest the gift of God, and who it is that saith to thee, Give me to drink; thou wouldest have asked of him, and he would have given thee living water."

There are teachers who advise that we adroitly introduce our Jesus; that we engage with men upon all the subjects in which they are interested and watch for an opportunity to work around to the great theme of the soul and its salvation. Seminary professors, whose memory we revere, great and good men of God, taught us after this manner! But there is no warrant in the Word.

Christ's example was also the apostolic method. Let us read the first chapter of John and see how the early disciples won their associates; or the second chapter of Acts or the fourth or the eighth or the ministry of Paul as recorded in that same book. Whatever else these apostles did, directness in appeal to men characterized every one of them who became a soul winner.

Andrew "findeth his own brother Simon, and saith unto him, We have found the Messias, which is, being interpreted, the Christ. And he brought him to Jesus." There is our sample for personal work. There is no indirectness suggested by that process, nor by any other Scripture. We believe the indisposition to speak to men frankly and at once about their souls is suggested by the adversary.

Dr. Wharton once addressed the students of the Southern Baptist Seminary. In the course of his remarks from the text, "Go out into the highways and hedges, and compel them to come in," he said:

> During the war I was attending Roanoke College at Salem, Virginia. For several days it was reported that General Averill, in command of a heavy force, was on a raid through Virginia and aiming at Salem to tap the Virginia and Tennessee Railroad at that point, and thus cut off the supplies coming to Lynchburg.
>
> One morning the cry was heard, "The Yankees are coming!" Looking up the street, we saw them riding pell-mell into town, horses' hoofs clattering, sabers rattling, men shouting, women and children flying to their homes, and fear and confusion falling upon all.
>
> A good number of us young fellows took to our heels for the woods about half a mile away. When nearly across the field, I heard several shrill, hissing sounds in my vicinity, followed by sharp reports of firearms. Looking back, I saw there was a man after me on horseback, and he seemed to be shooting at every jump.
>
> I reached the fence and fell over it and lay as flat on the ground as a lizard on a log. Presently I heard him say, "Come out of there, Sir!" I looked up, and he had a great big sharpshooter levelled at me, and the hammer of it was saying, "Be quick, or you are gone."
>
> "Come out," the fellow said. The end of the pistol was as big as a stovepipe. There was only one thing to do. "Yes, Sir," I said, "I am going to. Don't shoot!" and out I came. Now I call that personal work. He was after me, and he got me!

Why cannot we as Christian soldiers be as courageous and as direct in our methods, that we may capture men for Him?

How much we lose by indirectness, who can measure?

A pastor in New York City walked home with a druggist, watching for an opportunity to speak to him about his soul, but did not find it. Once at his door, the druggist urged the pastor to come in. He accepted, spent an hour in conversation, but saw no chance to speak of Christ. After he had put on his overcoat and was ready to leave, the druggist laid a hand on his shoulder and said, "Can't you stay a little longer and pray with us? I have been greatly interested for my soul and shall never be satisfied until I am a saved man."

There are those who have been in rebellion against Christ, who have grown tired of it and long for surrender and, like the Confederates at Richmond, will be exceedingly glad when the day comes when they are conquered and peace has been declared between them and Him whose right it is to reign.

Let Philip teach us:

"Philip findeth Nathanael, and saith unto him, We have found him, of whom Moses in the law, and the prophets, did write, Jesus of Nazareth, the son of Joseph. And Nathanael said unto him, Can there any good thing come out of Nazareth? Philip saith unto him, Come and see."

Directness in soul winning is after the Divine example and under Divine benediction.

With Whatever Success Be Dissatisfied

The man who is satisfied in soul winning is stultified in spiritual interest. We remember how it is related of the great Danish sculptor, Thorwaldsen, that, having finished, to his own satisfaction, a piece of work, he sat in gloom with a sob in his soul and declared that, having once realized his ideal, he feared that henceforth he should accomplish nothing.

The man who is satisfied in soul winning has better occasion for such fear. Paul had seen scores turn to God in consequence of his preaching before he ever penned the words, "I have great heaviness and continual sorrow in my heart. For I could wish that myself were accursed from Christ for my brethren, my kinsmen according to the flesh."

One may rejoice in the success given, but to be satisfied with it would be to grow indifferent to the dying about us.

At college we had a roommate who seemed sad and dispirited. One day we turned upon him and asked, "Why are you not more happy?

Your father provides you all the money you need. You have enjoyed good school advantages all your life. In person you are attractive, and you are popular, and yet there is a gloom over your spirit."

He answered by reciting an experience, the particulars of which were well known to me. It involved the rescue of three persons from drowning. But while he was about the work, three others went down, to be seen no more until the grappling hooks reclaimed the dead. And, concluding the story, he remarked, "Never since that day have I been entirely happy because the cries of those drowning ones are still in my ears."

Ah, beloved, is not one difficulty with the present-day evangelism the fact that our ears are deaf? The cries of the drowning are not in them. The men about us are going down, and we know it, but we are not deeply disturbed over it. If we were, our very distress would convert us into soul winners every one.

We have not forgotten Moody's report of his first impulse in soul winning. A young man, teaching a class of girls in Moody's Sunday school in Chicago, sickened with consumption and was about to die. He seemed in such distress that Moody sought to comfort him by saying that he had done better with that class of girls than anyone else. Under the hands of others they had seemed incorrigible. But he was so weighted down with sorrow because he had failed to bring even one of them to Christ that Moody hired a carriage and drove the young man to the distant homes of every one of those girls.

According to Moody's report, he entered each home and said, "I have just come to ask you to come to the Saviour." And then he prayed as Moody had never heard a man pray.

For ten days he labored, and at the end of the ten days every one of that large class had yielded to Christ. When the train was moving to take him to the South, they stood in the Michigan Southern depot, tearful at parting from this noble teacher, yet joyful in their newly-found hope.

And as he left for that Southland, to die there, as it afterward proved, he went, having illustrated what ten days' work for God can do when one converts his dissatisfaction into soul winning; yes, into inspiration in service!

TOM MALONE
1915-

ABOUT THE MAN:

Tom Malone was converted and called to preach at the same moment! At an old-fashioned bench, the preacher took his tear-stained Bible and showed Tom Malone how to be saved. He accepted Christ then and there. Arising from his knees in the Isbell Methodist Church near Russellville, Alabama, he shook the circuit pastor's hand; and this bashful nineteen-year-old farm boy announced: "I know the Lord wants me to be a preacher."

Backward, bashful and broke, yet Tom borrowed five dollars, took what he could in a cardboard suitcase and left for Cleveland, Tennessee. Immediately upon arrival at Bob Jones College, Malone heard a truth that totally dominated his life and labors for the Lord ever after—soul winning!

That day he won his first soul! The green-as-grass Tom, a new convert himself, knew nothing of soul-winning approaches or techniques. He simply asked the sinner, "Are you a Christian?" No. In a few minutes that young man became Malone's first convert.

Since that day, countless have been his experiences in personal evangelism.

Mark it down: Malone began soul winning his first week in Bible college. And he has never lost *the thirst* for it, *the thrill* in it, nor *the task* of it since. Pastoring churches, administrating schools, preaching across the nation have not deterred Tom Malone from this mainline ministry.

It is doubtful if young Malone ever dreamed of becoming the man he is today. He is now Doctor Tom Malone, is renowned in fundamental circles for his wise leadership and great preaching, is pastor of the large Emmanuel Baptist Church of Pontiac, Michigan, Founder and President of Midwestern Baptist Schools, and is eagerly sought as speaker in large Bible conferences from coast to coast.

Dr. John R. Rice often said that Dr. Tom Malone may be the greatest gospel preacher in all the world today!

VII.

Two-by-Two Soul Winning

TOM MALONE

"And he called unto him the twelve, and began to send them forth by two and two; and gave them power over unclean spirits."—Mark 6:7.

God's scriptural pattern for soul winning as established by Jesus Himself is a two-by-two method. This is certainly not saying that one person cannot win souls by himself, for this was also done many times in Bible days, like the personal work of Philip who won the Ethiopian to Christ, and of Jesus who won Nicodemus, and of the woman of Samaria, and many others!

It does seem, however, that God has established a scriptural pattern of two-by-two soul-winning work. Whenever churches are seeing great numbers saved, without exception you will find a great emphasis being placed on a two-by-two organized visitation program.

There is a great verse in the book of Ecclesiastes which bears out this emphasis on a two-by-two effort to win souls. "Two are better than one; because they have a good reward for their labour" (Eccles. 4:9). Here God says that two do a better job than one and the results of their labor are greater. When there are two, usually there is more prayer, more confidence and sometimes between the two, better answers can be given to questions often asked by sinners.

"For if they fall, the one will lift up his fellow: but woe to him that is alone when he falleth; for he hath not another to help him up. Again, if two lie together, then they have heat: but how can one be warm alone? And if one prevail against him, two shall withstand him; and a threefold cord is not quickly broken."—Eccles. 4:10-12.

Yes, two-by-two soul winning from house to house is God's greatest method of New Testament evangelism. "And daily in the temple, and in every house, they ceased not to teach and preach Jesus Christ" (Acts 5:42).

I. SOME BIBLE EXAMPLES

Now let us notice some instances in the ministry of Jesus where He sent out two people to get the job done.

1. Two Disciples Sent to Bring the Borrowed Colt

"And it came to pass, when he was come nigh to Bethphage and Bethany, at the mount called the mount of Olives, he sent two of his disciples, Saying, Go ye into the village over against you; in the which at your entering ye shall find a colt tied, whereon yet never man sat: loose him, and bring him hither."—Luke 19:29,30.

This is the occasion of His triumphal entry into Jerusalem one week before His crucifixion. Two disciples were sent to bring the little beast of burden upon which the blessed Son of God rode into the city of Jerusalem and wept as He entered the city of lost multitudes. "And when he was come near, he beheld the city, and wept over it" (Luke 19:41).

2. He Sent Two to Prepare the Last Supper

"Then came the day of unleavened bread, when the passover must be killed. And he sent Peter and John, saying, Go and prepare us the passover, that we may eat."—Luke 22:7,8.

"And he sendeth forth two of his disciples. . . ."—Mark 14:13.

Here two disciples are sent to locate and prepare the upper room and the passover supper for our Lord and His disciples. At this supper the betrayer Judas is revealed.

3. Two Men or Angels at the Empty Tomb

"And it came to pass, as they were much perplexed thereabout, behold, two men stood by them in shining garments."—Luke 24:4.

To help establish the reality of the resurrection, two angels were seen inside the empty tomb of Jesus by the first believers at the tomb.

4. Two Angels at the Ascension

"And while they looked steadfastly toward heaven as he went up,

behold, two men stood by them in white apparel; Which also said, Ye men of Galilee, why stand ye gazing up into heaven? this same Jesus, which is taken up from you into heaven, shall so come in like manner as ye have seen him go into heaven."—Acts 1:10,11.

What a sweet message these two had to give: "This same Jesus...shall so come in like manner as ye have seen him go into heaven."

5. Two Heavenly Messengers Appeared on the Mount of Transfiguration

"And, behold, there talked with him two men, which were Moses and Elias."—Luke 9:30.

Two men, Moses and Elijah, came from Heaven and met with Jesus on the Mount of Transfiguration. Why not only one man? Because God's Word is establishing the two-by-two method of witnessing.

6. Seventy Unnamed Disciples Sent Out Two by Two

"After these things the Lord appointed other seventy also, and sent them two and two before his face into every city and place, whither he himself would come."—Luke 10:1.

Many wonderful lessons are to be learned from these seventy.

(1) They were divinely appointed and sent out by Jesus. "After these things the Lord appointed other seventy also, and sent them two and two before his face into every city and place, whither he himself would come" (Luke 10:1).

(2) They were sent out into a great and fruitful harvest. "Therefore said he unto them, The harvest truly is great, but the labourers are few: pray ye therefore the Lord of the harvest, that he would send forth labourers into his harvest" (Luke 10:2).

(3) They were unnamed.

(4) They were untrained. "...lambs among the wolves" (Luke 10:3).

(5) They received great joy from their service. "And the seventy returned again with joy, saying, Lord, even the devils are subject unto us through thy name" (Luke 10:17).

(6) They were given power over the enemy. "Behold, I give unto you power to tread on serpents and scorpions, and over all the power of the enemy: and nothing shall by an means hurt you" (Luke 10:19).

(7) They had revealed unto them the truth of God, hidden from those who did not go out. "In that hour Jesus rejoiced in spirit, and said, I thank thee, O Father, Lord of heaven and earth, that thou hast hid these things from the wise and prudent, and hast revealed them unto babes: even so, Father; for so it seemed good in thy sight" (Luke 10:21).

7. Peter and John Went Out Two by Two

"Now Peter and John went up together into the temple at the hour of prayer, being the ninth hour."—Acts 3:1.

"Now when they saw the boldness of Peter and John, and perceived that they were unlearned and ignorant men, they marvelled; and they took knowledge of them, that they had been with Jesus."—Acts 4:13.

Peter and John are linked together after Pentecost, going out in this two-by-two soul-winning ministry.

8. Paul and Barnabas Went Out Two by Two

"As they ministered to the Lord, and fasted, the Holy Ghost said, Separate me Barnabas and Saul for the work whereunto I have called them."—Acts 13:2.

9. Paul and Silas and Barnabas and John Sent Out Two by Two

"And the contention was so sharp between them, that they departed asunder one from the other: and so Barnabas took Mark, and sailed unto Cyprus; And Paul chose Silas, and departed."—Acts 15:39,40.

II. WHY DOES GOD BLESS THIS NEW TESTAMENT TWO-BY-TWO SOUL-WINNING METHOD?

"Two are better than one . . . ."

1. Because It Uniquely Assures the Presence of Jesus

"For where two or three are gathered together in my name, there am I in the midst of them."—Matt. 18:20.

No one would say that Jesus is not with any one believer when he or she goes out to witness for Jesus and to win souls, but Jesus has promised a special consciousness of His presence when two soul winners go out together. There is a sweet and blessed confidence that comes to the heart of a Christian when he knows he is doing God's work in God's way. Mrs. Malone and I have been going out together in visitation work for many years, and I am certain there have been many, many instances where a soul was saved because there were two of us.

I recall one evening visiting a rest home where we had gone to see an 80-year-old lady who was lost and very ill and soon to die. I stood at her bed for ten or fifteen minutes and prayerfully tried to lead her to the Lord, but was not able to do so. Mrs. Malone stood by waiting and praying. When I felt I had said all that could be said and was about to leave, burdened that that poor lady was still lost, Mrs. Malone stepped up to the bed. She took the bony little hand in hers and in two or three minutes led the poor dying lady into the saving knowledge of Jesus Christ.

Yes, "Two are better than one. . . ."

Jesus has promised His glorious presence when two go out together to witness to those for whom Christ died. We read of two disciples who were walking from Jerusalem to the little village of Emmaus, after Jesus arose from the dead. "And, behold, two of them went that same day to a village called Emmaus, which was from Jerusalem about threescore furlongs" (Luke 24:13). After the revelation of His presence with them that day, they testified that their hearts burned within them. "And they said one to another, Did not our heart burn within us, while he talked with us by the way, and while he opened to us the scriptures?" (Luke 24:32).

We, too, can go out two by two with a burning heart because of His glorious presence.

2. Because He Has Promised in a Unique Way to Answer Prayer When Two Pray

"Again I say unto you, That if two of you shall agree on earth as touching any thing that they shall ask, it shall be done for them of my Father which is in heaven."—Matt. 18:19.

Prayer has a great part in soul winning. "Brethren, my heart's desire and prayer to God for Israel is, that they might be saved" (Rom. 10:1).

How many, many times have I gone with another to win souls and while one talked to the sinner, the other talked to God. Remember that in Bible times some great things happened when two soul winners prayed together and sought the salvation of the lost.

How true this was in the city of Philippi. "And at midnight Paul and Silas prayed, and sang praises unto God: and the prisoners heard them. And suddenly there was a great earthquake, so that the foundations of the prison were shaken: and immediately all the doors were opened, and every one's bands were loosed" (Acts 16:25,26). As they prayed the earthquake shook the prison, and deep and inescapable conviction came upon the jailer and he was saved, along with his whole family.

I recall going into a home some years ago with one of the young men of our church. The wife was a devout Christian, but for years the man of this home had rejected Christ and resisted being saved. Many had witnessed to him, but seemingly to no avail.

On this occasion his wife sat in the living room weeping while I pleaded for him to be saved. But he seemed unmoved. When it seemed that Satan would get the victory and keep him from being saved, something unexpected happened. That young man, my calling partner, suddenly dropped down on his knees in the middle of the room and began praying. As I pleaded with this poor lost sinner to be saved, he looked intently at the praying man in the middle of the room, then in a moment or two he began to weep and pray himself and beg God to save him.

"Two are better than one. . . ."

3. Because It Is the Way of Propriety

When two go together, under no circumstances can their good be evil spoken of. Generally it is not proper for a man to go alone to call on a lady or a woman to go alone to call on a man. However, when they are "two by two," together, any possibility of their motives being misjudged is virtually eliminated.

Certainly the Lord has thought of everything, and it is only reasonable and practical to believe that the Lord Himself knew that this two-by-two method of visitation would solve this problem.

Many times I have been keenly aware that I was gaining access into a home because there were two of us, when only one would have been refused an entry.

Had Joseph not gone into the house of Potiphar alone, he would not have been falsely accused and had to spend two years in prison.

"Two are better than one. . . ."

4. Two-by-Two Is the Way of Production

I repeat: the Bible does not teach that one person is not to witness;

and experience has taught us that one believer has often won souls all alone. However, the two-by-two method is more productive. In the case of the Ethiopian eunuch being won by Philip, the eunuch was ready to be saved. He was already reading the 53rd chapter of Isaiah, the chapter about God's Lamb dying for all our sins. Any one sincere Spirit-led Christian could have led him into the knowledge of Christ. But sinners are not always as ready.

God had two men, Peter and John, to go to the Gate Beautiful so that the lame man could be saved and healed. Why? God must have known this was a two-man job.

God had two men that night in the Philippian jail. Two men prayed, two men sang praises to God. Why? This work at Philippi was a two-man job.

Lydia was saved at the riverside; the demon-possessed girl was saved on the streets; the jailer was saved in the midst of the debris of the ruined prison; and all his family were saved in their home. This was a two-man piece of work. This is God's New Testament way of house-to-house evangelism through our Bible-believing churches.

Many times, by nature of the circumstances, there are more people than one person can talk to effectively.

"Two are better than one...."

5. The Two-by-Two Method Is the Way of Planning

It may take a little more planning for two to go out together. There must be a mutual time set to go, a mutual place agreed upon to meet. There must be a mutuality as to whom to call on. It involves more planning, more detail, more fellowship. This is all for a purpose. The unsaved are smarter than we think they are. Two coming together makes a greater impression on them. Which would impress you more: one salesman calling to sell you a vacuum sweeper, or would you be more impressed if two salesmen came together to your house to sell you a sweeper?

One night I went out calling with a new convert. In one house he gave a very good and effective testimony. But during his testimony he made this statement: "We just happened to be in your neighborhood and thought we would stop by and see you."

When we left the home, he said, "Pastor, how did I do? Do you have any suggestions?"

"Yes," I said, "I do have a suggestion. Don't ever say, 'We just happened to be in your neighborhood and just happened to drop by.' This was planned. You and I arranged to get together and purposely went to that man's house. To make him think it was rather incidental or even accidental is to destroy the effectiveness of the visit."

The two-by-two visitation is the planned method of soul winning.

It does take some definite planning to set aside a definite time, to prayerfully choose the right partner, to wisely use the time, to visit the most likely prospect. It is a planned method.

"Two are better than one...."

6. The Two-by-Two Method Is the Partnership Method

Paul said that Titus was his "partner" in the work of the Lord. "Whether any do enquire of Titus, he is my partner and fellowhelper concerning you: or our brethren be enquired of, they are the messengers of the churches, and the glory of Christ" (II Cor. 8:23).

The disciples were "partners" in the occupation of fishing:

"And they beckoned unto their partners, which were in the other ship, that they should come and help them. And they came, and filled both the ships, so that they began to sink.... And so was also James, and John, the sons of Zebedee, which were partners with Simon. And Jesus said unto Simon, Fear not; from henceforth thou shalt catch men. And when they had brought their ships to land, they forsook all, and followed him."—Luke 5:7-11.

Who will my partner be? It has been a sweet experience for many years to go with my wife. I believe that every preacher and wife should do a great deal of soul winning and visitation together.

It is good to take at least one new convert out each week and train him in this two-by-two, house-to-house, soul-winning work. It would also be effective if a pastor could go at least two hours a week with one of his deacons. Then a pastor should take one of his young people out for a period of soul winning each week. If this were done, our churches would be set on fire. Many precious souls would be saved, and many good soul winners would be trained. How wonderful for a father to take his son soul winning and a mother take her daughter!

What blessed fellowship, what sweet closeness there is between two believers when they go out to win lost souls to Christ! The Bible plainly teaches this togetherness in soul winning: "For we are labourers together with God: ye are God's husbandry, ye are God's building" (I Cor. 3:9).

We not only work "with God"—and what a privilege this is!—but we 'labor together.'

"Two are better than one. . . ."

7. The Two-by-Two Method of Soul Winning Is the Way of Proof

"But if he will not hear thee, then take with thee one or two more, that in the mouth of two or three witnesses every word may be established."—Matt. 18:16.

God's way of definitely proving something is to have not less than two witnesses attesting to that fact. This was not only true in the Old Testament days, "At the mouth of two witnesses. . ." (Deut. 17:6); it was also true in the New Testament times. Jesus even taught that besides His own witness concerning Himself, there was also the witness *of the Holy Spirit* concerning Jesus: "There is another that beareth witness of me; and I know that the witness which he witnesseth of me is true" (John 5:32). ". . .that in the mouth of two or three witnesses every word may be established" (Matt. 18:16). Even in the Tribulation, this principle will be true: "And I will give power unto my two witnesses. . ." (Rev. 11:3).

When two witnesses go to tell the sweet story of Jesus to a lost soul, then he will be without excuse at the judgment bar of God. The truth of the Gospel has been established before him from the mouth of two of God's witnesses. How often He reminds us that that is just exactly what we are, "his witnesses." "But ye shall receive power, after that the Holy Ghost is come upon you: and ye shall be witnesses unto me both in Jerusalem, and in all Judaea, and in Samaria, and unto the uttermost part of the earth" (Acts 1:8). "And ye are witnesses of these things" (Luke 24:48).

Yes, God's most wonderfully blessed way is the two-by-two, house-to-house, soul-winning way.

"And daily in the temple, and in every house, they ceased not to teach and preach Jesus Christ."—Acts 5:42.

"And how I kept back nothing that was profitable unto you, but have shewed you, and have taught you publickly, and from house to house."—Acts 20:20.

"Two are better than one. . . ."—Eccles. 4:9.

HYMAN APPELMAN
1902-1983

ABOUT THE MAN:

Dr. Appelman was born in Russia and was reared and trained in the Jewish faith. He could speak many languages. The family moved to America in 1914. Dr. Appelman graduated with honors from Northwestern University and from DePaul University where he was one of the highest in the class and was awarded a scholarship. He received his license to practice law from DePaul Law School and was a trial lawyer in Chicago before his conversion—from 1921-25.

At age 28 he was converted. His Jewish family, then living in Chicago, disowned him. His father said to him, *"When your sides come together from hunger and you come crawling to my door, I will throw you a crust of bread as I would any other dog."*

Feeling a definite call to preach, he attended Southwestern Baptist Theological Seminary in Fort Worth from 1930-33.

In 1933 he was elected to be one of the State Evangelists for Texas; he faithfully ministered for eight years in this capacity for the Southern Baptist Convention. Later he launched into larger meetings, both in Texas and outside, and soon was spending some time, year after year, in a foreign country. His meetings were large meetings, with hundreds, sometimes thousands, of conversions in each.

Dr. Appelman made eight or nine trips around the world and several trips to Russia as an evangelist.

His schedule left one breathless. It was hard to find a day in his long ministry of fifty-three years that he was not preaching somewhere. He averaged two weeks at home out of a year. That was the intenseness of a Jew! Of this Jew, at least! His prayer life, hard work and biblical preaching reminded one of the Apostle Paul.

Dr. Appelman was the author of some 40 books.

VIII.

Paralyzed People

HYMAN J. APPELMAN

(Sermon preached at Winona Lake Sword Conference on Evangelism, Winona Lake, Indiana, July, 1946)

"And again he entered into Capernaum after some days; and it was noised that he was in the house. And straightway many were gathered together, insomuch that there was no room to receive them, no, not so much as about the door: and he preached the word unto them. And they come unto him, bringing one sick of the palsy, which was borne of four. And when they could not come nigh unto him for the press, they uncovered the roof where he was: and when they had broken it up, they let down the bed wherein the sick of the palsy lay. When Jesus saw their faith, he said unto the sick of the palsy, Son, thy sins be forgiven thee. But there were certain of the scribes sitting there, and reasoning in their hearts, Why doth this man thus speak blasphemies? who can forgive sins but God only? And immediately when Jesus perceived in his spirit that they so reasoned within themselves, he said unto them, Why reason ye these things in your hearts? Whether is it easier to say to the sick of the palsy, Thy sins be forgiven thee; or to say, Arise, and take up thy bed, and walk? But that ye may know that the Son of man hath power on earth to forgive sins, (he saith to the sick of the palsy) I say unto thee, Arise, and take up thy bed, and go thy way into thine house. And immediately he arose, took up the bed, and went forth before them all; insomuch that they were all amazed, and glorified God, saying, We never saw it on this fashion."—Mark 2:1-12.

There is more to this tremendous story than appears on the surface. In addition to giving the Pharisees, the scribes and the rest of the critical Jews a sign of His power to forgive sins, the Lord Jesus Christ was teaching us a double lesson. First, He IS able to forgive all sin. Second,

He can also say to a man, "Arise, take up thy bed, and walk." The Lord Jesus Christ has the power to keep a man continuing to walk in the newness of life, in the carrying on of a spiritual, scriptural, separated, sanctified activity as a Christian.

I believe that the lesson contained in this wondrous passage may be covered by three words, all applicable to us today. They are the very essence, the very heart, the very soul of evangelism, of Christianity, of preaching. There is a much needed lesson here that every one of us must carry away from this place if we are to come back next year rejoicing, bringing our trophies with us, instead of being defeated.

The three things I wish to call to your attention are: THE PARALYZED SINNERS, THE POWERFUL SAVIOUR, THE PERSISTENT SAINTS.

There was this man sick of the palsy, a definite illustration and demonstration of the fact that every man, woman and child in the world who is not a Christian is paralyzed in sin. There is the powerful Saviour, the Lord Jesus Christ, able to save unto the uttermost all them that come unto God by Him. There are the persistent saints, willing, ready and anxious to press the battle to the gates, to keep on keeping on until they bring the seekers, the sinners, to the feet of Christ our Redeemer.

I. PARALYZED SINNERS

I sincerely wish we had time to go into full detail in this matter of paralyzed sinners. Very early in my ministry the Lord taught me a lesson, using a Baptist deacon to press it upon my heart. I was in a seminary and having a bit of a difficult time. There were problems there over which I had no control. For awhile I thought of leaving the seminary, of quitting the ministry. I am not at liberty to tell you what it was all about, for it reflects on people whom I love and admire. I was blue about it.

I came to my church in Oklahoma, the half-time church of which I was pastor. Something went wrong there, too. Instead of continuing to preach to them the beauties of the unsearchable riches of Christ, I scolded them—Christians and sinners—for not getting right and staying right with the Lord. I started scolding Saturday night, I scolded Sunday morning, I scolded Sunday afternoon, I scolded Sunday night. The more I scolded, the worse I felt and the worse they felt. But somehow I did not know how to stop. I didn't have sense enough to know how to turn away from the gloom that had possessed me.

I went home that night with a cotton farmer. (There was no hotel, of course, in that little country community.) While we were sitting around the table having a bedtime snack, I asked him some questions: "Brother Johnson, what was the matter with the services last night, this morning, this afternoon and tonight?"

"Preacher, will you listen to a plain word from a man old enough to be your daddy?"

"I surely will. That is why I am asking you. Make it plumb plain, too. Don't spare me."

"Son, you have never been on a farm, have you?"

"No. I do not know very much about a farm—I know nothing about it, to tell you the truth."

"Well, son, we farmers learned a long time ago that you can throw corn to a bunch of chickens and scare them into the next county."

That is all he said. I know that chickens love corn, so I couldn't understand how throwing corn at chickens would scare them away.

I thought about it most of the night. The next morning at the breakfast table I spoke to Brother Johnson again. "Brother Johnson, how can you scare chickens by throwing corn to them when that is what they love to eat?"

"Preacher, it's all in the way you throw it."

Even a Jew woke up! [The author, Appelman, was a Jew.] You must not be too critical of sinners. They are blind, sick, feverish. When they criticize and find fault with us, when they lash out and ridicule us, when they curse us, it is not the sinner speaking but his demon-possessed soul.

I remember a man in Vickery, Texas, where I was pastor—Lee Gering—a night watchman for the Texas Highway Department, caring for their supplies in a great barnlike structure a mile or two from where my church was. Almost every night when I was there, I would drive out to his place and while he was eating supper, talk to him about Christ.

Finally, he got so angry with me that he told his wife (you will forgive me, I am quoting him): "If that _____ Jew were lying in the highway with his throat cut and bleeding to death, I wouldn't stop to talk to him nor to help him even if I knew I could save his life. If I did, just as sure as sure is sure, that _____ Jew would start talking about his _____ church."

That was a compliment, in a way, wasn't it? At least a left-handed or a back-handed compliment.

He was the last man I baptized as pastor. He surrendered to the Lord

Jesus Christ a little before I resigned to become an evangelist. To him I am not a "_____ Jew" anymore. It is altogether different now. You see, it was not Lee Gering; it was the demon possessing him who was doing the talking. It was his sin expressing itself in bitter, biting, blighting language.

Sinners Are Paralyzed by Doubts

But how are sinners paralyzed? What do I mean by paralyzed sinners? First, sinners are paralyzed by doubts. They doubt themselves. How many times have you and I heard people say, "I'd like to be a Christian, but I am afraid I can't hold out"?

1. Sinners Doubt Themselves

They doubt themselves. They do not know what we Christians know. To us it seems dreadfully foolish, the whole argument, the whole excuse. We know that our dependence is not in ourselves, but in God. We know that the more we doubt ourselves and the less we depend on ourselves, the closer the Holy Spirit will draw us to the source of our strength, even the mighty Lord Jesus Christ. We know that pride goeth before a fall. We know that our very weaknesses are recommendations to the Lord God to protect us, to care for us, to sustain us in the ventures and adventures of our lives. But to these sinners looking from the outside in, it looks altogether different than from the inside out. After you cross over the line into the mighty love of the Son of God, into the fullness of the Holy Spirit, it looks entirely different.

2. Sinners Doubt Christians

They doubt the churches, and they doubt us Christians. I wish we could find some new word, some new appeal as we go to plead with ourselves, to plead with our church members, to plead with each other to live holy, sacrificial, separated, spiritual lives, to express our Christianity in such manner and fashion that no one can doubt us.

Permit a personal reference.

I am a graduate of a Protestant university and of a Catholic university. I belong to four fraternities, one of them a scholarship fraternity; and the other three are Greek letter fraternities. One is exclusively Jewish, and the other two are universal. The ritual of these last two fraternities is based on the New Testament.

I spent five years in those universities. Ninety percent of my schoolmates were Gentiles. Most claimed to be Christians. My teachers were all Gentiles, and they all claimed to be Christians.

My heart aches when I say this. When it came my turn to face out the problem of accepting the Lord Jesus Christ as my personal Saviour, next to the fact that I had to give up my father and mother, the greatest obstacle that stood in my way was the lives of those fellow students, of those college professors with whom I had spent weeks, months, years. To their shame and to mine, be it said that we companied together in all sorts of sin, that never was there a word spoken about the Saviour of salvation.

I was in a revival in Tyler, Texas. Morning and night services were being fully broadcast. The station manager, a member of one of the churches, gave us the time free. The Jews of that town began to call me up, to invite me to their homes and to their stores.

One day the pastor and I walked into the store of a wholesale grocer. After we had talked to him about Jesus Christ, he said to me, "What do you want me to do?"

"I want you to give your heart to Christ."

"What will it do to me?"

"It will make you a better man."

Turning to the preacher, this Jew said, "Brother Robinson, tell him what kind of man I am."

"Brother Appelman," said the preacher, "he is one of the choicest, cleanest, finest citizens in this town."

"Still," I said, "if you will give your heart to Christ, it will make a better man out of you."

Angrily, the Jewish man said, "Listen, fellow, I want to tell you something. I belong to the Odd Fellows Club. Every Thursday night we have a meeting. After the meeting, some of us meet in the anteroom for a game of poker or pinochle. Every Thursday night for the past nine years, ever since I have been a member of that lodge, my partner in the game has been a member, a deacon in this preacher's church. Do you want to know his name?"

I looked at the preacher. The preacher said, "No."

What chance did I have of winning that Jew for the Lord Jesus Christ? None. I was stymied. I was stopped. I just blushed and said, "Come to church," and walked on to talk to someone else.

We face this everywhere. We are going to continue to face it, unless an extraordinary revival sweeps across our country. We have to contend with this terrible declension on the part of God's people.

But the thing that breaks my heart is that, when these poor, perishing Jewish or Gentile sinners stand before the Lord Jesus Christ on Judgment Day, they are not going to be able to point to these hypocritical church members and use them as an excuse for their sins, to keep them out of Hell, to save them.

3. Sinners Doubt Christ

You surely would be surprised at the great multitude of sinners who are paralyzed by doubting not only themselves, not only us and our Christianity, but also the Lord Jesus Christ.

When I first started on my Christian journey, I used to believe that the way for me to grow in faith was just to keep on repeating morning, noon and night, "Day by day, in every way, I'm getting to be a better and better Christian. I am getting more and more faith."

It would not work. One day I came across that wondrous passage of Scripture, "Faith cometh by hearing, and hearing by the word of God."

What gives us the assurance of the power of the Lord Jesus Christ to save us, to keep us? Is it experience? That definitely is not enough. The thing that gives us full assurance is the fact that in God's holy Word are His promises. We know that God's Word has never been broken, is not being broken now and never shall be broken. But these unsaved millions are not reading the Bible. They know very little about the full truths concerning the Lord Jesus Christ. They know mighty little about His Person. They are hazy about His passion. They are seemingly stopped in their consideration about His power. They cannot quote very many of His promises.

You and I, when the Devil comes to tempt us, can take a bit of God's Word and smash him between his eyes with it. These unsaved people cannot do it. They doubt it. There is always a question in their minds as to whether Jesus Christ loves them or not. Have you ever heard any of them say, "I am not good enough," forgetting the fact that they never will be good enough until the Lord Jesus Christ makes them so?

4. Sinners Are Paralyzed by Discouragement

Another way in which sinners are paralyzed is by discouragement.

Here is a man sitting in the congregation before you Sunday morning and Sunday night. Here is a person in one of your Sunday school classes, a class that you are going to teach. You are pleading with that soul, telling him what Jesus can do for him, or for her. You are beseeching him to be reconciled to God.

Here is what that person is thinking: *Supposing I came down the aisle and gave my heart to Christ this morning, or tonight. I have to go back to my job tomorrow morning. All I shall hear all day long will be cursing and dirty stories. I won't be able to hold out. Why, I would just make a fool of myself.* Thus they are discouraged by their surroundings, by their circumstances.

We have husbands in our churches whose wives are an abomination of desolation standing in a hundred places where they ought not. They begrudge their husbands every minute these dear men spend in the service of the Lord.

On the other hand, we have wives in our churches who have to do everything but lie and steal in order to get a little extra money or a little extra time once in awhile for the Lord.

We have children in our churches, in our Sunday schools who never hear a word about Jesus or God or the Holy Spirit or Christianity, except as a curse word.

All of these things are frightfully discouraging. And the Devil uses them.

Think further of the multitudes who at one time have tried, at least so they say, the Lord Jesus Christ. Have you ever had a sinner say to you, "I tried it once, and it just doesn't work. I have been there before. I used to be a member of a church"?

You may not agree with me. Today I am not interested in the theology of the thing. What I am interested in is getting that soul right with God and by God's grace helping him stay there.

Do not spend too much time arguing about the final perseverance of the saints. Get them to make a surrender or a re-surrender to the Lord Jesus Christ. Get them to make a dedication or a rededication to the Son of God. It will not hurt them to confess the Lord Jesus Christ half a dozen times, half a hundred times, for that matter, a thousand times each day, for so long as they live. If they do make a mistake, let them make it on the right side of the fence, on the side of confession and salvation rather than on Satan's side.

I speak from humble experience when I say that in my observation, in the greatest majority of cases, a person who is seriously and honestly uncertain about his salvation has never been saved.

May I be permitted to call your attention to one outstanding incident in my own poor ministry? It happened in the first great revival in which the Lord used me, in Philadelphia, in 1942. The Lord poured out His Spirit in a mighty Pentecostal tidal wave of power, when beyond 2500 came to claim Christ in the pardon of their sins.

Night by night I pled with people to accept the Lord Jesus Christ as their Saviour, to make certain of their salvation, or to dedicate their lives to the service of the Lord. Thank God they came in droves! The inquiry rooms were not of the best, although we had the most matchless set of personal workers that I have ever seen. As they crowded to the front, it was difficult to handle them in the inquiry rooms.

After a few nights, with hundreds still coming, some of the personal workers and preachers urged me to divide them at the front—that is, to send those who were seeking salvation one way and those who were seeking complete surrender another way. I did not feel led of the Spirit to do so. I tried to explain my feeling, but they would not let me. I insisted, and they insisted. It looked like there was going to be some difficulty there.

Dr. McPherson, that great Philadelphia pastor, came to my rescue. Putting his arm around me and drawing me to himself, he said, "Let this boy alone. He knows what he is doing. He is being led of the Spirit. I have been doing personal work in the inquiry room. Two out of every three who come down for consecration have never been saved."

I have never forgotten that lesson. Whenever I speak to anyone who comes into the inquiry room, my first question is not, "Why did you come?" but, "Are you a Christian?" When I instruct personal workers— and that is many times in each revival—my insistence is always that they do not ask the person why he or she came but that they make sure of that person's salvation.

You will find multitudes of backslidden Christians and multitudes of unsaved souls who are further paralyzed by the fact that they were not given a proper welcome when they came into the church.

When you and I come to church, to whom do we speak? Whom do we approach? Generally it is somebody we know and like, somebody about whom we have been thinking all week. But we ought to exceptionally greet the person we do not know, the stranger in our midst. If you love those who love you, what reward have you? Do not the heathen do the same thing?

So people come to our churches and are not welcomed properly. An atomic bomb is almost needed to break into some of the cliques in our churches. There is no warmth there. No fire. No enthusiastic greeting.

You all recall that classic story that D. L. Moody told again and again. You recall how he established a Sunday school on Illinois Street in Chicago. You recall that little boy who walked halfway across Chicago— and Chicago even in those days was a large city—passing church after church to go to the Illinois Street Sunday school.

One day a superintendent of one of the Sunday schools he passed asked him, "Why do you go all the way out there? Why don't you come here? It is right next door to you."

Looking up at the superintendent, the lad said, "I go where they love a fellow."

My friends, they need love. When a child gets sick, he wants love more than he wants medicine. He is afraid. He is unhappy. He does not know what is happening to him or what is going to happen to him. His heart is trembling within him. He wants to be surrounded by a fence, by a wall of love.

It is the same way with sinners. It is the same way with drifting Christians. They want our deepest affection to draw them to the Lord Jesus Christ.

5. Paralyzed by Sin

There is another paralysis that is common, that you and I are constantly facing out there in the world and shall have to come up against as we go from these sacred grounds. That paralysis is a disease—the disease of sin.

Hear me! Don't you dare stand in the pulpit, don't you dare, in private conversation, criticize a drunkard unless you know the agony of that soul for the drink that is in him. Do it with tears, do it in love—or don't do it at all.

Oh, how many times in my ministry have men come to me sobbing their hearts out, even as do little children, because the galling habit, the slavery of sin, has taken hold and they can't break loose. Don't you dare criticize the drunkard unless you do it out of a broken heart, with tear-stained face, unless you know the awful anguish in his soul because he cannot give up the drink. If you have never been tempted with the red demon of lust, let your heart be broken by the impact of the Holy Spirit before you lash out at the unfortunate victims of that emissary of Satan.

All of these, enthralled and enslaved by sin, are not to be criticized, but they are to be loved and cherished. They need help. They are sick, feverish. The way some of us exercise ourselves towards these bond-servants of sin makes just about as much sense as if we were to walk into a hospital, take our Bibles, beat the patients over the heads and cry to them, "Get up! Get up! You are not sick. Get up!"

My beloved friends, these people who are diseased by sin, ensnared by some evil habit, need our help, our compassion, our grace.

When I was Staff Sergeant, a Sergeant in the station hospital at Fort Sill, Oklahoma, I knew a Master Sergeant in the Quartermaster Department, a veteran of the war between 1914 and 1918. He had gone just as high as a noncommissioned officer could go. He had a wife and a small child.

I was discharged from the Army—perhaps I ought to say I purchased my discharge—to go to the seminary in 1930. I came to Lawton, Oklahoma, the nearest town to Fort Sill, three years later for a revival meeting.

Something had happened to the Master Sergeant. He had begun to drink. He had lost his rating. He had been busted down to a private. He had given up his drink for awhile and had gone back up again to become a Technical Sergeant. When I got to Lawton he had been busted all the way down again. I knew him, and he knew me. His wife was converted in that revival. She called my attention to the friendship of the man for me and my friendship with him.

"Brother Appelman, will you come down and see my husband?"

"What's the matter with him? He used to be a good soldier."

"Yes, he used to be; however, he always drank a little. It got worse with the passing of the years. Drink has got him. He is now a buck private."

"When does he come home?"

"Tomorrow is Saturday, Brother Appelman. He will be home about two o'clock."

The next day, before two o'clock, one of the pastors and I were in that home. There was the former Master Sergeant. In self-defense (as sinners so often do), taking his little baby girl up in his arms, he played with her all during our conversation. You have seen sinners do that. They use some such scheme as a defense mechanism.

I talked to him about old times, about the joys and troubles we had shared as soldiers, about the time we had come to Christian Endeavor together. I talked to him about the numbers of times we had sat at the feet of the chaplain in the Bible class that we called the "Cauducean." He was an interloper in those classes because he was in the Quartermaster Department while it was primarily for the Medical Department.

As we kept talking, I could see his eyes beginning to mist over with unshed tears.

"Fellow," I said to him, "your wife has told me the story of your troubles. She has told me what happened. She gave her heart to Christ last night. Now she is praying for you."

"I know," he grunted. "She kept me awake half the night crying and telling me about it."

"Thank God for that! Man, you can't go on doing like you are doing. You have wasted your life. You have thrown your rank away. You have dissipated your ability as a soldier. You've got nothing left but your sin."

"Yes, Hyman, but I just can't give it up. I just can't."

"I know you can't, but I also know Someone who can take it away from you."

"Who?"

"Jesus Christ, the Son of God."

"I wish I thought so."

"Buck, I know so. Will you give Him the chance right now to show you what He can do?"

"Fellow, I'll just make another mess of it. If I give Him the chance, I shall promise not to drink, then in a little while I'll go right back to that rotten stuff."

"You don't have to promise a thing. Just let Jesus come into your heart."

You could almost see the struggle in his soul as the perspiration stood out in great drops on his face. He wanted to come to Christ badly. I could see his aching heart. I could see the last vestige of manhood in him protesting against his weakness, against his cowardice. All I could do was to sit there and watch him and try to push back my own tears.

"Buck," I said after awhile, "there is just one more thing to do. Let's pray about it."

"I don't know how to pray."

"I will pray for you. Will you let me?"

"Sure. I believe in you. I wish I had what you have."

I knew I had him then. We got down on our knees. I said, "Preacher, pray!"

Brother Wilcoxson lifted his voice in supplication to God. I crawled over on my knees to Buck's side. I took that little child away from him and put her down on the carpet. I put my face on my hands on his lap and I began to pray, to cry aloud for God to save Buck. As I prayed, I could feel him tremble. I kept on praying. He broke down.

"Preacher!" he cried, "I will! Hyman, I will, I will!"

Thank God, he is a Master Sergeant again! Thank God, the Lord has restored unto him the years that the locusts had eaten. Jesus Christ has given him back his sanity, his manhood, his chances at life.

But suppose I had come to him and said, "Buck, you are thus and so, and this and that and the other kind of a rat for abusing your wife, for drinking up the money that belongs to your child." I would not have gotten to first base with him. You cannot talk to these sinners that way. They are sick, paralyzed. Remember that when you leave here to face them out yonder in your workaday world.

II. THE POWERFUL SAVIOUR

The next thing in this story is the powerful Saviour. Thank God a million times over for that!

I'm just as sorry as I can be for you folks who are not preachers. I am just as sorry as I can be for you preachers who are not called to be evangelists. I thank God for you pastors. But how glad I am that the Lord has seen fit to make an evangelist out of me. I go from one end of this continent to the other. When I tell Jews, Gentiles, black folk, white folk, the rich, the poor, "Behold, the Lamb of God which taketh away the sin of the world," I know I am telling the truth. I know that the Word of God will back me up. I know that Jesus can save them from every sin.

You know these things also. Keep telling them to all you meet. Do not let Satan tear these truths away from you. Remember that Jesus, the Christ of God, is able to save to the uttermost all that come unto God by Him. There is no sin, no sinner that is impervious to His mighty power. His blood can cleanse from every sin. His blood can remove every stain. His Spirit can regenerate every soul.

When we stand before a congregation or before a class or before one person, let us not be apologetic. Every word spoken by us that is true to the Word of God is more definitely true than the sun is even now shining in the heavens and that, by God's grace, the stars will twinkle aloft tonight. God's glory, God's power, God's person, God's authority are back of what we tell them when we say to them, "Come to Jesus and He will save you."

It is not, "Perhaps He will save you." It is not, "If you will join this, that or the other church, He will save you." It is not, "If you are able to hold out, He will save you." It is that He will wash away all your sins if you will but come to claim your part and portion in His precious shed blood.

Let us believe and experience it ourselves; then let us pass it on to others. I cannot tell you how many Jews and Gentiles have come to me to say, "I think you are as crazy as you can be. I don't believe a word you say, but you certainly believe it." I certainly do, with all my heart, with all my soul and with all my might, with all my life. I believe every bit of it because of what it has done for me in my own personal experience.

What Christ has done for me, He can do for others. I have seen Him do it.

Some of us put our feet in the way of the cross through faith in the Lord Jesus Christ and walk the straight and narrow path without ever straying. But most fall into some sort of sin before we are very long on the journey. There are some of us who sin even more grievously after we are converted than we ever did before. However, there is provision in God's mercy for us erring ones. If we confess our sins, the Lord is faithful to forgive us our sins and to cleanse us from all unrighteousness, either before conversion or after.

Do not misunderstand me. I am not suggesting that a Christian will keep on sinning, will keep on stumbling, will keep on falling. It is absolutely possible, in the demonstration and power of the Holy Spirit, to be constantly victorious over sin. Nevertheless, when the Devil does catch up with us, when he causes us to stumble, there is no need to wallow, no need to lose our faith in God or in ourselves and doubt as to whether there is anything to the religion of our Lord and Saviour, Jesus Christ. Permit an illustration.

I knew a man named Jeff. I cannot tell you his last name. He is very much alive out yonder in the hill country of Texas. He was converted in the very first revival the Lord used me in, in that great state. At that time he was in his early thirties. His wife had been a Christian since she was a child and an active member of the church. They had two little children.

Jeff was an irritable person. He was wealthy, with much land, a great deal of stock and loads of equipment. He was a murderously tempered man. Curse? Why, he could curse until the cotton tops blistered. When he was converted, some commented, "Wait until spring and he starts plowing some of that new ground he has been buying up."

Spring came. Jeff was plowing one day with a mule. All of a sudden, his plow struck a stone, or a stump, and the mule pulled the wrong way.

Jeff got terrifically mad. He started thrashing the mule with his lines and cursing at the top of his voice. The men plowing with him laughed gloatingly.

Finishing the row, Jeff unharnessed the mule and let it graze. He left the plow, went back to his barn, threw himself on his face and sobbed out his repentance and regret to God. How do I know it? His wife and some of the men found him there late that evening sobbing his soul out to God. They believed in his religion after that.

You may not agree with me that that man was saved. I wholeheartedly believe he was. He was trying to live right. This is my kind of holiness, my kind of sanctification. This is what I mean by victory over sin. I say as did William Jennings Bryan: I cannot keep buzzards from flying over my head, but I surely can keep them from building nests in my hair.

Holiness means letting God, in the Holy Spirit, save and keep you. If you stumble and backslide, then fall to your knees in penitential confession before the throne of grace, claiming once again the cleansing power of the Lord Jesus Christ.

He Is Powerful to Keep

Jesus Christ not only is the powerful Saviour because He can save, but He is also the powerful Saviour because He can keep.

You recall what Jude has to say in his book, the 24th and 25th verses:

"Now unto him that is able to keep you from falling, and to present you faultless before the presence of his glory with exceeding joy, To the only wise God our Saviour, be glory and majesty, dominion and power, both now and ever. Amen."

Brother MacArthur told us the other evening on the hillside that he liked Peter. I like two men in the Bible, David and Peter. I am afraid of Moses and Paul because they are so mighty, while David and Peter are right down my alley. Every time these brethren turned around, they got into a jam! I guess misery loves company. That is why I like them so well.

Catholics say Peter was the first pope. If the Catholics want to claim him, let them. The Lord knows we have enough Simon Peters in our churches. There they are, hot and cold, on the mountaintop one time, in the valley and slough of despair the very next time. If ever there was a man tested by God, if ever a man tested God, that one was Peter. Yet at the end of his lifetime, he could cry for the ages,

*"Blessed be the God and Father of our Lord Jesus Christ, which according to his abundant mercy hath begotten us again unto a lively hope by the resurrection of Jesus Christ from the dead, To an inheritance incorruptible, and undefiled, and that fadeth not away, reserved in heaven for you, Who are kept by the power of God through faith unto salvation ready to be revealed in the last time."—*I Pet. 1:3-5.

Thank God for the keeping power of the Lord Jesus Christ! We may let go, but He never lets go.

I can take you to the place in the Central Christian Church of Denver, Colorado, where I was converted. I can take you down to the basement where I would lock myself in hour after hour reading my Bible. I can show you the place and tell you the time of day, and the exact month—April, 1925—when first I read that wonderful promise of Paul, "If we believe not, yet he abideth faithful: he cannot deny himself" (II Tim. 2:13).

Being Jews, my father and mother both disowned me when I became a Christian. I am still daddy's son, still mama's son. I was born of their blood, of their flesh, of their bone. When I became a child of God, or when you become a child of God, we all become part of the kith and kin of the Lord Jesus Christ. It will take a great deal more than the Devil has to tear those bricks loose from the building that the Holy Spirit is erecting in the church in the kingdom of God!

He Is Powerful to Use

The Lord Jesus Christ is the powerful Saviour because He is able to use.

Think of men whom you and I know. Think of great Anthony Zeoli. Talk about a miracle of grace! Why, he can quote more Bible than any five of us. He himself told me that he was converted in a jailhouse. If I remember correctly, he was led to Christ by a black man in a state penitentiary. Think of the mighty way in which God, for Christ's sake, is using him! Think of the multiplied tens of thousands of souls he has brought to a saving knowledge of the Lord Jesus Christ!

Go on then to study how God will use even our own poor selves.

I had a friend in the seminary—you will know his name when I finish telling my story. One day as he and I drove to our churches in Oklahoma, he told me of his conversion. He told how he was almost driven away from home because of his drunkenness, how he was kicked out of a Christian school in Mississippi, how he became a traveling salesman, how he went from bad to worse.

Then he told me of a night in a hotel room in Vicksburg, Mississippi, recovering from an awful bout of delirium tremens after a terrible period of drunken debauchery. He made up his mind then and there that there was but one more thing for him to do—commit suicide. Starting towards the Vicksburg bridge across the Mississippi, he walked up on the bridge and stood leaning over the railing watching the swelling, dark, muddy waters of the father of rivers.

Reaching into his pocket and taking out his package of cigarettes, he put one in his mouth but couldn't find a match. Perhaps he did not have any or was too hazy to find it.

A man came along. This young fellow of my story stopped him to ask, "Mister, do you have a match?"

"Yes," said the stranger, and gave him a box of matches.

Scratching the match with trembling hands, he tried to light his cigarette. One after another, match after match went out. Finally he succeeded in lighting the cigarette.

The stranger was carefully watching him. After awhile he said to him, "What are you doing here at this time of night?"

"Oh, I'm just walking along."

"You look kind of sick. Are you?"

"Well, I have been."

"Let's go have a cup of coffee."

Something about the stranger appealed to the man in question. "All right, let's go." In his mind he said to himself, *I can commit suicide anytime.*

After the coffee and perhaps a sandwich, the stranger would not let this young fellow go. "Come with me."

"Where?"

"Never mind, just come along. Come on. You can go home after we're through."

They went to church. A revival meeting was going on. The two of them sat in the very back. Somehow, to the befuddled brain of the man in question, there came the story once again of the love of God, of the death of Christ on the cross. Apparently he was impressed, but he made no move.

He went back to his room. He stayed a few more days in Vicksburg to straighten out; then he went home. His people did not seem too glad to receive him.

On Sunday he went to church without saying a word to them. When the preacher gave the invitation, this young fellow walked slowly down the aisle, made a public profession of his faith in the Lord Jesus Christ, then followed the Son of God in baptism.

He felt the Lord calling him to preach, and in a bit his church ordained him. It was then that he went to the seminary in Fort Worth, Texas to become my classmate.

One day he was sitting in the Texas Hotel in Fort Worth when another traveling salesman came along and greeted him. "Charlie, I haven't seen you lately. Have you changed jobs?"

"Yes."

"Are you still selling?"

"Yes."

"Before we talk, Charlie, let's go upstairs and have a little refreshment."

Going upstairs to the man's room, they sat down. After a bit, the man, opening his valise, took out a bottle of Scotch, got two glasses and started pouring, saying, "How much?"

"As much as you want to give me."

Pouring out half a glass of whiskey for himself and half for Charlie, the man handed the glass to his visitor. "All right, fellow, bottoms up!"

Reaching for the glass of liquor, Charlie spoke up: "Before we drink, I want to tell you about my new job."

Slowly, carefully, prayerfully, Charlie told his old friend the story about Christ and Him crucified. The tears came to both of them. The room grew quiet as Charlie brought his fellow traveling salesman face to face with the cross.

They got down on their knees. The miracle of grace came to pass right there in that room. They thanked God for their salvation. Getting up from their knees, the salesman took the glasses and bottle, walked into the bathroom and poured the liquor down the drain.

I am sure you recognize the name of the man of whom I speak, because in a brief while he became one of the outstanding religious characters of the United States of America. God saved him for Christ's sake, kept him for Christ's sake, and used him for Christ's sake.

III. THE PERSISTENCE OF THE SAINTS

The last item in this story is the persistence of the saints. I suppose you expect me to say persistence in holy living. I suppose you expect me to say persistence in praying. With your permission, I should like to take a little different track and suggest a different thought or two.

First, there must be persistence in loving. We get frightfully blue. We drive ourselves, and after awhile we almost hate to stand in front of a crowd. Thank God, however, we can always get warm again at the feet of the Lord Jesus Christ.

I don't know what you do when your heart, your passion, your soul gets cold. I don't know what you do when you get tired of dealing constantly with hard-hearted sinners. I don't know what you do when you almost have to drive yourself to do the work of God.

I go away somewhere by myself, get down on my knees, read again what the Bible teaches about Hell and Heaven, read again what the Bible teaches about the Lord Jesus Christ. Then I close my eyes as tightly as I can. Once again I see the body of the Lord Jesus Christ torn by the cruel laceration of Pilate's judgment whip. Once again I see the steps that He trod between the judgment hall and the cross, marked with His own blood. Once again I see Him hanging in bitter loneliness, in heartache and heartbreak, on that cruel tree.

I get up from my knees aflame for Jesus, aflame to tell the story of His mighty love. I go back and preach with renewed zeal and enthusiasm. I am burning up with the desire to tell people about what happened long ago on Calvary. I feel that if He loved that much, I am going to love and keep on loving everyone for Jesus' sake.

Yes, there must be persistence in loving. There is no power in loveless preaching. There is no power in loveless evangelism.

Dr. A. N. Hall in Muskogee, Oklahoma, pastor of the First Baptist Church there, a great man of God, did me a wonderful turn one day. It was a rainy Saturday morning. I had come to the church to get my mail. It started to rain, and, not caring to slosh back to my hotel, I went into his study, closed the door, got down on my knees, opened my Bible and decided I would have my prayer season right then and there.

I was praying and crying, so did not hear the pastor come in until he dropped down on his knees by my side. He asked me to pray again. I did. He prayed also.

When we got up, he commented, "You have been crying?"

"Yes."

"What about?"

"It is a personal matter."

"Is it about your home or your loved ones?"

"No, it's about myself."

"Can you tell me?"

"I don't want to worry you."

"Tell me. I am an old man. You will not worry me. I love you. Perhaps I can help you."

"All right, Dr. Hall. Forgive me if I presume upon your goodness. I want you to tell me how to keep from being a professional preacher. You know, Dr. Hall, I preach all the time, three and four times a day, 350 days a year, sometimes even more than that. I am afraid of getting dry and mechanical. I am afraid of getting professional. How can I keep from these sins of the flesh?"

Putting his hands on my shoulders and drawing me to himself until our bodies almost touched, he said, with tears, "Son, I am glad you asked me. We all have that problem. I'll tell you, son. Just keep Jesus sweet on your soul. Just keep on making love to the Lord Jesus Christ." He meant—get down on your knees.

Think of the beauty of the Son of God. Think of His holiness. Think of His young manhood, His young vitality. Think of what He had to go through in order to make our salvation possible. Think of the price that He paid for our redemption. Do this and I'll guarantee you it will break your hearts, melt your souls, drive you to your faces in agony of re-surrender, then up from your knees and your faces into the harvest field to witness to and win lost souls to Christ. I'll guarantee you there will then be no question of professionalism, no question of dryness, no question of having to drive yourself to tell the story of Christ and Him crucified.

Some weeks ago, as President of the American Association for Jewish Evangelism, I was in a mid-year conference of that Association in Chicago, in the great Moody Church. Among the speakers on the platform were a doctor and his wife, refugees from Germany. She also was a doctor. They were working under the great R. G. LeTourneau Foundation. Their work was almost exclusively among Jewish refugees.

The lady doctor told us a story that broke my heart. She said the refugee children brought to New York—those orphan children with the marks of the German concentrations camps upon them—were taken by them (the doctor and his wife) out of New York City's sweltering heat to summer camps. She said she would never forget the first group she took. There were those tiny children with their pale faces and extended little stomachs, with their rickety little legs and thin arms. There they were—with the marks of fear and despair upon them, their eyes big and heavy in their tiny faces. She tried to tell them about the Lord Jesus Christ, but they did not seem to be able to understand. She didn't know what to do.

One day at dinnertime she was walking around watching them eat when she saw a little tiny girl holding a glass of milk in her hands but not touching it. Bending over the child, the lady doctor said: "Darling, why don't you drink it?" Of course, she spoke in German.

Looking up into the face of the questioning lady, the little girl, her eyes splashing over with tears, said, "How much of this milk can I drink?"

The lady doctor reached for that child, lifted her out of her seat in her own arms, hugged and kissed her, crooned to her, sobbing out, "You can drink all of it, sweetheart, and as much more as you want."

When she finished telling us that story, our own tears keeping company with hers, she sobbed out, "We may not be able to preach or teach them into Christ, but we have determined to love them into Christ."

These unsaved people can stand anything, almost, in the way of preaching and teaching and witness-bearing. The mightiest weapon we have in our arsenals is the weapon of a broken heart, the weapon of a tear-stained face. Oh, may God give us the grace of tears to weep over these perishing souls and sinners!

Not only must there be persistence in loving, but there must be persistence in lifting. We must lift them to God by our personal testimonies. We must lift the Lord Jesus Christ before their eyes by our ceaseless pleading with them to be reconciled to God. We must lift them by visitation, by our gifts and by the spread of every sort of sound Christian literature.

What will happen when we have loved them, when we have led them, when we have lifted them to the Saviour? Listen to me and I am finished.

Years ago there was in this country of ours a great temperance evangelist by the name of John D. Gough, a mighty man of God. Thousands crowded to hear his passionate appeal for Christ and holy living. Thousands were turned into the way of righteousness by his pleading appeals.

He held a revival in a great auditorium in one of our eastern cities. At the end of each service, the crowds flocked to him to shake his hand, to express their gratitude and appreciation.

One night, when he was standing there shaking hands with the folks, a woman came up to say something to him. She was holding up a bit of lace handkerchief. He did not quite understand what she was saying.

Bending down he asked, "What is it you are trying to tell me?"

"I want you to have the handkerchief."

"Why?"

"I cannot tell you in one word. It will take a little time."

"Come up here," he suggested, pointing to the platform.

The woman walked around the rear and got up on the platform. Turning his back upon the thronging people, the preacher said, "Now tell me your story."

> May I start at the beginning? I was very young when I married a young attorney in Virginia. He and I were childhood sweethearts. He was very brilliant. He began to grow by leaps and bounds in his chosen career. He was invited to New York to become partner in a great company of lawyers.
>
> We had a fine home. God gave us four children. After awhile we had two homes, one in the country and one in the city. We

had everything that our hearts could desire. Our children were all in a private school. When they were not, we had governesses and nurses for them. We were rich beyond the dreams of avarice.

The government took my husband over on special work. He began to make more and more money. His work necessitated traveling across the country. I could not always go with him.

First thing you know, he began to company with the wrong crowd of men. There was a social drink here and there. He got a taste of liquor for the first time in his life. It ruined him. He went down and down and down. He lost his job with the government. He lost his practice. We lost our home in the country, then in the city. We moved to cheaper and still cheaper rented places.

One night I found myself in a one-room shack on the riverbank, my four children stretched out on a pallet fast asleep. We hadn't had supper. We had nothing in the house for breakfast. My husband had not been around for almost a week.

I did not know which way to turn. I did not know what to do. I decided there was but one thing to do, and that was to take my children and myself and throw ourselves into the Hudson River.

Sitting there that night, I took this little wisp of a handkerchief, the last pretty thing I had left (the rest of it had been sold or pawned to provide food for the family) and saturated it with my tears.

Suddenly the door opened, and my husband stumbled in. Starting towards him to reprove him, he reached for me and fell face down on the floor, vomiting all over himself. I sat there and sobbed aloud. The children woke up. They cried with me. It took me awhile to quiet them down. I straightened out my husband the best I could, washed his face, undressed him, washed up that awful filth on the floor and put him to bed.

He fell asleep. I sat there through the hours of the night. What to do I did not know. It came to me again that there was but one way out, and that was to take my babies and throw ourselves into the river, to die, to be done with it.

I sat there crying and praying. The morning sun came up. I didn't notice it. I was sitting there at the table, leafing through the old album of our former days, when I felt somebody breathing hard behind me. I looked up and there was my husband looking over my shoulder, his face puffed up with his dissipation, his eyes bleary. I kept on turning the pages and came to the picture of my husband and myself on our wedding day.

He bent over me. I saw his great hot tears splash down on that picture. I just didn't have the heart to talk to him. I was too broken up. My children would wake in a minute. There was nothing for them to eat. I didn't know what to do.

Somehow we scraped something together and passed that day. That night my husband asked me if I wanted to go anywhere. I told him I should like to go and hear Dr. Gough speak.

We came that night. We heard you speak. The next night I couldn't come because one of the children was ill, so he came by himself. The third night he came alone also. The fourth night he came home to tell me he had made a public profession of faith in Jesus Christ.

Dr. Gough, we started back. We have not yet reached where we were before all this happened, but we are not in that shack anymore. My children and I have good clothes. My husband is practicing again. He's climbing up in his profession. I want you to have this handkerchief as a remembrance.

The preacher was weeping with the woman about that time. Stepping back, he lifted his golden glorious voice to cry, "Wait, people, I want to tell you a story." He told that giant congregation the story as I am telling it to you. Waving that handkerchief before the crowd, his voice choked with his own emotions as he sobbed out: "The Devil is in the business of making handkerchiefs like these wet with the tears of wives and children, but the Lord is in the business of drying them again."

Thank God for that! We have a powerful Saviour. There are paralyzed sinners. It is for us, as persistent saints, to go out in the name of the Lord, in the power and demonstration of the Holy Ghost, to love, to lead, to lift these souls to the saving Son of God.

God give us the grace to do that, for Christ's sake. Amen.

JOE HENRY HANKINS
1889-1967

ABOUT THE MAN:

"He was a weeping prophet" is the way Dr. Hankins was characterized by those who knew him best—one of the 20th century's great soul-winning preachers.

BUT—Hankins preached sharply, strongly against sin. Would to God we had more men of his mettle in a ministry today that has largely been given over to namby-pamby, mealy-mouthed silence when it comes to strong preaching against sin.

Dr. John R. Rice wrote of him: *"His method and manifest spiritual power would remind one of D. L. Moody. He has the keen, scholarly, analytical mind of an R. A. Torrey, and the love and compassion of soul of a Wilbur Chapman."*

Hankins was born in Arkansas and saved as a youth. He graduated from high schol in Pine Bluff, then from Quachita Baptist College. He held pastorates in Pine Bluff, Arkansas; in Whitewright, Greenville and Childress, Texas. His last and most productive pastorate was the First Baptist Church, Little Rock, Arkansas. There, in less than five years, 1,799 additions by letter, 1,144 by baptism—an average of 227 baptisms a year—made a total of 2,943 members added to the church. Sunday school spiralled to nearly 1,400; membership mushroomed to 3,200 despite a deletion of 882 to revise the rolls.

In 1942, Hankins gave up the pastorate for full-time evangelism.

In 1967, Dr. Hankins passed on to the Heaven he loved to preach about. Be sure that he was greeted by a thronging host of redeemed souls—saved under his Spirit-filled ministry.

IX.

Visualize, Agonize, Evangelize

JOE HENRY HANKINS

(Preached in 1942 at Sword of the Lord Conference on Evangelism, Chicago)

"But when he saw the multitudes, he was moved with compassion on them, because they fainted, and were scattered abroad, as sheep having no shepherd. Then saith he unto his disciples, The harvest truly is plenteous, but the labourers are few; Pray ye therefore the Lord of the harvest, that he will send forth labourers into his harvest."—Matt. 9:36-38.

I will center my message on three words: *visualize, agonize, evangelize.*

I. VISUALIZE

If this great multitude of humanity that makes up the population of this world could see what Jesus saw, it would be easy to get people out after souls. I am sure that the disciples who were with Jesus when the crowds thronged to hear His teachings during those three years, saw only a great crowd of milling, curious humanity. But the Lord saw what I am praying you may see tonight.

1. Jesus Saw Them as Lost Souls

The Lord saw a great host of souls without hope and on the road to eternal night, to spend eternity separated from God in a Devil's Hell.

I wonder sometimes if we who call ourselves Christians really believe people are lost. As I have talked with the Lord, time after time I have asked myself, *Joe Hankins, do you really believe that every person old enough to know right from wrong who has not been born of the Spirit of God is a lost soul and on his way to Hell?*

A few times in my own ministry I have experienced the awful agony of a burdened soul that seemed to bring me almost to the point of death.

The first time I had that experience, I was in a revival meeting in Fort Worth, Texas. One Saturday night, just as I started to the pulpit to preach, such a burden came on my soul that I couldn't speak another word after reading my text. I just stood there, sobbing. In a little bit the thing got hold of the congregation, and many out there were also weeping. None knew why I had broken down, but somehow the Holy Spirit took hold of other hearts.

When I could speak, I said, "People, you are wondering about this. God has placed on my heart such a burden for some soul here tonight that I am about to die!"

There were times in that sermon when I felt I couldn't go on. I said to those present, "I cannot interpret it any other way than that God is saying to my heart, 'There is a soul in the balance, and that soul must be reached tonight or go to Hell.' The Spirit of God seems to be saying to me, 'With some soul here tonight, it is now or never.'"

After I had spoken those words, the very hush of death fell on the congregation. Again many broke into sobs.

When I had stumbled my way through that message and made the altar call, people began coming down all the aisles. Still that burden was there. I said, "The soul for which God put that burden on my heart hasn't come yet. When that one does come, God will take away this burden."

I kept on pleading, kept on calling—but the burden stayed. Finally I fell to my knees in that pulpit, and I said, "Lord, if that soul doesn't come, I believe I will die right here!"

When I got up and looked out over the congregation and saw a man coming, I said, "Praise the Lord! There he is!" The burden then was lifted.

It was the strangest experience of my life. I believe the Lord took me through Hell that night after a soul in order to teach me a lesson I would never forget—that when God's preacher and people have a broken heart for the lost, they are going to get saved.

The second time this happened was in Little Rock one night, in a tent meeting. Again I felt it. Again I said, "A soul is in the balance tonight. That soul must be saved tonight or go to Hell, just as certain as there is a God in Heaven."

After I had preached and made the call for sinners to accept Christ, many came; but that burden remained. I held that crowd until I felt I could hold them no longer. "I will make one last call. It is now or never with some soul," I said.

An old, gray-haired man at the back of the tent threw both hands up over his head and started out of that tent in a run. As he ran into the dark he screamed, "My God, I am that man!"

When the service had been dismissed, a man came running. "Pastor, we stopped him out at the corner. One of the men is holding him. I came to get you."

I went to him. The man had his foot on the running board and his hands up on top of the car, with his head leaning on its top, trembling like a leaf.

When I placed my hand on his shoulder, he said, "Preacher, I knew from the very minute you spoke those words, I was the man!"

There by the side of that car God gave me that man for Christ.

That night the total count: twenty-three saved, including this man for whom I had such a burden.

I tell you, when we really believe that souls are lost and that truth is pressed home to us to the extent that our hearts break, people are going to get saved. The Lord has promised it. "He that goeth forth and weepeth, bearing precious seed, shall doubtless come again with rejoicing, bringing his sheaves with him."

The reason the world is going to Hell is that not enough people care.

I repeat: I wonder if we believe they are lost. Oh, I know mentally we have accepted the fact that people without Christ are lost; but has it ever gone right down into our hearts?

That precious little girl in your home who is old enough to know right from wrong—she may be the most beautiful child in the land, fine and sweet, lovely and obedient—but as surely as God's Word is true, if that child is old enough to know right from wrong, but is still unsaved, she is a willful, lost sinner and on her way to Hell.

When you see the milling multitude, what do you see? When you walk down the streets of this city, streets jammed with humanity, what do you see? Just a lot of people going here and there? Oh, God help you to see that six out of every ten are on their way to Hell! When you think about these millions who have never heard about Jesus, what do you see?

When we think of those millions—over a thousand million who have never heard the name of Jesus, look at them and visualize them as a great army on the march. Can you hear the tramp, tramp, tramp of a thousand million? Listen to the tramp of those feet!

And to that mighty army add another five hundred million who have heard the Gospel but are still on their way to Hell, and what do you have? Oh, it is a death march, a death march! Tramp, tramp, tramp into Hell they go, without God, without hope! Do you see that? Do you believe that? I wish we could see what Jesus saw.

2. Jesus Saw Their Heart-Hunger

Jesus not only saw them lost; He saw hungry hearts, hungry souls famished to the fainting point.

We never know, we can't know how hungry many hearts are whom we pass every day. We sometimes criticize the unsaved man because he doesn't come to church; but if you get out there and get close to his heart, you will find it hungry.

What do you see when you see crowds rushing to the places of amusement, crowds rushing to the dance halls, crowds at the night clubs, crowds at the places of sin? Do you see just a crowd who seem to have lost their heads and are going pell-mell after this thing, that thing and the other which look so foolish to us? Is that what you see?

That isn't what Jesus saw. He saw a crowd of hungry-hearted people trying to find something to satisfy. They don't know why that heart-hunger. They think they can find something to satisfy. But we know they will never find it until they find it in Jesus Christ. That is what Jesus saw.

I went into a home one day to see an unsaved mother with two children. I told her the story of Jesus and His love. On our knees together there she called on the Lord, and He came into her heart.

Then she got up off her knees and asked, "Why didn't somebody come to me before this! Seven years ago my baby died, leaving me a broken heart: now for seven years I have carried the hungriest heart anybody ever carried in a human breast. This is the first time in seven years I have had peace." Then she added, sadly, "Had somebody come to me anytime during those seven years with what you brought tonight, I would have been saved!"

Oh, hungry hearts will never be satisfied until they find satisfaction in Jesus.

A missionary to China, Miss Blanche Groves, told this story one day. There was a young Chinese, a graduate of Yale University. He had gone back to his homeland after graduation and was saved in a mission. Miss Groves said:

> I asked the Chinese Christians to stand and in a few words tell the one thing about Jesus that had meant the most to them. One after another said this, that and the other thing. Finally this brilliant Chinese graduate stood and said, "Miss Groves, I will tell you how Jesus has meant the most to me. For the first time in my life I have found that which satisfies. I thought I would find it in education, so I went to Yale. The best teachers taught me. But when I came out, my heart was still as hungry as when I went in. But when I found Christ, I found that which satisfies."

3. Jesus Saw Their Helplessness

He not only saw them with hungry hearts, but He saw they were as sheep scattered abroad without a shepherd. Can you see that?

What is more helpless than a lost sheep? Out on our farm where I was reared, we used to have a little flock of sheep. We had much wooded land in that country. So when we turned them out, they would wander into the woods to graze. On one we put a bell so we could find them if they didn't come home.

Every now and then, when the flock came home in the evening, one or two would be missing. Sometimes one would come right up to the back of the field where we could see him from the house running up and down the fence back there.

My father would say, "Son, you had better run over and get him."

"But dad, he's right over there in sight of the house. Don't you reckon he will come home by himself?"

"No, son, he will never find his way home. And if he stays out there tonight, a wolf will get him or some prowling dog will come along and tear him to pieces. Better go get him."

Listen! Lost souls are just that helpless. They will never find their way home, never, never, until someone who knows the way goes and brings them in. That is why Jesus instructs us: 'Go into the highways and hedges, and bring them in.' "Go ye into all the world"—go out where they are, in our own America and to the uttermost parts of the earth. The great need today is for those who care enough to go.

I repeat: The reason so many souls are lost all around us, those we rub elbows with every day, is that not enough people care.

II. AGONIZE

Jesus told us to pray. But if we ever see what Jesus saw, nobody will have to tell us to pray. When your heart breaks, when the burden presses in on your soul until it haunts you, until you lie awake and wet your pillow with tears, there will be a prayer in your heart night and day.

Oh, how we need intercessors at the throne of grace weeping over souls!

Dr. Oswald J. Smith's book, *David Brainerd, a Man of Prayer,* is made up of excerpts from Brainerd's diary. Brainerd tells how, on his knees before God, he prayed and wept until he prayed scores of Indians into the kingdom of God, when he couldn't speak their language and it was necessary to preach through a drunken interpreter!

I heard that great evangelist, Hyman Appelman, tell this story:

He was preaching in a revival when a mother came up to him one night after service and said, "Brother Appelman, I have two boys unsaved. Other mothers' boys are being saved in this meeting: I don't understand why my boys are not saved."

That great man of God looked her in her face and said frankly: "I think it may be because your eyes are still so dry."

The next day when he saw that woman, her eyes were swollen from crying. Now she said, "Brother Appelman, last night you drove home the truth that I hadn't really been agonizing in prayer for my boys, hadn't been weeping over their lost condition. But last night I prayed and wept the night through. Now this morning I feel as if I will die if they are not saved in this meeting!"

You can guess what happened.

That night when he gave the invitation, the first two to walk the aisles were her sons.

When our hearts break, when we agonize before God, souls will be born into the kingdom.

III. EVANGELIZE

The Lord instructs us to "go," which means evangelize. "Go" with the message. You will search in vain for a Scripture where the Lord commands the unsaved to come and hear the message or where the Lord gives a command to build nice church buildings and put in a pipe organ. I like those things. It is fine to have a beautiful temple of worship, but you will search in vain for any command from the Lord to build a temple of worship and get a trained choir and a good preacher, then open the doors and say to the unsaved, "Come."

On the other hand, the Lord commands us, "Go out into the highways and hedges, and compel them . . . ." He tells us, "He that goeth forth and weepeth . . . shall doubtless come again with rejoicing, bringing his sheaves with him." It is always go, go, go.

Why go? First, because the Lord commanded it, and that is reason enough for any Christian. I marvel at the ways we many times treat His commands. If you are born again, the very fact that in His Word He has said "go" ought to be enough for every one of us. It ought not take any persuading, any coaxing, any pleading to get us to go after souls.

Another reason we ought to go is that God says if we don't and people go to Hell we could have won, then their blood will be on us. Do we believe that? What does God mean when He says their blood will be on our hands? I don't fully understand the meaning, but I know He means that we will be guilty of soul-murder.

We speak of the murderer as having the blood of his fellowman on his hands. God says if you fail that poor lost soul, you will stand before the judgment seat of Christ guilty of soul-murder. His blood will be on your hands. Very few believe that.

Oh, if I let them slip through my fingers through neglect, get too busy about other things and let them go to Hell, God will require their blood at my hands. I believe that. And this belief has driven me away from my home, away from my family; this thing has driven me out, while I was a pastor, to preach in small rural churches, in schoolhouses, on street corners—everywhere I could find a place to preach. I believe the Lord meant exactly what He said: "If you don't warn them, their blood will I require at your hands." I don't understand that fully, but I want to deliver my soul of the blood of lost souls.

Even if you don't win them but warn them faithfully, you have delivered your soul, and their blood will be on their own heads. You will not win all you go after—maybe one out of every twenty or one out of fifty—but you will deliver your own soul when you go and warn the lost.

I would rather win souls than do anything else. I look back on my ministry and see some the Lord has helped me win to Him. I wouldn't take anything on this earth in exchange for that privilege.

When I was pastor in North Texas, I went out beside the Red River and built a little brush arbor. There I preached the Gospel. Night after night I called people to the altar.

One night when I made the call, a great group came. I dealt with them one by one, every one personally, and led every one to victory in Christ.

I preached on Heaven that night. And how Heaven came down to bless us! As I stood ready to pronounce the benediction, I saw a little girl sitting on the end of the second seat just sobbing her little heart out. I had never seen a more neglected child. Poor, thin, her hair matted, dirty hands and bare feet, dirty dress, scaley feet and legs because she hadn't been cared for.

There she was, crying her little heart out.

I went down, put my arm around her and said, "Sweetheart, what's the trouble?"

She replied:

> Brother Hankins, you said the sweetest things tonight. You were talking about Heaven, how you and your mother were going to walk the golden streets together. Brother Hankins, I am an orphan. Nobody in the world loves me. Nobody cares anything about me. I am living with grandpa, who is 85 years old, but he doesn't want me. My daddy died when I was two, and mama died last year. Mama was a Christian, and she is in Heaven. I want to know Jesus. I want to go to Heaven so I can be with mama. I want to see mama again.

I opened my Bible and taught that child the way of salvation. I found her mind had been as neglected as her little body. It took nearly an hour to lead that child to the light. After awhile, the Holy Spirit opened her little heart to receive the truth. When she saw it and accepted the Saviour, she jumped up from that pine board bench, clapped her hands together and shouted all over that brush arbor, "O Jesus, I thank You that You have saved me! Now I can see mama again!"

I would rather have won that child to Christ than to have made a million dollars.

The greatest thrill a child of God can experience is to go out after souls and bring them to Jesus! Why don't we do it? Oh, why don't we do it? We will, when we see what Jesus saw; when we feel what Jesus felt.

How many of you would have to lift your hand and say, "I, as a Christian, am guilty before God of neglecting souls. Pray that I may be a real soul winner"? Let's be honest with God and face our own failure. Let me pray for you, that God may burden your soul and make you a winner of souls.

(After prayer, more than a hundred came to the altar publicly dedicating themselves for soul winning.)

WILLIAM ASHLEY SUNDAY
1862-1935

ABOUT THE MAN:

William Ashley (Billy) Sunday was converted from pro baseball to Christ at twenty-three but carried his athletic ability into the pulpit.

Born in Ames, Iowa, he lost his father to the Civil War and lived with his grandparents until age nine when he was taken to live in an orphanage. A life of hard work paid off in athletic prowess that brought him a contract with the Chicago White Stockings in 1883. His early success in baseball was diluted by strong drink; however, in 1886 he was converted at the Pacific Garden Mission in Chicago and became actively involved in Christian work.

Sunday held some three hundred crusades in thirty-nine years. It is estimated that a hundred million heard him speak in great tabernacles, and more than a quarter million people made a profession of faith in Christ as Saviour under his preaching. His long-time associate, Dr. Homer Rodeheaver, called him "the greatest gospel preacher since the Apostle Paul."

Billy Sunday was one of the most unusual evangelists of his day. He walked, ran, or jumped across the platform as he preached, sometimes breaking chairs. His controversial style brought criticism but won the admiration of millions. He attacked public evils, particularly the liquor industry, and was considered the most influential person in bringing about the prohibition legislation after World War I.

Many long remembered his famous quote: "I'm against sin. I'll kick it as long as I've got a foot, and I'll fight it as long as I've got a fist. I'll butt it as long as I've got a head. I'll bite it as long as I've got a tooth. And when I'm old and fistless and footless and toothless, I'll gum it till I go home to Glory and it goes home to perdition!"

Those who heard him never forgot him or his blazing, barehanded evangelism.

The evangelist died November 6, 1935, at age 72. His funeral was held in Moody Church, Chicago, the sermon by H. A. Ironside.

X.

How Much Do You Care if Souls Go to Hell?

BILLY SUNDAY

"No man cared for my soul."—Ps. 142:4.

Life and nature seem to be made up largely of contrast. Midnight, midnoon. . .summer, winter. . .heat, cold. . .hills, valleys. . .famine, plenty. . .rain, drought. . .sickness, health. . .vice and virtue walk the street. . .joy and sorrow look from the same window. . .the hearse follows quickly after the bridal procession. . .the funeral dirge is heard mingling with the wedding march. . .tears follow laughter.

All lives are more or less of a contrast. But to me, no life, no history, sacred or profane, presents a larger number than that of David, the author of my Psalm and text.

I am first introduced to him as a shepherd lad when he herded his father's flocks and when Samuel was sent of God to anoint him king of Israel.

The next vision I catch of David is that he has thrown the shepherd crook on the ground, picked up the crown, climbed up and sat down on the throne and swayed a scepter instead of a shepherd's crook.

The next vision I have of David is that he has become a sinner. He forgot God, to whom he was indebted, and trailed and dragged His name in filth; then, by crying unto God, who granted him pardon, he became a saint.

He was also a poet of no mean ability.

He was a musician, too, and early he charmed King Saul in his melancholy moods. He was a warrior and led the hosts of God to victory. His son Absalom had rebelled. Saul, jealous of his popularity and success, sought to kill him and chased him from the mountains like a partridge.

David went from pillar to post, and at last took refuge in the cave of Engedi. Then it was that the words of my text were wrung from his heart:

"I looked on my right hand, and beheld, but there was no man that would know me: refuge failed me; no man cared for my soul."

It seems strange that any man, at any period of the world's history, should be compelled to use words like these and that such words should be the honest expression of the lack of interest manifest toward him by those whom he knew and with whom he came in contact.

But it is more than passing strange to me that any man in your day and mine, with such opportunities to know God, with all the inducements that he has, his knowledge of Christianity—and he has seen that bigotry and superstition have been swept aside and we stand on a foundation of common sense—I say, it does seem to me staggering and astoundingly strange that any man could use words like these and that they would be the honest expression of the lack of interest manifest toward him by those who profess to love and know the Lord.

Yet it is true. "No man cared for my soul." It is as true in Pittsburgh as when David, from the cave in the mountains, cried it out.

We Care About Physical Distress

Did you ever stop to think of the great concern which is manifest for people in times of physical distress? Let the cry of a child be heard, and we will drop our money, we will turn from the counter, we will stop discussing politics or talking religion, we will forget our differences of creed and color and rush to the aid of the helpless whose cry has called us.

A friend of mine told me that as he sat one day in the Russell House in Detroit, Michigan, the fire alarm sounded. Soon the 4-11 rang out which summons all the apparatus except the reserve. He hurriedly finished his meal and, with others, followed the people down the street. They stopped in front of a building nine stories high, which was reputed to be fireproof. The flames had started in the second story and had driven the inmates to the top of the building.

They had shut off opportunity for escape. Many jumped from the windows. The fire apparatus came and coupled onto the stand pipe. That is where they put five engines onto a huge stand pipe and from the nozzle throw a stream of water six inches in diameter. But with all those engines they could not get force enough to break the windows, the hydrants were so nearly frozen.

When people were driven out by the heat, they raised the windows and stood on the ledge. My friend counted seventeen men and women as they toppled over and over and struck the street below.

Scores of lives were lost. Detroit was in mourning. Business was suspended. Schools were closed. Money poured in like water to supply the needs of those who had been prematurely deprived of the bread winners. D. M. Ferry, the seed man, gave $5,000 and in a few minutes sent $5,000 more; and in less than an hour $50,000 had come in during this time of physical distress!

When the message came telling us that San Francisco was lying in ruins and the hungry flames were licking up hovel and palace, we ran our hands into our pockets to our elbows; and an endless stream of gold poured to the Pacific coast to supply the people with their needs. You were proud you were an American and had some part in alleviating human misery and suffering.

Many Could Honestly Say, "No Man Cared for My Soul"

It is a solemn thought when it may apply to people who come to your own church. Every church has a standard. Certain men in this town, when they go to church, go because their mother went there or because their wife is a member or because their children are in that Sunday school. Every church has a standard.

A friend of mine told me (and he was pastor of one of the largest churches in this country), that a man and woman came regularly to his church, neither of whom was a Christian. They gave more to the current expenses than any member. He personally had never talked with them about God, and he didn't know that any of his members had.

The Lord troubled him for their salvation, and he said, "God, the next time I see them I will ask them."

It proved to be on Sunday morning as they sat in their accustomed place. When the sermon was over, he hurried down and said, "Mr. and Mrs. Towne, I have come to ask you to be Christians." My friend told me that the tears trickled down their cheeks. They thanked him and said, "That is the first personal invitation we have ever had. We have had it through sermons, we have attended socials and receptions of your members, we have contributed to the current expenses of your church; but not one has ever asked us to be a Christian."

Certainly they had a right to say that no one cared for their souls.

Think. It may apply to your own home. I don't know but there are boys and girls in your home—to young men and women they have grown—and you have never spoken to them about Jesus Christ.

I will never forget one time in a town in Illinois when I was leaving the tent where we were holding the meetings. Among those who went out last was a young man to whom I was especially attracted by his keen, bright appearance. I walked down the street with him, and we engaged in conversation. Presently I put to him the inevitable question, "Are you a Christian?"

"No, I am not."

"Father and mother alive?"

"Yes, sir."

"Father a Christian?"

"I don't know; he is a steward in the Methodist church."

"Is your mother a Christian?"

"I don't know; she is superintendent of the Sunday school in the same church."

"Have you a brother or a sister?"

"I have a sister."

"Is she a Christian?"

"I don't know; she teaches in the primary department in the Sunday school."

"Do you have family prayer in your home?"

"No, sir."

"Ask the blessing at the table?"

"No, sir."

"Has your father or your mother or your sister ever asked you to be a Christian?"

The tears trickled down his cheeks as he answered, "Mr. Sunday, as long as I can remember, neither my father, mother nor sister has ever asked me to be a Christian."

Certainly that young man had a right to say, of his own flesh and blood, the mother whose breast he nursed, the father whose name he bore and the sister he loved, that they didn't care for his soul.

Before I go any farther, this may need a little explanation. You may think you are unworthy. People estimate religion by what they see in the lives of the people who profess to be Christians. Your life may be far from what you desire it to be, yet I believe your life is just what you want it to be. If you are an old cusser, it is because you would rather cuss than pray. If you are an old boozer-fighter, it is because you would rather be a boozer-fighter than be sober. If you are an old libertine, it is because you would rather be that than be pure. You are what you are because you would rather be that than anything else.

If you are not a Christian, it is because you would rather be that way than to be a Christian. You can be what you want to be. If you are not a Christian, it is because you don't want to be. You know that Christ will change a lot of things in your life and you do not want Him to do it. You may feel, "No man cared for my soul."

If it is scriptural, a sermon dropped in an audience will do its work. God says, "My word," not Shakespeare's, not Emerson's, not Browning's, not Carlisle's—"My word," not some man's opinion about God's Word, not your theories about God's Word—"My word" (with no apologies), "shall not return unto me void." And it won't. A sermon dropped in an audience will do its work. But if this world will ever be won to Jesus Christ, it will not be by an unaided clergy. And when a preacher or an evangelist thinks his sermons are going to save the world, God Almighty will have to call in another Martin Luther and have another Reformation.

There may be those who will use the words David used in the past tense and put them in the present tense and say: "No man cares for my soul."

Let us not betray Jesus Christ with a guilty silence. How have you influenced people today in your home, on the street or wherever you have met them?

Will it be possible for anybody to say in the day of judgment, "You came to the store, and I sold you dry goods. Yes, we talked about religion, about politics, about the meetings"; or, "You paid me my wages. I worked for you in your home [or in your store or your office or your shop, on your farm], but you never talked to me about Jesus Christ. You never asked me to be a Christian." I wonder if it will be possible, on the day of judgment, for anybody to say that to you? What is the trouble? I'll tell you. You fail to realize that without Jesus Christ they are lost.

There is a man by your side. You bear his name. He is a good man.

He pays his debts. As long as he will buy you a new hat, a new dress, pay the house rent or the installment on the house or the taxes, you are perfectly satisfied; but once you begin to awaken to the fact that that man is lost and if he were to die tonight, you would never see him again, you would begin to pray and work for his salvation. Neither is there salvation in any other way but by accepting Jesus Christ.

I was at one time in a town in Iowa. People kept telling me about the mayor of the town. I said, "Haven't any of you been to see him?"

"No."

I said, "Well, I'll go to see him."

I went to his office and said, "Good morning, Mr. Seibe. My name is Sunday. I am down at the tent helping in the meetings. So many people have talked about you that I have come to ask you to be a Christian."

He looked at me, thanked me and invited me to sit down.

I sat down. We talked a little while. Our conversation led me to quote to him John 3:18: "He that believeth on him is not condemned: but he that believeth not is condemned already, because he hath not believed in the name of the only begotten Son of God."

He said, "Do you believe that, Mr. Sunday?"

"Yes, that's the reason I have come to you."

"Do those people down there in the tent, the church members, believe it?"

"They profess to."

"Will you explain to me, then, how it is that I have lived in this town fourteen years and nobody has ever asked me to be a Christian before? You are the first man ever to ask me that question. Mr. Sunday, if I believed that Scripture, I would get on my knees and ask you to pray for me."

I said, "That wouldn't do you any good. You'd as well ask me to eat or sleep for you or go to the pump and drink water for you when you are thirsty." I said, "You will have to pray for yourself before God will save you. God will save you, but He won't save you by just my prayers for you. You have something to do with that."

He did pray, and God saved him.

Certainly he had a right to say those in that town did not care about his soul.

We Fail to Comprehend that the
Unconverted are Lost.

We fail to realize that without Christ, people are lost. Everywhere they are waiting for someone to come.

In one of our large cities a mother had a little child with afflicted eyes. The mother had been trying to doctor the child herself. Finally someone suggested she take her to an oculist.

Mother finally took her to the oculist. Taking her into his private office, the doctor looked her over carefully. The mother said, "Now doctor, if worst must come to worst, tell me. Don't hold out hope when there is none. I am prepared for the worst."

The doctor examined the child's eyes carefully, then led the little one out and said to the mother, "I am sorry to tell you, but the optic nerves are affected, and it is beyond the skill of man to cure your child. In three months—at the longest—she will be stone blind."

The mother threw her arms around her little one, and her shrieks of agony rang through the hall as she cried, "My God, my baby blind!"

God says you had better be maimed and halt and blind than to go to Hell. I would rather lose my eyesight and grope and stagger my way to the coffin than to stumble into Hell. I would rather hobble through life with one limb and one arm and go up and look Jesus in the face and hear Him say, "Well done," than to walk to Hell.

Christians fail to realize that people are lost.

Sometimes you might think people don't care to talk about religion. Now listen! Where you will find one man or one woman who will treat you disrespectfully, you will find one hundred who will listen to you and thank you because you came. Then let the one go to Hell and try to get the one hundred. If a man is so low-down and good-for-nothing and Godforsaken that he would treat you disrespectfully when you go and talk to him about Jesus Christ, I have no patience with him. You will find some harebrained people just like that, but there are not very many. They are in such a sad minority that they are scarcely worthy of passing attention.

But I believe people will be disappointed if you don't talk to them. You must have your eyes in the back of your head if you can't see that God's Spirit is sweeping over Pittsburgh as you never saw Him before. You have never seen the time when it was easier to talk religion than it is today. Why, that's all you can hear. Go into any store, into any office; the conversation will open and immediately switch, and they will go to talking religion.

Many Would Come to Christ if Invited

Every town has a few leaning posts, moral and immoral. Every town has a few men that, whatever they do, the town will do. If they go to Hell, the town will go. The trouble with a good many towns is that the wrong gang got there first and settled it. So God will have to wait until He can get them and their offspring out of the way before He can do much.

In a town in Nebraska the people kept telling me about one man there. A section of that country is as rotten as Hell. The Republic Valley in Nebraska was settled by infidels, from Portage Junction down to the Missouri River, and the lower end of it, Nebraska City. Don't go out there. The wrong crowd got there first. Well, in this town in Nebraska they said, "There is one man here—if you can get him, he is good for one hundred men for Christ."

I said, "Who is he?"

"John Champenoy, the miller."

I said to Mr. Preston, then the minister, "Have you been to see him?"

"No."

I asked another minister if he had been to see the fellow. No. I asked the United Presbyterian preacher (they have a college out there). No, he hadn't been around to see him. I said, "Well, I guess I'll go around to see him."

I found the fellow seated in a chair teetered back against the wall, smoking. I asked, "Is this Mr. Champenoy?"

"Yes, sir, that's my name." He got up and took me by the hand.

I said, "My name is Sunday; I'm down at the church preaching. A good many have been talking to me about you, and I came down to see you and ask you to give your heart to God."

He looked at me, walked to a cupboard, opened the door, took out a half pint flask of whiskey and threw it out on a pile of stones. He then turned around, took me by the hand and, with tears rolling down his cheeks, said, "I have lived in this town nineteen years, and you are the first man who has ever asked me to be a Christian." He continued: "They point their finger at me and call me an old drunkard. They don't want my wife around with their wives because her husband is a drunkard.

Their children won't play with our babies. They go by my house to Sunday school and church, but they never ask us to go. They pass us by. I never go near the church. I am a Mason, and I went to the church eleven years ago when a member of the lodge died, but I've never been back, and I said I would never go."

I said, "You don't want to treat the church that way. God isn't to blame, is He?"

"No."

"The church isn't to blame, is it?"

"No."

"Christ isn't to blame?"

"No."

"You wouldn't think much of me if I were to walk up and slap your wife because you kept a dog I didn't like, would you? Then don't slap God in the face because there are some hypocrites in the church you don't like and who are treating you badly. God is all right. He never treated you badly. Come up and hear me preach, will you, John?"

"Yes, I'll come tonight."

I said, "All right, the Lord bless you, and I will pray for you."

He came; the seats were all filled, and they crowded him down the side aisle. I can see him now standing there with his hat in his hands, leaning against the wall looking at me. He never took his eyes off me.

When I got through and gave the invitation he didn't wait for them to let him out, but he walked over the backs of the seats, took his stand for Jesus Christ, and in less than a week seventy-eight men followed him into the kingdom of God. They elected that man chairman of the civic federation, and he cleaned the town up for Jesus Christ and has led a host to righteousness from then until now.

Men do care to talk about Jesus Christ and about their souls. "No man cares for my soul" is the trouble. They are anxious and waiting for someone to come.

In time of trouble, go to a man who has lost his property. He has tried hard to make things go, but he has gone to the wall and is up against it. When he was prosperous and successful, men would cross the street to shake his hand and say, "How do you do?" Now he goes to the post office, gets a bundle of letters and, like Shylock of old, they demand 100 cents on the dollar. He goes home, reads the letters, throws himself prostrate and cries, "No man cares for my soul, only 100 cents on the dollar."

No Answer but Jesus When Death Comes

Professor Knox was telling me an incident that happened in a town in Iowa. One winter a plague of diphtheria was in the city, and sixty-three children died in less than three weeks, mostly all from the homes of nonprofessing Christians.

At last the dread scourge reached the home of a man who edited an infidel paper. His wife had gone to a premature grave, brokenhearted over his scorns. He had two children, a boy associated with him in his business and a little girl eight years old whom he idolized and who was stricken.

Of course the home was quarantined. She kept begging her papa to send for Dr. Knox. She used to go to the Presbyterian church to Sunday school. Her dad had never allowed a preacher in his home, and he cursed the little one when she asked for him.

Finally the father's heart softened, and he sent for my friend, Dr. Knox, who told me the incident. He said that as he walked up the steps, he met Dr. Butler coming down. He asked, "How is Mabel?" The doctor said, "She is very ill. She may live until midnight, but she will not see the sun rise again, Dr. Knox."

My friend nerved himself and went in. The little girl's father met him with a handshake. He walked to the bed, and Mabel looked up and smiled faintly. As he brushed her hair back, he said, "You sent for me; well, I've come. What do you want me to do?"

She said she wanted him to talk about Heaven.

He said, "Why, that's the place where little girls go who love Jesus." She smiled and said, "I'm going."

Her papa said, "No, honey, you're not going to leave me. I know I'm a big swearing, cursing, drinking man, but honey, you'll not leave papa; I couldn't live without you."

She smiled and said, "I'm going, papa. I see mama with Jesus and the angels, and I'm going to go."

My friend told me that as he stood there, Mabel turned her face to the wall, breathing regularly and seemingly asleep. The clock struck two, and still Mabel had her face to the wall, breathing regularly.

My friend said, "I guess I'll go, Mr. Preston. It is midnight, but the doctor told me she can't get well, so you had better prepare for the worst."

The father bit his lips. With tears rolling down his cheeks, he said to my friend, "I beg of you, don't go. I think I'll die! The stillness will kill me. Nobody is allowed in but the doctor and you preachers. Don't go."

My friend said he stayed until one o'clock. Mabel still had her face to the wall, breathing regularly. He said, "Mr. Preston, I'm very tired. I must get some rest. I'll just lie down to rest. If I can help, send for me and I'll come."

He couldn't have gone more than four blocks when Mabel turned and almost leaped out of the bed. Her father caught her, and she wrapped her arms about his neck, her teeth chattering. Shivering, she said, "Papa, don't let me get in the river! I'll freeze. Look at the big cakes of ice."

Her papa said, "There, there, honey, you're not in the river, you're in papa's arms. Don't you feel my hand on your head?"

She smiled and said, "O papa, when did you come?" She clung to him and said, "Papa, don't let my feet get in the river! Don't let me fall; I'll freeze!"

She shivered. Her teeth chattered. He said, "Honey, you're not in the river. Don't you hear papa's heart beating?"

He laid her ear against his heart. She said, "Papa, where did you come from?"

He looked at her. Now her little fingernails were blue. Pretty soon she loosened her clasp from around his neck and reached her arms out to an imaginary person. Her face lighted up, she smiled and whispered, "Papa, you needn't care. Yonder comes mama with Jesus and the angels. They will take me over the river."

They bore her away on their snowy wings to their immortal home.

He laid her on the bed and sent for Dr. Knox. Why didn't he send for the president of the infidel club? Why didn't he send for the saloonkeeper or the dancing teacher or the progressive euchre prize winner? A board of trade failure or anti-expansion, evolution, sociology, Mrs. Neptune, Venus—all make a good text when one is well and alive and there are no empty chairs around the table, no newly made graves in the family lot; but when the death rattle is in the throat and the lurid lights of the farther shore are in the face of your loved ones, then it is that you want the consolation of the old-time religion.

Nothing on earth can help you like the Gospel of Jesus Christ in time of trouble, sir. The old gospel ship will go down the streets of Pittsburgh.

Look yonder, businessman. There are your wife and children standing on deck and begging for you to come and get on board. Get on board, it is going by! In times of a great awakening like this, ring every doorbell and say, "Listen! Hear me! The world doesn't care for your soul. It will give you money, it will give you fame; but it doesn't care for your soul."

What Else Really Matters When Death Comes?

How melancholy have been the last days of some whom the world has called great! Caesar was stabbed to death. Alexander the Great sat down and wept as he wrapped the drapery of his couch about him. Godfrey languished in jail. Charles V got a melancholy streak and locked himself up. Napoleon spent his last days on St. Helena's barren rock. How sad have been the later days of many who have climbed to the very pinnacle and looked down!

The world doesn't care. The mind of many a man is perplexed when he takes his dinner bucket and goes to work in the store, in the mill or on the farm. He knows a few brief years will wind up his earthly career, and he wonders how much of the Bible is true. He wonders if it is figurative; how much is literally true. There are men in Pittsburgh who would pull out their checkbook and write a check for $1,000 or $5,000 if they could have it proven that the Bible is the Word of God, Jesus the Son of God, Heaven for the saved, Hell for the lost, salvation only through Jesus Christ.

But it won't cost you a cent. You can come and listen, and I will tell you in five minutes that it is true "because the mouth of the Lord hath spoken." The world doesn't care.

Did you ever hear or read that story told by Count Tolstoi? He tells of a man to whom the government would give a piece of land as long as the distance he could traverse and retraverse between the rising and the setting of the sun.

As the sun came tripping over the banks, the signal was given and away the man ran, over the hills and valleys, on and on. In the distance he looked and saw what at first he thought was a mirage but what proved to be a lake. He leaped into a canoe and paddled to the farther side; he leaped out and said, "Ah, that is mine."

On he ran. He saw a woodland along the edge of which trickled a stream and, like the hare panting after the water brooks, he plunged in, waded the stream, clambered up on the farther bank, dripping and exhausted, said, "That is mine."

On and on he ran, over the hills and valleys, driven by cupidity, avarice and greed. When at last he raised his eyes, he staggered back. The sun had passed the meridian. He said, "I must retrace or I will lose it all."

So he ran. From the bank into the stream he leaped and, swimming, wading and floundering, he clambered up the bank; and on he hurried. Reaching the lake he leaped into the canoe and paddled to the other side. Then on he ran.

Friends came to meet him. They saw he was about to lose. He threw off his coat, his hat and his vest. With his hair streaming in the wind and the perspiration rolling down his face, eyes bloodshot and almost bursting from their sockets, like Damon of old he rushed on. Just as he reached the starting point he stumbled and fell at the stake, and as he did he cried, "I have won!"

He remained motionless. They looked at him, then running to his side, gazed upon his face and found he was dead. He had won, but had paid the price with his life.

Your Companions in Sin Do Not Care for Your Soul

Yes, you will win that political office, but Hell will be the price you will pay. Yes, a gang of fellows in Pittsburgh will come and pat you on the shoulder, laugh at your dirty, rotten story and say, "You're a dead game sport, pal," but Hell will be the end of it.

God pity you! What a price you pay for it! The politician doesn't care for your soul; he only wants your vote. Vote for him today and you can go to Hell tomorrow for all of him.

The saloonkeeper doesn't care for your soul. All he wants is your dollar, and you can have his booze. The world doesn't care, and the Devil doesn't care. He will flatter you, lie to you, cheat you, lead you by his subtlety and intrigue to indulge; and when at last you have gone I venture every man in this tabernacle would give his right arm if you could be free.

The Devil doesn't care. He leads you on to indulge, and when at last you awaken to your peril, you will cry out, "O wretched man that I am; who will deliver me?" God pity you! The Devil doesn't care.

But I want to tell you, Heaven, earth and Hell are all interested in this tabernacle. Earth wants to lead you, Hell damn you and Heaven save you. Above your heads are the angels of light, snow white from the throne of God. And around you are the devils of darkness, black pinioned from Hell, that rip and tear with beak and talon; you have it to say who will win—Heaven or Hell. You have it to say whether with a shriek they grab your soul and go to perdition, or whether the angels will take you and mount up with wings of love and burst through the gates of Heaven.

How Foolhardy to Go on With No Care for Your Own Soul!

All earth and Hell are interested in these meetings. But I tell you, you are like a ship at sea. Yonder she goes, careening in her way, when they discover a fire in her hold. They rush to the captain and say, "Captain, the ship's afire! Let's fire the gun; let's wave the signal."

The captain says, "No, no. I'm captain of this ship. Close the portholes and put out the lights. I'll put this ship in the harbor at Liverpool, or I'll put her at the bottom of the sea."

But they say, "Captain, that is foolhardy! The flames will soon be through, and down we will go. Captain, yonder goes a Cunarder, the *Majestic;* there goes the *Lusitania;* there goes the *Cedric;* there goes the *St. Paul* of the American line. Yonder goes the *Kaiser Wilhelm.* Captain, shoot the gun, fly the signal, wave the flag. The watchman will see us, and they will pick us up."

"No!" commands the captain. "I'll put this ship in the harbor at Liverpool or down at the bottom of the sea."

There are men like that. If you would lift your head, walk down the aisle, tell your wife and the people you want to be a Christian; if you would just fly the slightest signal of distress, just give God the slightest indication that you want to be a Christian and want to do right, all Heaven would hurry to your aid. The Devil doesn't care, but Christians care.

Friends, hear me! If I didn't care, do you think I would come all this distance, with all these helpers and put all the money I have in these meetings? Do you think I would stand up here and work as hard as I do—study until 2:00 or 3:00 in the morning—do you think I would do it if I didn't care? Every board in this tabernacle, every nail, every electric light, is an evidence that people care and want to see you saved.

There are men who have always been in the soul-saving business. There are thousands of preachers praying and sweating and dying to bring men to Jesus Christ. Yes, they care. God cares or He would never have given you the plan of redemption. Every thorn in His brow, every nail in the cross, every drop of blood that He shed puts it square up to you and tells you that God wants you to go to Heaven instead of to Hell. He is anxious; He cares. That's the reason Jesus came.

It was only six miles from where Jesus was born to where He died on the cross, six miles. On He came, denounced, damned, stoned, vilified. They hurled and belched out their maledictions, but on He came. They stoned Him, drove Him out of their cities. He had to lie down with nothing but the ground for a bed and the canopy of God for a covering, hair wet with the dew and drenched with rain. No man gave Him to eat, but He kept on and on.

What for? To open up a plan to keep you out of Hell. Yet men will pass it up with indifference. I wonder that God has not given up the task and let some go to Hell.

God Cares So Much: We Should Do All We Can

Go out and work. The trouble is a lot of you take it too easy. You rub elbows with people, and never a prayer goes from your lips. You never had a drop of sweat go down your face trying to keep people out of perdition. No wonder you sit there with a curl on your lip when someone is trying to preach. Jesus Christ cares, my friends.

A friend of mine told a story, and the man who he said told it I met one day in Chicago. I said, "Hello, Mr. Brown, I heard a friend of mine tell a story that you told. Now I want you to tell it to me." He said, "Come up to the Y.M.C.A., and I will." This is the story:

He was preaching in a town in Wisconsin, and the last night, or next to the last night, there was a young fellow, cashier in one of the banks, whom they had tried to get to give his heart to God. He wouldn't listen to them. He was a leader among the young men.

My friend closed the meeting. Shortly after that he received a letter from this boy's father saying that he had left home. The father said, "We had a letter from him, saying he would come back sometime, but for us not to bother, that we wouldn't know where he was, but that when he made up his mind to come home, he would come. I have written to you to ask you, if you see or hear anything of him, tell him we love him. Mother is just dying."

My friend told me that two years later he went back to that town, and the first man he met when he got off the train was James Stewart, the father of this boy.

It was a cold day, and my friend said, "Why, Mr. Stewart, what are you doing down here today?"

The father said, "My boy."

"Hasn't he come home yet?"

"No, sir."

My friend transacted his business and left.

Eleven years after he went back to that town. On the train he saw a great, stalwart, young fellow. He would walk nervously up and down the aisle, would pick out the landmarks as they came along and then sit down and talk to himself. When the train stopped, he followed the crowd out of the front door, and my friend went out the rear; and as he stepped from the platform the first person he saw was James Stewart.

His hair and beard were whiter than snow. The old man's eyes were dim, his brow wrinkled and his form bent.

My friend said, "Hello, Mr. Stewart. What are you doing down here today?"

The old man failed to recognize him, and said, "Who are you?"

My friend told him.

"Oh, yes, I remember you."

My friend said, "What are you doing here?"

The old man said, "My boy."

"Do you mean to tell me that he hasn't come back yet?"

The old father said, "No, sir; he ain't come back yet, and we haven't heard anything from him—only that letter. I don't know but that he might come."

The old man hobbled along and looked in the car window and caught sight of a face he thought he knew. Presently the stalwart young fellow got to the front of the car. The old man started, dropped his cane and ran as fast as his tottering limbs would carry him. His hat flew off, and his hair blew in the wind. He stumbled and would have fallen, but strong arms went around him and held him up.

He threw his arms around the young fellow's neck and said, "My boy, I knew you would come! I knew you would come sometime!" For thirteen years he had gone to the station, and at last his face lighted up, and he said, "I knew you would come! I knew you would come!"

God has been waiting for some of you men for thirty, forty, fifty, sixty or seventy years, and you haven't come. He cares. Listen! God cares. Jesus cares, and the Christian cares. Don't you think you ought to care a little bit? If there is so much interest manifest for you, I think it is the height of manhood and womanhood to show your appreciation, and I think the most unmanly or unwomanly thing you can do is to not care when Heaven cares and Hell doesn't.

FRED M. BARLOW
1921-1983

ABOUT THE MAN:

In 1959 Dr. Fred M. Barlow was elected National Sunday School Consultant for Regular Baptist Press and the General Association of Regular Baptist Churches. He held pastorates in New York, Ohio and Michigan. Then he began a ministry to local churches and multi-church Sunday school conferences; held evangelistic campaigns; gave addresses to Bible colleges and seminaries; and was active in summer Bible camp evangelism and youth rallies.

His sermons have been prize winners in sermon contests held by the Sword of the Lord. He was the author of several books, including: *Vitalizing Your Sunday School Visitation. . . Special Days in the Sunday School. . . Timeless Truths. . . Profiles in Evangelism. . . Revival for Survival. . .* and several smaller booklets, including a biography of Dr. John R. Rice.

Dr. Barlow was a native of southeastern West Virginia.

He graduated from Baptist Bible Seminary (now Baptist Bible College of Pennsylvania, Clarks Summit, Pennsylvania) and received an honorary Doctor of Divinity degree from Western Baptist Bible College, Salem, Oregon.

Dr. and Mrs. Barlow were parents of four children.

Dr. Barlow died in 1983.

XI.

Look at Your Hands – Are They Bloody?

FRED M. BARLOW

(Preached in 1965)

"Son of man, I have made thee a watchman unto the house of Israel: therefore hear the word at my mouth, and give them warning from me. When I say unto the wicked, Thou shalt surely die; and thou givest him not warning, nor speakest to warn the wicked from his wicked way, to save his life; the same wicked man shall die in his iniquity; but his blood will I require at thine hand."—Ezek. 3:17,18.

Look at your hands! This very moment hold your hands, palms toward your eyes. Look at those hands. Look at them carefully. Look at them critically! Although those hands may look clean—rubbed, scrubbed—I witness to you from the authoritative Word of God: your hands may be foul and filthy hands; yes, BLOODY HANDS—hands that are dripping, drenched—stained with the blood of sinners!

For our text—again repeated in Ezekiel 33:7,8 to give multifold and manifold weight in its warning—is one of the most gripping, commanding pronouncements in God's Word of our individual responsibility in personal soul witnessing and soul winning, for it points to that inescapable day of judgment when we Christians shall stand before the Lord Jesus Christ to give an account of our evangelism!

Lest some reader imagine this text is only dispensational (Old Testament, age of the Law); or, only individual (son of man, Ezekiel); or, only racial (to the Jew, Israel); may I sincerely suggest that you read prayerfully some New Testament texts that tell the same terrible truth: when men, women and youth die unsaved, unprepared to meet God, but unwarned, unreached by Christians, their blood will be required at our hands!

Hebrews 13:17 warns,

"Obey them that have the rule over you, and submit yourselves: FOR THEY WATCH FOR YOUR SOULS, AS THEY THAT MUST GIVE ACCOUNT, that they may do it with joy, and not with grief: for that is unprofitable for you."

This text and truth in Ezekiel, chapter 3, were among the motivating powers that impelled, compelled, propelled the Apostle Paul to plead daily, nightly, publicly, personally, passionately with every sinner to get saved!

"And how I kept back nothing that was profitable unto you, but have shewed you, and have taught you publickly, and from house to house, Testifying both to the Jews, and also to the Greeks, repentance toward God, and faith toward our Lord Jesus Christ. . . . Therefore watch, and remember, that by the space of three years I ceased not to warn every one night and day with tears."—Acts 20:20,21,31.

So testified this soul-seeking apostle as he rehearsed his ministry in Ephesus to the elders of the church. Then Paul, gratefully aware that he had seen and seized every opportunity to evangelize; had fulfilled his every responsibility to witness of God's saving grace to every soul in that city; and that he would stand guiltless in that day of account-ability (II Cor. 5:10), thrillingly testified,

"Wherefore I take you to record this day, that I am pure from the blood of all men."—Acts 20:26.

I believe Paul held his hands high, opened and extended, as he sobbed out with tears of unquenchable joy, "I am pure from the blood of all men"! There would be no blood of unreached, unwarned Ephesians dripping from his stained hands—he was pure! He was free!

Oh, I pray to God that when you and I stand before Christ our Lord at that judgment throne, that we, too, like Paul, may be able to hold up stainless, sheaf-filled, soul winner's hands and with rejoicing, sob out to our Saviour, "I am pure from the blood of all men!"

But, hear me, my friend, the tragedy is that this triumphant scene will not be true of many of us. Rather, most of us will stand in sorrow, stricken with grief, smitten in shame before the Lord, holding out blood-soaked hands! Why?

I. LOST OPPORTUNITIES!

Look at your hands; are they bloody? Indifference to the obligations of our opportunities cries out, "Yes!"

Opportunity! In one of our midwest art museums is a sculpture by that title. It is a man, face turned away, eyes concealed by hair that has fallen over his face, and feet that have been fitted with powerful, poised wings.

The first impression one gets upon viewing this museum piece is that this sculpture is a monstrosity. But actually this statue preaches a sobering sermon. It speaks out, in the first place, that men are not seeking opportunities. It says that men do not recognize opportunities even if they are seen. Third, the statue states that once an opportunity has sped by, even with winged feet, it can never be caught nor re-captured.

The analogies to soul winning are all too awfully apparent. We Christians are not even looking for the limitless whitened fields of opportunities to witness. Second, our eyes are too much blinded by the cares, the affairs, the pleasures of this world to seize these opportunities to win souls. Third, when we fail to see and fail to seize these opportunities to witness for Christ, these opportunities are gone for good, never to be recalled nor recaptured!

In light of these terrible truths, consider the criminality of our 20th century Christianity that is not earnestly evangelizing sinners for the Saviour, iniquities that indict us with bloodguiltiness!

1. Laxness in Evangelism in Light of a Lost World!

The population of this earth has now spiraled until nearly two and three-fourth billions of people live upon this planet. [Now, in 1989, there are 5 billion.] Yet it is stated that nearly 65 percent of these souls are unreached, untouched with the saving story of Jesus Christ. It is further stated that over one thousand tribes have never once heard the saving name of Christ in their own tongue. It is further declared that of the 2,974 different languages and dialects in the world, 1,789 of these peoples have not one verse of Scripture that tells them of Christ's soul-saving sacrifice at Calvary.

These startling statistics scream out the terrible truth about "evangelism" over the seas. But what about our "evangelism" across the street? Read these statistics and blush, my friend, for they scream out the same, sad, sickening story: 37 million of our youth are unreached with the gospel good news. These are pagan youth who have never seen the inside of a church nor the inside of a Bible! Small wonder, but with the amoral teaching in the public schools, along with banned Bibles and prohibited prayer, that we have on our hands a generation of immoral youth who prefer pornography to Bible biography, lust to love, abstraction to art, and lawlessness to liberty!

And adults are just as untouched with the Gospel! Although there are churches on almost every corner, who attends? Only three out of ten on any given Sunday morning are in attendance in anyone's Sunday school; only eight out of one hundred attend any preaching service in the morning, and incredibly, only two out of a hundred are found in the evening service. Any tour around your city, out in the suburbs, up to the mountains and out to the beaches, the ball parks, etc., will confirm these conclusions!

Yes, multitudes are being born, live and die in urban and suburban areas of America unreached with the Bible message by us who profess to be Bible-believing and Bible-practicing! The lie to this kind of living is made light by this palling pronouncement recently made by a nationwide broadcaster: "Of the 4 million babies being born in America annually, at our present dying rate of evangelism, only 300,000 will be reached with the Gospel!"

We Christians claim to believe that we have a great and glorious Gospel! We proudly prate after the Apostle Paul: "For I am not ashamed of the gospel of Christ: for it is the power of God unto salvation to every one that believeth . . ." (Rom. 1:16). We claim to believe our Gospel is soul-saving, life-transforming, social-ills-correcting, every-human-need-meeting, Devil-defeating and Christ-glorifying! But we do not even bother to propagate it! We do not snap two fingers together, pronounce two syllables one after another, put two feet, one a step ahead of another, to get this miracle-working Gospel into our communities!

But if we born-again Christians are feebly, futilely failing in evangelism, you be sure no other gospel is! Other isms, cults, sects are tirelessly tramping the streets of our cities, fanning out further into the highways and hedges, passing out their literature, starting classes, organizing preaching and teaching centers, training their converts with poisonous doctrines that deceive and, at the last, damn the souls of multiplied millions of men, women and youth in infernal, eternal Hell!

There is a reason for the super successes of these satanic-inspired isms, and that reason is stated in Ezekiel, chapter 34. For today, even as in the day of Israel, idolatrous and infidelistic religions flourish like a green bay tree because of the heartless, faithless and careless ministry, the "easy-come, easy-go" brand of evangelism by the "Bible-believing" pastors and teachers.

May the condemning charges spelled out in these Scriptures speak to our too calloused, careless ministries:

"... Thus saith the Lord God unto the shepherds; Woe be to the shepherds of Israel that do feed themselves! should not the shepherds feed the flocks? Ye eat the fat, and ye clothe you with the wool, ye kill them that are fed: but ye feed not the flock. The diseased have ye not strengthened, neither have ye healed that which was sick, neither have ye bound up that which was broken, neither have ye brought again that which was driven away, neither have ye sought that which was lost...."—Vss. 2-4.

Now read the woeful results in verse 5,

"And they were scattered, because there is no shepherd: and they became meat to all the beasts of the field, when they were scattered."

I trust these scathing sentences, charges of criminal and spiritual neglect of souls committed to your care, are not true of any pastor, teacher, father, mother, yes, any Christian who reads this message. For if these indictments are true of you, there is one more pronouncement from the pen of the Lord: the charge that your crimes will cause you to stand before the Lord one day bloodguilty and bloody-handed:

"Therefore, ye shepherds, hear the word of the Lord; As I live, saith the Lord God, surely because my flock became a prey, and my flock became meat to every beast of the field, because there was no shepherd, neither did my shepherds search for my flock, but the shepherds fed themselves, and fed not my flock; Therefore, O ye shepherds, hear the word of the Lord; Thus saith the Lord God; Behold, I am against the shepherds; AND I WILL REQUIRE MY FLOCK AT THEIR HAND, and cause them to cease from feeding the flock...."—Vss. 7-10.

You believe it! When denominations, when churches, when individual Christians lose their vision, their passion, their purpose for soul winning: when they cease from their intercession and visitation for souls, you be sure the Lord God will write "Ichabod" over that ministry, take away the light of that testimony, and souls, as sheep without a shepherd, will become strayed, stolen, prey for every beast of the field: every ism, every sect, every cult that deceives, deludes and damns souls to a Devil's Hell!

The Scriptures have decreed it. History has demonstrated it! Jerusalem, the cradle of Christianity, lost its vision, its passion for souls, and, as a result, succumbed to ritualism and paganism; so God marked "Ichabod" over its once mighty missionary ministry and moved its testimony to Antioch.

Denominations and churches have deteriorated in the same way. The Methodists, the Congregationalists, the Presbyterians, the Baptists once were aflame, fervent, zealous in soul winning. But these old-line denominations have lost the vision, the passion for souls and have substituted formalism and a social program for one time earnest personal evangelism. So God has, in some measure, given up these old-line organizations and raised up some independent fundamental fellowships and independent fundamental churches here and there that are passionately reaching, teaching, preaching and winning lost souls. You only have to look to yourself personally, and at members of your family, to see this same tragedy is true of individuals also!

But don't you forget the rest of that doom-declaring decree in Ezekiel 34:10, *"And I will require my flock at your hand."* Ah! That is the other price that must be paid: bloody, stained hands and the awful regret, remorse—repentance without any opportunity of restitution or recovery at the judgment seat of Christ!

O Christian, what a lamentable price to pay for laxity and lethargy in trying to evangelize a lost world!

I suggest another reason for bloodguiltiness on our hands—the charge against

2. Christian Criminality That Fails to Warn the Lost in the Light of Limited Opportunities!

"But this I say, brethren, the time is short. . ." (I Cor. 7:29) is the sobering statement of Scripture to stir us to soul winning today. No one can dispute nor deny that call to urgency in evangelism in the light of the all-pervading and always present death in the harvest field of sinners.

A hundred thousand souls a day
Are passing, one by one, away

Into Christless guilt and doom.
O Christian, what will you say,
When in that awful judgment day
They charge you with their doom?

This is the powerful plea of the poet to warn us to seek souls today before they die unreached and we are declared responsible for their doom! His plea was well put, for souls are dying daily, dying unsaved and unwarned.

Such a tragedy was told me recently. A teacher had taken a class of junior high girls. The church, at the time, had no requirements that teachers must visit absentees and prospects, so this teacher was naturally careless in her calling. She was a saved woman, loved the Lord and prepared her lessons, and doubtless prayed some for her pupils. However, she did not appeal for decisions nor call upon her absentees.

One night some of the neighborhood young people went joy-riding. Suddenly the car got out of control, clipped a fence and crashed! One girl was pulled out dead, a pupil in this teacher's class.

The teacher went to the funeral. She apologetically introduced herself as their dead daughter's Sunday school teacher. You can be sure it was a bitter and embarrassing experience. She had been her teacher, but never once had she visited in her home; her teacher, but never once had she personally dealt with her about her soul; her teacher, but she did not know the true spiritual state of this dead pupil; her teacher, but a bloody-handed teacher! Be sure, although she was repentant and regretful, this teacher could never recall nor make any restitution for being amiss in her soul winning. The death of her pupil had forever ended every opportunity to evangelize! May we not be similarly sinful and shameful at the judgment seat of the Saviour!

Realize this, my reader: the death of the unreached is not the only death that will necessitate that fearsome facing of blood on Christian's hands. What if YOU were to die today? It was this sense of peril that prompted one pastor to promise on his hospital bed, "When I get up from this sickbed, I am going to concentrate on soul winning." This godly pastor had prayed much, had prepared his messages well, and he had preached them with spiritual profit to his people. But he had never emphasized soul winning in his messages nor in his personal ministry. On his sickbed he ruefully realized how he had failed in his greatest responsibility. "When I get up from this sickbed, I am going to concentrate on soul winning," was his passionate prayer of repentance.

But he never became a soul winner; for, alas, his sickbed turned out to be his *deathbed* and he never got up so he could get out and go after the lost. He died as he had lived—a fruitless, yes, a bloody-handed preacher!

But there are reasons for bloody-handedness besides death destroying the hope of harvest. I refer to:

3. Delinquency of Soul Winners to Seize the Ripe-Unto-Harvest Opportunities to Evangelize, Opportunities Usually Once-and-for-All

You be sure that, if you don't warn the sinner the first opportunity you get, you don't often, if ever, get a second chance. Even as I write these words, my heart rises up to smite me of the multiplied times I have shamefully sinned in neglecting to speak to someone about the saving, satisfying Saviour. At that time I conveniently comforted my conscience with such conclusions as: "I don't have time now," or "I don't have a tract with me," or "It's not the right time (or place)," etc., etc. But, you believe me, I never had those opportunities again. They were once-and-for-all opportunities; they are gone and gone forever! Even as I suggested earlier of the sculpture entitled "Opportunity," even with winged feet I cannot recover a lost opportunity to witness.

Nor can you! May the Spirit of God be pleased to burn into our so dulled brains and our so often calloused souls this terrifying truth: we shall stand bloodguilty at the judgment seat because of criminal neglect, the failure to witness at the first, fleeting, yea, sometimes the last opportunity.

This awesome reality was vividly brought to my attention again recently in Southern California. I was preaching on a beautiful mid-March Sunday morning. After a message on our responsibilities and accountabilities in the light of our opportunities to win souls, a man came forward at the invitation. I dealt with him. He was a Christian, a member of that fundamental church, and a Sunday school teacher. "Do you really believe God will hold us responsible, bloodguilty for sinners if we have had opportunity to warn them and failed to, and no one else ever speaks to them?" was his probing question. I read to him the verses of our text:

"Son of man, I have made thee a watchman unto the house of Israel: therefore hear the word at my mouth, and give them warning from me. When I say unto the wicked, Thou shalt surely die; and thou givest

him not warning, nor speakest to warn the wicked from his wicked way,
to save his life; the same wicked man shall die in his iniquity; but his
blood will I require at thine hand."—Ezek. 3:17,18.

To ask the question was actually to answer it, and he knew it. He
looked at me tearfully, "May I tell you my story?"

"I would like to hear it," I suggested.

This is what he told. He and his family had gotten in their car and
started for Sunday school. On their way to church they rounded a corner. Dozens, perhaps fifty or more, children were in the street playing
ball, roller skating, flying kites and playing other games. He slammed
on his brakes, at the same moment honking his horn. The children scattered to the sidewalks and lawns. With his car stopped, it seemed as
though the Lord said, "You should give these children some tracts, invite them to Sunday school and tell them how to be saved." "I don't
have time," was his argument. "I have to get on to church; some other
time," was his alibi. It seemed the Lord insisted, "Tell them now. Now
is the acceptable time." But he refused, released his brakes, repeating
his alibis, and sped on toward Sunday school.

"While you preached," he confessed, "God spoke to my disobedient
heart. I'm guilty. I am guilty! Oh, what can I do?"

I read to him I John 1:9: "If we confess our sins, he is faithful and
just to forgive us our sins, and to cleanse us from all unrighteousness."
"Confess your sin to the Lord right now," I suggested. "Ask His
forgiveness. Claim His promise." Then I added, "Get in your car. Go
back to that corner. Take some tracts. Get out and tell those kids how
to be saved. And pray you don't get there too late."

We had a time of prayer. He confessed his disobedience. He called
for forgiveness. He asked for a second chance. He seemed satisfied.
Then he left.

I left the area to begin a meeting in another church that evening, so
I did not learn immediately the results of this brother's efforts.

Three months later I was back in Southern California. While walking
across the lobby to enter the auditorium of the building I was in, I heard
a voice calling, "Brother Barlow! Brother Barlow!" I turned and saw
this good brother approaching. "Do you know me? Do you remember
me?" were his anxious questions.

"I sure do," I replied as I extended my hand. "How did you make
out with those boys and girls at that street corner?"

"You do remember me," he stated. Then he dropped his head to his chest. Suffice it to say, I had my answer. Then he looked up at me with tear-filled eyes and sobbed out, "Brother Barlow, it's incredible. It's unbelievable. When I arrived, the corner was deserted. I went back that afternoon. I have been back mornings, afternoons, evenings, but I have never found more than a handful. O brother, their blood is on my hands! I had a chance. I failed! I failed! I sinned!"

Then he leaned over to me: "Brother Barlow, will you promise me something? Will you promise to tell my story everywhere you go? Will you tell Sunday school teachers, preachers, deacons, all Christians, when God tells you to talk to sinners and you don't, you may get only one chance, and their blood will be upon your hands!"

I could not promise him that I would tell his story everywhere, but I tell you right this moment this passionate plea of a tortured soul, a Sunday school teacher who found out too late, and the hardest way, this tragic truth: when you neglect to witness to souls, whether it be in stubbornness or because of fearfulness or indifference, it is SIN, the sin of bloodguiltiness and bloody-handedness! May you not have to stand chargeable to this crime of crimes!

But there are reasons more than these why we should look at our hands—

II. INCONSISTENT CHRISTIAN CONDUCT MAKES US GUILTY

Look at your hands—are they bloody? Inconsistency of Christian conduct cries out, "Yes!"

Inconsistent church members, inconsistent Christians! They are the corrupters of Christendom, the plague of pastors and people who sincerely seek to win souls, the millstone around the neck of militant and evangelistic churches, yes, a curse to Christ and His cause.

Only eternity will truly total the legions of lost sinners who stumbled into Hell over the inconsistent lives of professing Christians. Mirrored in my mind are the many times I have heard some unsaved sinner eagerly excuse his rejection of Christ by claiming, "I don't want to be a hypocrite. When I get saved, I mean to live like a real Christian. I can't really see any difference in your church members and myself. I know a lot of Christians who do things I don't even do."

Every Christian worker knows the heart-rending reality of that experience, and every soul winner knows there is sometimes no availing argument to down those oft-given alibis of sinners. As Dr. Joe Henry Hankins once poignantly preached:

> When they tell me that, it breaks my heart. If I cannot convince them, I just have to hang my head in shame and walk off, because they are telling the truth, and I know it.
>
> Sometimes you cannot answer that. Oh, you can say, "You are responsible to God for yourself," but down in your heart you often know you are not getting anywhere with them. The hardest task anybody ever had is to win unsaved people over a crowd of ungodly church members. . . . People are going to Hell by the millions that way, stumbling over inconsistent church members! They see their lives. They hear their talk. They see where they go. They see that they are outwardly no different than anyone else.

Dr. Hankins posed the problem rightly. And he pictured the price tag of such poisonous influence of unsaintly living saints when he witnessed:

> Oh, listen! One day some church members will wake up and see somebody sent to Hell, somebody damned from the presence of God, somebody who, as he is cast into outer darkness, will point a damning finger at those church members and say, "If you had lived as you ought to have lived, I would have been a Christian. I stumbled over you into Hell!"

This is bloody-handedness: sinners stumbling into Hell over sin-loving, sinful-living saints!

A foretaste of that fateful day was experienced one night in a calling program where I was pastor. I was handing out the "calls" and re-marked to one of our teachers, "You sure won't have to use much gasoline tonight. These two calls are your neighbors." The teacher took the cards, eyed them carefully, then flung them back to me protesting with words weighed with finality: "I will not make these calls!"

Momentarily, I was stunned. No such scene had ever happened before in my ministry (and it was a scene that never happened again, I sug-gest). I handed the cards back to the worker and insisted, "I believe you *ought* to make these calls." The teacher returned them again, declar-ing, "It is not that I won't make any calls tonight. I just won't call at these homes! Give me some cards anywhere else and I will gladly go. But these are my next-door neighbors. *They know me too well!* Why, pastor, they would laugh in my face if I asked them to be saved."

I stood there stunned in utter unbelief. But it was true, too bitterly, bitingly true! What could I say? Only this—and I say the same to all of you: If there is one person anywhere—neighbor or near of kin—that would laugh in your face because of inconsistent Christian conduct, go to that home, knock at that door, get down on your face, confess your sinfulness, ask their forgiveness, at the same time assuring them of your repentance to the Lord. Then plead with them as with a brother to get saved before it is eternally too late. If they hear you, if they believe you, praise God a thousand times over because you have delivered your soul and you can plead clean hands at the judgment day. But, oh, if, as Lot, you "seem as one that mocked," then realize you "have wounded their weak conscience. . . sinned against Christ" (I Cor. 8:12); and that you will stand bloody-handed, bloodguilty in the light of your inconsistent Christian testimony!

May I suggest further, the final, the unequivocal reason why there will be blood on believers' hands and that because of the crowning crime committed by Christians against the Christ.

III. INSUBORDINATION TO CHRIST: HOW GUILTY!

Look at your hands—are they bloody? The iniquity of insubordination against the commands of Christ to win souls cries out, "Yes!"

Every argument I have used in this message, every burden I have bared from my heart, every challenge I have cited, every declaration, every entreaty, every fact, yes, all the gamut of reasons from "A" to "Z" I have given for soul winning, may be disdained, discredited, yes, even disobeyed by you. But you be sure that these declarations, these demands by the Lord Jesus Christ to warn, to witness to, to try to win the lost are beyond any debate, discussion and disobedience on your part!

For you see, *Christ has commanded every Christian to win souls!* Read these commands of Christ and realize your responsibility to these charges. Hear them! Heed them! Believe them! Behave them!

"Go ye therefore, and teach all nations. . . ."—Matt. 28:19.

". . .Go ye into all the world, and preach the gospel to every creature."—Mark 16:15.

". . .Go home to thy friends, and tell them how great things the Lord hath done for thee, and hath had compassion on thee."—Mark 5:19.

"After these things the Lord appointed other seventy also, and sent them two and two before his face into every city and place, whither he himself would come. Therefore said he unto them, The harvest truly is great, but the labourers are few. . . . Go your ways: behold, I send you forth as lambs among wolves."—Luke 10:1-3.

". . . Go out quickly into the streets and lanes of the city, and bring in hither the poor, and the maimed, and the halt, and the blind. . . . Go out into the highways and hedges, and compel them to come in, that my house may be filled."—Luke 14:21,23.

". . . as my Father hath sent me, even so send I you."—John 20:21.

". . . and ye shall be witnesses unto me."—Acts 1:8.

"Ye have not chosen me, but I have chosen you, and ordained you, that ye should go and bring forth fruit, and that your fruit should remain. . . ."—John 15:16.

I have cited these Scriptures to show you the plain facts: every Christian is commanded, commissioned and called by Christ to win souls. Realize it, my reader. That is exactly what these Scriptures are: COMMANDS! These are not some suggestions from the Saviour on the subject of soul winning; nor are they counsels from Christ to encourage us to witness if and when it is convenient to our schedule; this is not even advice from the Almighty One. These Scriptures are the demands, the dictates, the decrees, the dictums of Deity. As Dr. John Rice correctly commented,

> Christian, did you think Jesus was only giving advice when He stood on that little hill that day and explicitly said that every convert should be taught to carry out all the commands He gave the apostles? Did you think it was only a mild suggestion when Jesus said that you are to help carry the Gospel to every creature, that you are to save people from Hell by your earnest entreaty? Jesus was not giving advice; He was giving orders. And there is only one thing for any Christian to do who acknowledges the authority of Jesus Christ—that is, he is to obey orders and put soul winning in its primal place in his life.

For a Christian to disobey these orders from heavenly headquarters must be counted as cardinal criminality; for disobedience in soul winning is the crime of anarchy—anarchy against the authority of Christ who affirmed, "All power is given unto me in heaven and in earth. Go ye therefore and teach all nations. . ." (Matt. 28:18,19).

Disobedience in soul winning is the crime of mutiny—mutiny against the mandate of the Master who remanded, ". . . as the Father hath sent me, even so send I you" (John 20:21).

Disobedience in soul winning is the crime of insubordination—insubordination against the injunction of Jesus Christ who indicts, ". . . ye shall be witnesses unto me" (Acts 1:8).

Disobedience in soul winning is the crime of spiritual manslaughter—the wickedness of a watchman who warns not the lost in light of this warrant from the Lord,

". . . therefore hear the word at my mouth, and give them warning from me. When I say unto the wicked, Thou shalt surely die; and thou givest him not warning, nor speakest to warn the wicked from his wicked way, to save his life; the same wicked man shall die in his iniquity. . . ."—Ezek. 3:17,18.

But the rest of that passage spells out the price of such disobedience: "but his blood will I require at thine hand."

May I sincerely suggest that every bloody-handed saint at that tribunal will stand defenseless before the Saviour, for He not only ordered us, He also ordained us and thus obligated us to win souls when He cited, "Ye have not chosen me, but I have chosen you, and ordained you, that ye should go and bring forth fruit. . ." (John 15:16). There is absolutely no alibi, no argument that a Christian can possibly offer for failure to witness and to win souls that will be allowable and acceptable to Christ in the light of this obligation-involving enlistment.

Which causes me to consider, not only are Christians chargeable to win souls because of the commands of Christ, they shall stand accountable because *He is counting on them to fulfill those commands!*

Mrs. C. H. Morris in her scriptural, sobering song, "His Plan," relates this responsibility:

> **There's only one way that this lost world can know**
> **That Jesus for sinners hath died;**
> **To spread the glad tidings He's bidden us go,**
> **And no other way doth provide.**
> **He's counting on us—the story to tell,**
> **His scheme of redemption for man;**
> **He's counting on you; He's counting on me,**
> **The Master has no other plan.**

If Christ's first disciples had silently gone,
And been to their great trust untrue;
God's plan of salvation we could not have known—
His mercy for me and for you.

Oh, consider the bloodguiltiness, the wanton wickedness of Simon Peter, or beloved John, or the Apostle Paul, if they had disobeyed and would "have silently gone, And been to their great trust untrue!" But, beloved, these same condemning charges will be just as true of our 20th-century Christians who will not heed the Saviour's high behest by covenanting—

Dear Master, we hasten the story to tell
And pass on the life-giving Word;
Then they must tell others, and they, others still,
Till all the glad message have heard.
For He's counting on us, the story to tell,
His scheme of redemption for man;
He's counting on you; He's counting on me.
The Master has no other plan.

In conclusion, consider this question: Who is commanding and counting on Christians to seek souls? To ask the question is actually to answer it: *The crucified Christ by right of redemption has consummate claims to command Christians to witness to the world!*

Will you look back to Calvary and see that stretched-out, spiked-to-the-cross, smitten-of-God Saviour? Will you see His body bathed in blood—blood that spilled from a thorn-pierced brow, spike-rent hands and feet and a lash-torn back, blood that is sin-canceling and sin-cleansing? That blood-soaked Saviour is the One who commands Christians to call!

Will you see that sin-bearing Saviour, He, who ". . . bare our sins in his own body on the tree. . ." (I Pet. 2:24)?

Sum up your every sin: your sins of omission and commission. See your every sin defiantly done against Deity, damagingly done against society, disgracingly done against your family, dissolutely done against your own body. Smitten with every one of these death-dealing, heart-breaking, Hell-dooming, Calvary-causing crimes, Christ has the supreme right to command His converts to witness!

Will you hear that Hell-fire-and-brimstone-soaked Saviour as He sobs out, "My God, my God, why hast thou forsaken me?" (Matt. 27:24). Can't you realize in some sense the price Christ paid for your salvation—that final, fatal lostness and loneliness of a soul separated from God, banned from Heaven, baptized in Hell fire? Realize He has the right to count on you to warn others to be saved from baneful Hell to blessed Heaven!

In the light of the claims of Christ upon Christians by reason of Calvary (". . . ye are not your own? For ye are bought with a price. . ." [I Cor. 6:19,20]); and in the light of the all-compelling commands of Christ for Christians to seek souls in His stead; for a Christian to fail Christ is to insure facing Him in the judgment guilty, yea, grossly guilty, bloodguilty and bloody-handed of base ingratitude and brazen insubordination!

L. R. SCARBOROUGH
1870-1945

ABOUT THE MAN:

L. R. Scarborough, a pastor-evangelist-educator-author, left an indelible impact for soul winning upon America, especially among Southern Baptists.

Dr. George Truett likened Scarborough to the Apostle Paul. Another said that "he was the most compassionate Christian I ever met."

Scarborough was born in Louisiana in 1870 in a Baptist minister's home, but was raised in West Texas, spending his youth as a cowboy. He dated his conversion at the age of 17. Having been encouraged to get an education, he graduated from both Baylor University and Yale. It was at Yale that he surrendered to preach.

Upon completion of his seminary work at Southern Baptist Theological Seminary in Louisville, in 1900, he pastored in Texas for the next eight years. In 1908 he went to Southwestern Baptist Theological Seminary, Fort Worth, as professor in the School of Theology where he served until elected president of the seminary in 1915. He served in that capacity for the next twenty-seven years until he retired in 1942. During this period he also served as president of the Baptist General Convention of Texas (1929-31); and president of the Southern Baptist Convention (1938-41).

Soul winning was Scarborough's consuming passion. "I have won somebody to Christ every way Jesus did except up a tree and on a cross. And the first chance I get I'm going after them"—a statement made by one who had such compassion for lost sinners.

Some of America's great evangelists, including Dr. John R. Rice and Dr. Hyman Appelman, caught much of their fire for lost souls from this great Christian.

Dr. Scarborough was also the able author of fourteen books, which excel in the field of evangelism. Personal revival results in reading such books as: *With Christ After the Lost* (on personal evangelism); *Endued to Win* (on evangelism in Acts); *How Jesus Won Men; Prepare to Meet God*, etc. The challenge to compassion, conquest for Christ, conversion to the lost cry out from almost every page and paragraph of this man's pen.

He died in Amarillo, Texas, on April 10, 1945.

XII.

How Jesus Used Others in Soul Winning

L. R. SCARBOROUGH

"... he entered into Capernaum after some days; and it was noised
that he was in the house. And straightway many were gathered together,
insomuch that there was no room to receive them, no, not so much
as about the door: and he preached the word unto them. And they
come unto him, bringing one sick of the palsy, which was borne of four.
And when they could not come nigh unto him for the press, they uncovered the roof where he was: and when they had broken it up, they
let down the bed wherein the sick of the palsy lay. When Jesus saw
their faith, he said unto the sick of the palsy, Son, thy sins be forgiven
thee. But there were certain of the scribes sitting there, and reasoning
in their hearts, Why doth this man thus speak blasphemies? who can
forgive sins but God only? And immediately when Jesus perceived in
his spirit that they so reasoned within themselves, he said unto them,
Why reason ye these things in your hearts? Whether is it easier to say
to the sick of the palsy, Thy sins be forgiven thee; or to say, Arise, and
take up thy bed, and walk? But that ye may know that the Son of man
hath power on earth to forgive sins, (he saith to the sick of the palsy,)
I say unto thee, Arise, and take up thy bed, and go thy way into thine
house. And immediately he arose, took up the bed, and went forth
before them all; insomuch that they were all amazed, and glorified God,
saying, We never saw it on this fashion."—Mark 2:1-12.

In Mark 2 Jesus has hung in God's Hall of Fame a most beautiful
picture of soul winning.

He had been busy around the shores of Galilee with the glorious tasks
which filled His wonderful ministry. His headquarters were Capernaum.
There was some hospitable home in the city by the sea which welcomed

Him on His visits to Capernaum. We do not know whose home it was, neither the name, the number in the family, the comforts and apartments of the home, the furniture, the food; we only know that it made a glorious welcome for Jesus. It was noised abroad that He, the Messiah, was in this house.

A great crowd gathered. Four men, evidently His disciples who knew His power and believed in His saving and healing strength, thought of their friend who doubtless for months or years had been under the frightful power of paralysis. Wanting to see him healed and saved, they went to his home, put him on a bed, took hold of the four corners of the couch and carried him through the streets to the home where Jesus was preaching. The curious and anxious crowd was so great that they could not get their man in the door in to Jesus, so they carried him to the roof, tore it up and by some sort of contrivance, let him down on the bed just in front of Jesus.

It is said that Jesus, when He saw their faith—the faith of the four personal workers and the faith of the paralyzed man—said unto him, "Son, thy sins be forgiven thee."

He saved him, afterwards healed him, rebuked the doubts in the hearts of some of the crowd, rewarded the faith of those who believed, sent the man back to his home well in body, saved in soul, to rejoice with his family in the blessings of God.

A Look at This Case

The study of this case brings out many a glorious gospel truth.

1. It is a case of home evangelism. This hospitable home for Jesus not only welcomed the Saviour but sinners as well. The man who owned the home allowed Jesus to turn it into a preaching place, a hospital for the sick and a center of evangelism for the lost. He was willing for them to tear up the roof of his house if need be to get a soul to Christ. He had nothing too dear to sacrifice for the salvation of the lost and the glory of the Saviour.

What a wonderful illustration of the power of domestic evangelism! What a beautiful example of a home welcoming Christ and sinners together!

2. The presence of Jesus is and will continue to be the drawing power of every church, every Sunday school, every young people's group and all other groups worshiping God and seeking to win the lost. "It was

noised that he was in the house." Whenever it gets out on our churches or other groups of worshipers that Jesus is in the midst, the multitudes
are sure to come, and acts of benevolence, of healing, of soul winning
and kingdom building are sure to follow.

3. Picture in your mind these two homes, the one which welcomed
Jesus and the sick sinner and was willing to tear the roof off in order
for the two to get together. Picture the Saviour preaching in this home,
the sick man healed and the lost man saved.

Then contrast this home with the home of the paralyzed man. He
certainly had a home because Jesus sent him to it after He healed him.
He doubtless had a wife and children. Think of the long vigils, of the
lonely, patient wife caring for her sick husband and her little children.
He was unable to work. She must care for him at night and work for
him in the day to provide food, clothes and other necessities for him
and the children. Think of what a blessing Jesus brought in healing the
breadwinner and saving the husband and father.

When I was in Capernaum in 1923, standing on the tessellated
floor of the synagogue of Capernaum, my heart went out in loving
gratitude to God for the blessing Jesus brought to the home of the
paralyzed man. Age and destruction had blotted out all signs of other
houses then in Capernaum, except the synagogue. But the records
eternal have left the sign of the glory of Christ in His benevolent
evangelism and healing power in the home where Jesus healed this
sick sinner.

4. This paralyzed man is revelation's photograph of lost men
everywhere. Paralysis to the body is a picture of sin's paralysis to the
soul. Paralysis is incurable—was then and usually is today.

I took my brother to all the doctors in reach. He was paralyzed;
and every one of them, after the diagnosis, shook his head and said,
"No cure."

No doctor can cure paralysis except the great Physician; and there
is no remedy for sin except the power of Jesus Christ. This paralyzed
man was helpless and hopeless without Jesus; and so is every lost man,
every unbeliever in the world.

5. The cure of Jesus both for the soul and for the body was instantaneous and immediate; and they both came in response to faith. Jesus
has power over the bodies of men to heal their diseases, and the souls
of men to forgive their sins.

These Four Immortal Men

I want us to look at Christ's plan of personal cooperation in winning men to life eternal in the conduct of these four men. Let us itemize the case.

1. They evidently believed in and loved Christ. He was the central and compelling motive in their hearts; they believed in His power to heal and His power to save; and they put hands and feet to their faith.

2. They planned carefully and faithfully to bring this man to Jesus. The purpose was born in the heart of one of them, who evidently mentioned it to a second and the second to a third and the third to a fourth; and their plans were perfected that they should meet at a certain time, at a certain place, and lend their strength to the helpless man in order to carry him to Jesus.

3. They not only planned but pushed their plans. Many a plan dies in the purpose of the heart; but these plans were realized in the activity of their beings. They went for their man after they had planned and prayed for him.

4. They were willing to get under the man's burden and feel his weight and share his load. And this is one of the necessities of evangelism today. We must feel the weight of the sinful souls of men and have as a resultant a burning compassion for their salvation.

5. They had faith in Christ, His power to heal and to save. They were not carrying their man to an experiment. The Galilean shore and hills had rung with the praises of the power of Jesus Christ, and their faith in Him was implicit and confident. We can be as sure today of Christ's healing and saving power in every case of soul-sickness the wide world around; and our faith in His power to save is one of the moving motives to get Him to save.

6. These men faced, fought and won over and against all their difficulties and embarrassments. Nothing could hinder them nor halt them. The derision and ridicule of the crowd on the streets, the embarrassment of carrying a man on a bed in public, the crowds that blocked the door at the home where Jesus was preaching, the difficulty of carrying a sick man upstairs and tearing up the roof and letting him down through the hole in the roof, the excitement and embarrassment of such a sensational thing—none of these difficulties halted these men.

7. The wonderful statement when "Jesus saw their faith" gives a picture of the condition of evangelism, the personal faith of the soul win-

ner in the power of Christ to heal the sick and save the lost. Thank God, Jesus did not say He saw their clothes, their pocketbooks, their scholarship, their social standing, their political power, their personalities; He said He "saw their faith," and seeing their faith, He moved His arm in power to heal and to save.

I have not a doubt but that my mother's and father's and sister's faith and the faith of dear Brother and Sister Blair—the pastor and his wife—had much to do with my salvation. The faith of the faithful preacher who was conducting the meeting, Rev. Will James, evidently had much to do in drawing and winning my soul to Christ. The consecrated schoolteacher, Professor Witt, who, when I asked him for an excuse to leave school and go to church, put his hand softly on mine as he consented for me to go and said, "Lee, I am praying for you." The faith of this fine group had much to do with my salvation. I was converted that day before I got to the church house.

When He saw their faith He said to me, the wandering, wild cowboy, "Son, thy sins be forgiven thee." Thank God for the cooperant faith of soul winners as a helpful agency in winning souls to Jesus!

8. What a pity that there are two sad black spots in this wonderful photograph of evangelism! One was the crowds that blocked the door and kept the seeking sinner from getting to Jesus; the other was the silent doubt of the scribes and Pharisees who sat within the crowd where Jesus preached.

He said, "Why reason ye these things in your heart?" They doubted the power of Christ to save souls. The greatest difficulty in the way of evangelism is the doubts of God's people. The block of unfaith kept Jesus from doing mighty works in Nazareth and in a thousand places since.

9. Look at the method Jesus used. He first saved the soul of the seeking sinner. He regarded that the lost man's salvation was preeminent above the healing of his body. The interests of the soul are primal with Christ and should be with all His people. Hospitals, orphans' homes, rescue stations and other benevolent institutions, social service, the proper housing and feeding and clothing of the poor, all laws governing child labor and such like are important indeed; but the salvation of the souls of the people is the first matter; and in whatever benevolent and social service we render, we must have regeneration as the foremost objective. We must heal and help the bodies of men, train and culture the

minds of men, but our primary purpose and objective must be the salvation of the souls of men.

10. Here comes from this wonderful incident one of the greatest truths ever revealed and demonstrated to men; and that is that "the Son of man [Jesus] hath power on earth to forgive sins."

Nothing is gladder news to a lost world. Nobody else has that power. Jesus has a monopoly on forgiveness, the power to save souls. Isn't it glorious that He has that power? He is the only Person who ever traveled this earth who could stop and turn and beat back and defeat the power of sin in the souls of men. But He can. He is able and willing and ready to forgive sins. He is God's message bearer of a lost world's best truth, the power to save from sin. We should ring it around the world, from mountain to valley, from shore to shore, that "the Son of man hath power on earth to forgive sins."

Young Charles Spurgeon, the embryo of probably the world's second greatest preacher, sat on an elevated seat in the back of a little Methodist chapel one snowy Sunday morning in London. The simple exhorting cobbler arose and said, "Look unto me, and be ye saved, all the ends of the earth." "Though your sins be as scarlet, they shall be as white as snow; though they be red like crimson, they shall be as wool." This double message of the truth burned its way into the soul of the penitent boy sinner. He was saved, Jesus forgave him of his sins, called him to preach, elevated him to one of the greatest pulpits in the world and for forty years and more made him God's mightiest evangel to win men to Christ. Through his preaching multiplied thousands have looked unto Jesus, had their scarlet sins cleansed and their souls made white as snow in the blood of the Lamb.

11. Next, I would have you look at the joy of the reaper. Look in the faces of these four men looking down through the hole in the roof. Their faith moved the arm of Jesus, and the moved arm of Jesus healed and saved the penitent, sick sinner.

They see him now rising, picking up his bed and going out of the crowded room. They come down from the roof; they meet him just outside the door. They clasp hands. They embrace him. They congratulate him. They rejoice with him. I imagine they went with him and took him back home and carried him to his wife and children and delivered him well and safe. Can you not imagine the happiness of that home and those four soul-winning personal workers?

There is no joy like it in all the world. Would it not be glorious if in every church and Sunday school and young people's and women's and laymen's organization, in every seminary, in every college, hospital, orphans' home, rescue home or mission station in all the world, there were such a combination of personal workers and spiritual soul winners as are here shown in this wonderful photograph of evangelism?

Jesus said when He won the woman at the well, as He pushed back the food offered by the disciples, "I have meat to eat that ye know not of." This is the food of spiritual joy to winners of souls. And, thank God, there is plenty of it, and it is accessible to all winners of men. There is more joy in the winning of one soul in one hour than can possibly come in all resorts of pleasure the world around.

Here is a great lesson in personal work, in spiritual combinations to win men, in the power of faith, in the beauty of a hospitable home welcoming Jesus and sinners, in the primacy of the soul's interest above our physical needs, in the power of Christ to save sinners, in the joys of soul winning, in the inexpressible peace and power of Christ's harvesters and reapers around the world. Jesus preached the Word unto them, the saved brought the lost and they all—Jesus, the saved and the newborn soul—rejoiced together in the triumph of sins forgiven.

May this picture be repeated in every community until Jesus comes. This is how Jesus used others in winning the lost.

(From the book, *How Jesus Won Men,* now out of print. Published by George H. Doran Company. Copyright holder, Sunday School Board of the Southern Baptist Convention. Used by permission of copyright holder.)

TOM WALLACE
1930-

ABOUT THE MAN:

Dr. Tom Wallace has had a very busy and successful ministry.

After his conversion at General Motors Corporation in Wilmington, Delaware, he held noon services until he entered the ministry. And a busy, busy ministry it has been.

Dr. Wallace attended Tennessee Temple Schools and later was on the staff of Highland Park Baptist Church, Chattanooga; pastored Baptist Bible Church, Elkton, Maryland, for 17 years. While there he founded Elkton Christian Schools; established a bus ministry with 18 routes; led the church in eight major building projects, increasing property values from $15,000 to $1,140,000; conducted two daily radio broadcasts; edited *The Visitor*, a monthly church newspaper.

Dr. Wallace served and is serving on many boards.

In 1971 he accepted the pastorate of Beth Haven Baptist Church, Louisville, Kentucky and remained there until 1986. Here many were saved. And in one year alone, he baptized more than 2,600 converts. While in Louisville, he founded Beth Haven Christian Schools and had six daily radio broadcasts.

In 1986 he went into full-time evangelism.

This warmhearted evangelist and conference speaker is widely sought after as speaker at Bible conferences, banquets, workers' meetings, soul-winning seminars, youth events, etc.

XIII.

Jesus, the Soul Winner's Example

TOM WALLACE

(Preached in the Second Baptist Church, Festus, Missouri, August 30, 1982, in a
Sword of the Lord Conference on Soul Winning and Revival)

I would like to read in John 4:1-26, the entire twenty-six verses:

*"When therefore the Lord knew how the Pharisees had heard that
Jesus made and baptized more disciples than John, (Though Jesus
himself baptized not, but his disciples,) He left Judaea, and departed
again into Galilee. And he must needs go through Samaria. Then cometh he to a city of Samaria, which is called Sychar, near to the parcel
of ground that Jacob gave to his son Joseph. Now Jacob's well was
there. Jesus therefore, being wearied with his journey, sat thus on the
well: and it was about the sixth hour [about twelve o'clock]. There cometh a woman of Samaria to draw water: Jesus saith unto her, Give me
to drink. (For his disciples were gone away unto the city to buy meat.)
Then saith the woman of Samaria unto him, How is it that thou, being
a Jew, askest drink of me, which am a woman of Samaria? for the Jews
have no dealings with the Samaritans. Jesus answered and said unto
her, If thou knewest the gift of God, and who it is that saith to thee,
Give me to drink; thou wouldest have asked of him, and he would have
given thee living water. The woman saith unto him, Sir, thou hast
nothing to draw with, and the well is deep: from whence then hast thou
that living water? Art thou greater than our father Jacob, which gave
us the well, and drank thereof himself, and his children, and his cattle?
Jesus answered and said unto her, Whosoever drinketh of this water
shall thirst again: But whosoever drinketh of the water that I shall give
him shall never thirst; but the water that I shall give him shall be in him
a well of water springing up into everlasting life. The woman saith unto
him, Sir, give me this water, that I thirst not, neither come hither to*

*draw. Jesus saith unto her, Go, call thy husband, and come hither.
The woman answered and said, I have no husband. Jesus said unto
her, Thou hast well said, I have no husband: For thou hast had five
husbands; and he whom thou now hast is not thy husband: in that saidst
thou truly. The woman saith unto him, Sir, I perceive that thou art a
prophet. Our fathers worshipped in this mountain; and ye say, that in
Jerusalem is the place where men ought to worship. Jesus saith unto
her, Woman, believe me, the hour cometh, when ye shall neither in
this mountain, nor yet at Jerusalem, worship the Father. Ye worship
ye know not what: we know what we worship: for salvation is of the
Jews. But the hour cometh, and now is, when the true worshippers
shall worship the Father in spirit and in truth: for the Father seeketh
such to worship him. God is a Spirit: and they that worship him must
worship him in spirit and in truth. The woman saith unto him, I know
that Messias cometh, which is called Christ: when he is come, he will
tell us all things. Jesus saith unto her, I that speak unto thee am he."*

The setting is very familiar, and I will point out one thing that you
might or might not have thought of. We have a privilege in this setting
which the Lord Jesus did not allow His disciples to share. He picked
a time when they had gone to get physical provisions before He came
to the setting of this woman at Sychar, depriving them of the opportunity of witnessing her salvation. But we are not deprived of that
privilege. We see what they didn't see. Something here makes me feel
sort of privileged of God.

Jesus had said to His disciples before this, in Matthew 4:19, "Follow
me, and I will make you fishers of men," or "I will teach you, show
you—I will make you into. . . ." It is not, "I will touch you and cause
some miraculous thing to happen," but "I will expose you to various
examples." But for some strange reason He deprived them of this
example.

"Make" in this verse means something I have heard Dr. Curtis Hutson say over and over again: soul winning is *caught,* not *taught.* Once
we get around it and it is talked about and we begin to experience it
and see it take place, it gets hold of us. Then soon we begin thinking
in that direction. The fever builds up, and something exciting begins
to happen.

Now in these verses just read Jesus is showing us how He did it. In
verses 35 to 38 He tells us to go out and do it.

"Say not ye, There are yet four months, and then cometh harvest? behold, I say unto you, Lift up your eyes, and look on the fields; for they are white already to harvest. And he that reapeth receiveth wages, and gathereth fruit unto life eternal: that both he that soweth and he that reapeth may rejoice together. And here in is that saying true, One soweth, and another reapeth. I sent you to reap that whereon ye bestowed no labour: other men laboured, and ye are entered into their labours."

Some people have sown a lot of seed, and we have come to the point when reaping is right before us. "The fields are white unto harvest," the Bible says. What a thrilling time in which to live, when we can reap the benefits of all the preaching that has been done, all the books that have been written. We are sort of going along on the coattails of Dr. John R. Rice and all the others who have set the pace for us!

In Matthew 28:19 and 20, we are reminded that Jesus gave us a general commission to go out into all the world and preach the Gospel to every creature, baptizing them in the name of the Father and of the Son and of the Holy Spirit. And He promises, "Lo, I am with you alway, even unto the end of the world" (Matt. 28:20).

He came here for that purpose—"to seek and to save that which was lost," says Luke 19:10. We may be talking to a different person than the woman at the well—or it may be a different time or place or setting; yet there are some similarities in this story that relate to every one of us. And this should help us to see how easy it is to bring someone into the family of God.

On one occasion Dr. Bob Gray got so burdened about winning someone, he prayed early in the morning that the Lord would give him a soul that day. He had that on his heart as he drove to his early morning radio broadcast. As he got out on the expressway in Jacksonville and headed downtown, he saw a fellow sticking out his thumb. The Spirit of the Lord seemed to say, *There's your man.* So Dr. Gray pulled over and said, "Jump in, fellow. Where are you going?"

"I'm going downtown."

As Dr. Gray started back out on the expressway, he said to him, "I didn't mean, 'Where are you going *today?*' but 'Where are you going when you die?'"

The fellow said, "I haven't thought much about that."

Dr. Gray engaged him in conversation about it. The man listened intently. Then Dr. Gray asked, "Do you mind if I pull off the highway and explain this to you?"

"I'll be glad for you to," he answered.

They did so; and Dr. Gray took out his New Testament, showed him some verses and led right up to the point where he said, "Why don't you bow your head and let's both pray. Then you can receive Christ as your Saviour."

The fellow did it. Then as he wiped a little tear out of his eye, he reached into his pocket, pulled out a revolver, laid it on the seat and said, "Sir, as I hitchhiked I had determined that whoever picked me up, I would make him pull off the highway. Then I would kill him and steal his car, dump his body and go on my way to another state. Sir, if you hadn't talked to me about this, you could have been a dead man by now!"

Dr. Gray said, "It pays to be a witness, doesn't it!"

Now I want us to see in this story:

I. JESUS HAD A GREAT INTEREST AND CONCERN FOR *ONE* INDIVIDUAL

He was not concerned that there be a great host of people like this. Jesus was interested in one, solitary, isolated, individual soul all by herself—one on one. When going through the book of Matthew, I was amazed to find sixteen private interviews between the Saviour and one individual. In the book of John I found seventeen places where the Saviour talked to one isolated individual. In Luke 15 there is *one* lost sheep that gets all the attention. Ninety-nine others are left over there, but just *one* do we give our attention to. Though there were several other coins, the *one* coin got the attention. The *one* son who wandered away from home got the attention. The other good boy stayed home and minded his own business and did what he should; yet the one individual, the prodigal, got the attention. In Mark 8:36, the Bible says, "For what shall it profit *a* man [one man], if he shall gain the whole world, and lose *his own soul?*"—one individual.

I read again this week the wonderful story about Ed Kimball, a Sunday school teacher. He won a young fellow to the Lord and got that one stirred up. The new convert got the secret of the Lord's power upon his life. He became the well-known D. L. Moody.

The story says that after evangelizing America, D. L. Moody started on England. There in England Frederick B. Meyer heard his message. One of the illustrations that Moody used did not at first stir Brother Meyer. Then one of his Sunday school teachers came to him and said, "Brother Meyer, the illustration that that preacher gave in our church the other day stirred my girls so much that there has been a lot of weeping, confession and testimony. We are sure that the Holy Spirit has come among us; and we have had an experience in our class that you won't believe!"

F. B. Meyer was so affected by the testimony of that teacher and those girls that he got off by himself, and soon it began to grip him in the same manner. His ministry began to open up and spread, and as it did, he was invited to come to America.

He came and went to Furman University to preach. One young fellow in the student body had decided to quit the ministry and go back to a secular job. But the message by F. B. Meyer was given with such fervor and flame that the young fellow stepped out, came forward and renewed his vow to his calling. He became the great R. G. Lee.

Then F. B. Meyer went on to preach at another location. In that service a young fellow caught fire and began to evangelize. His meetings spread out all over the areas of New England and the mid-Atlantic coast, until they were bulging at the seams. J. Wilbur Chapman, set on fire of God through the preaching of F. B. Meyer, began to stir up the whole northeastern coast.

Then, because of Chapman's preaching, he was invited to speak at a certain place. His ministry was changing, and he needed someone to move in on those citywide crusades that he was holding. Someone said, "The man you want is the young convert, Billy Sunday."

Billy Sunday, influenced by J. Wilbur Chapman, got into the ministry and went to Charlotte, North Carolina. There a group of laymen got so inspired and so stirred up that they organized a committee to invite other evangelists back. One invited was Mordecai Ham from Louisville, Kentucky. He preached in a meeting, and Billy Graham got saved. Billy Graham became a renowned evangelist around the world—all because Edward Kimball—one nobody—won one other nobody and started a series of dominoes falling that ended up with millions saved in Moody's ministry, hundreds of thousands in Meyer's ministry, hundreds of thousands more in Chapman's ministry, hundreds of thousands more in Lee's ministry, and hundreds of thousands more in Graham's ministry. All because one fellow won one soul to Christ!

That is why Jesus spent so much time talking to this one poor woman at the well. This story needs to be indelibly impressed upon our minds so that we might be influenced and affected, and some will catch fire by this one story and go out blazing to win one hundred thousand more to the Lord.

So it's a matter of one on one here. A chain reaction starts, and no one knows where it will end. Let's take time for just one.

Then notice:

II. JESUS HAD TO GO OUT OF HIS WAY

It was not convenient for Him to go through Samaria. All the Jews went across the Jordan, up through Moab, then back over the Jordan into Galilee again. They did not go through Samaria primarily because the Samaritans were the scum of the earth to the Jews. To go through Samaria meant one had to stop and eat at their homes, sleep in their homes; and the Jews wouldn't do that under any circumstances. They felt toward the Samaritans then somewhat like the Jews feel toward the P.L.O. today. They had no dealings with them at all. Yet Jesus went through that area because He had something pressing upon Him. It was a matter of taking the time, working it into a situation regardless of whether He had the time or could afford to go that way or not.

I am saying this: we are not going to win anybody if we wait for them to stumble across our path. We must make a point to go out of our way and give of our time and energies. We have to be concentrating and hunting for the experiences just like Jesus was.

Then think also about:

III. THE COMPULSION THAT WAS IN JESUS' HEART

The Scripture says here, "And he *must needs* go through Samaria." That word *must* is the same as the word in II Corinthians 5:14 where it says, "For the love of Christ *constraineth* us."

There was some sort of pressure on Jesus, a leading of the Holy Spirit. And let me say that nobody can be an effective witness without being under the influence and direction of the Holy Spirit.

A fellow was giving out tracts. He would knock on a door; and when the people came to the door, he would smile, hand them a tract and say, "I would be very grateful if you would read this," then knock on the next door and the next and the next.

He came to one house; and when he knocked, nobody came to the door. He knocked again; nobody came. He knocked a third time; nobody home. So he put the tract in the screen door and walked away.

But something compelled him. It seemed that the Spirit of God said, *Don't go off this porch! Go back up there and knock again.* He felt silly, but he walked back and knocked again. Still no answer. As he started to walk away this time, the feeling came stronger. So he went back and knocked again.

This time the door suddenly opened, and there was a man standing there saying, "WHAT DO YOU WANT?!"

"I got the wrong house." He was shaking when he handed the man the tract. "Sir, would you please read this?"

The man snatched it out of his hand and slammed the door.

He walked off the porch unnerved. It took him two or three houses before he got his composure back. Then he finished that block and another block and went home.

His name, address and phone number were on the bottom of each tract.

Late that evening the phone rang. "Sir, are you the man who was giving out the little papers over in a certain area today?"

"Yes, I was."

"Is it possible for you to come by and talk with me?"

"Sure. Give me the address."

He copied down the address and quickly made his way over there. It was the same house where he had knocked several times!

The fellow said, "Come in. I want to show you something." He took him up in the attic. The man said, "I was getting nervous for sure then!" There in the attic, on the rafters, hung a rope with a noose; and a basket was sitting right under the noose. He didn't know what to think about it.

The fellow said, "This afternoon I heard your first knock. I was standing on that basket with that rope around my neck, planning to end it all. When I heard you knock a second time, I thought, *I'll wait just a moment; and when the man goes away, I'll jump.* You knocked a third time. Then it got quiet. I was ready to jump when I heard you knock again! I figured I had better go see who it was. After you gave me that tract, I sat down and read it in its entirety. I must have read it fifty times this afternoon before calling you. I need what that is talking about."

I am glad that one in the tract ministry was sensitive to the leading of the Holy Spirit in his life. Jesus "must needs go." He had no choice. If somehow we, too, can understand the impression and the guidance and the leading of the Holy Spirit, it would greatly help us. Romans 8:14 tells us, "For as many as are led by the Spirit of God, they are the sons of God."

There is another thing for us to see:

IV. JESUS WAS FRIENDLY AND SYMPATHETIC TO THIS WOMAN

He didn't walk up to her and say, "Look here, you wicked harlot!" He didn't walk up to her and say, "You're the lady who has had five husbands and are now living with a fellow who's not your husband! What kind of a wicked soul. . .! You're going to bust Hell wide open!" He didn't use that approach. He was friendly and sympathetic.

Neither was He reserved and distant. He was friendly. It wouldn't hurt fundamental Baptists to be friendly, would it? He was not arrogant or curt or blunt toward her. He was not too busy, not too preoccupied. He was just simply, in an everyday way, friendly, sympathetic and understanding. The poor soul was a sinner who needed something, and He knew what. So He approached her in a kind and friendly manner.

Then I want you to see:

V. JESUS ENTERED INTO AN ORDINARY SITUATION

He took advantage of the ordinary, everyday circumstances to open the conversation. He said, "Excuse me; could I bother you for a drink of water?" It was just beautiful.

She said, "Why, Sir, I will be glad to give You a drink of water. . . but aren't You a Jew?"

"Yes."

"Well, why would Jew like You be asking of me. . .? Don't You realize I'm a Samaritan?"

"Well, that's all right."

There was an ordinary setting in which Jesus stepped in and used it to an advantage. Jesus was weary. He was thirsty. And she came along. It was an ordinary thing—just like all of us live in our everyday routines. That is the place to win souls, the place where we get folks saved. He turned a disadvantage into an advantage.

Dr. Walter Wilson wrote a book in which he gave several examples of how he personally went at this. This medical doctor later preached more than he practiced medicine. I guess he was like the two Dr. Browns. One was the preacher; one, a medical doctor. One was the father; the other, the son. The phone rang. The grandson answered it. The caller said, "I would like to talk to Dr. Brown." The grandson asked, "Do you want the one that preaches or the one that practices?"

Dr. Walter Wilson said that when he would get on an elevator, it was his custom to say to the elevator operator, "Do you go up and down like this all the time?" To which that person would usually say, "All day long, eight hours a day—up and down." "When you die, are you going up or down?" He said the operator would open his or her mouth and gawk at him. Then he would usually be able to lead that one to Christ on the elevator.

To a bookkeeper he would ask, "Are your books balanced?" Then he would talk about the books, then ask about his or her eternal books.

When he would meet a lawyer, he would usually ask him, "What will the verdict be for you at the Great Judgment?" Boy, he probably hadn't thought much about it, but he started to, then.

Then when he met a laundryman, he would take an old dirty shirt or a pair of trousers that had a big spot, show it to the laundryman and say, "Do you think you can get this spot out of this pair of trousers?"

The person would usually say, "Why, sure, we can handle that."

He would say, "Do you think maybe blood would take that out?"

The person would say, "No, I don't suppose it would."

"Blood removes stains. The Bible says. . . , " and Dr. Wilson would give a verse of Scripture and win the laundryman to Christ talking about how blood cleanses from sin and takes care of the stain.

When he would meet a policeman, he would usually ask, "Do you realize that you are a minister of the Lord?" Then he would quote Romans 13:1. This was his way to win souls.

When he went with an undertaker on one occasion, he looked over at him and asked, "Sir, would you have any idea what that verse of Scripture means when Jesus says, 'Let the dead bury the dead'?" He won the man to Christ.

Jesus just went right into the situation of a well, some water, and a poor woman with a bucket when He didn't have a bucket. It was ordinary, an everyday circumstance.

Then He did another thing:

VI. JESUS ASKED HER FOR A FAVOR

What a beautiful lesson—just to open a conversation with a simple question! People usually like to be asked questions: "Could you tell me the way to the post office?" Nine out of ten would be so happy to tell you.

My wife and I were traveling through a little town in Indiana. The highway came into this little town and went right back out the other side of it; and we were hungry. I said to my wife, "Pull over right there where that man is." Here was a sharp-looking businessman. She wheeled over to the curb. I opened the door, stepped out and said, "Excuse me, sir. Could you help me find a real good family restaurant?" He smiled real big and said, "Just a block and a half down there is the best restaurant in town." That fellow was delighted to help me find a restaurant. People will always help us find restaurants, post offices, etc.

One preacher checked with a little boy one day and said, "Excuse me, son. Do you know where the post office is?"

The boy said, "Yeah. It's two blocks down this way."

"Now you have helped me. Let me help you. Son, let me tell you how to get to Heaven."

"Oh, no. You don't even know the way to the post office!"

I don't know how many times I have asked people for change for the telephone when I had plenty of it in my pocket. People like to help you. If I can find some way to ask somebody for something, then I can get the conversation started and break the ice. It's a matter of practicing and working at it. "You've been kind to me. Let me be kind to you . . . , " and we could do what Jesus did here.

Then I want you to see another little thing, and that is:

VII. HE TALKED TO HER ALONE

He didn't wade into her while two or three people were there. When people are with their peers, they are different from when they are by themselves. If you see four teenage boys out playing, there is no use walking up to them and saying, "Hey, boy, let me ask you something. Where are you going to spend eternity?" You will get wiseacre answers.

Don't talk to folks when they are in crowds. Isolate them and get them out. Jesus got this woman when she was by herself. He made sure that the disciples had gone before He touched this woman's life. Otherwise she would have been supersensitive. Can you imagine Jesus' talking to this woman with twelve disciples all gawking and staring, seeing what her reaction would be? Each time Jesus asked a question, she would have looked at all twelve. But He talked to her when she was alone.

I think there are exceptions. When there is death in the family, sometimes you can deal with the whole family because everyone is affected by that same mood. In the hospital where two or three people are around, perhaps you can talk to them together.

One occasion was a delightful exception for me. My phone rang; I answered. The fellow on the other end said, "Tommy? Is that you?"

I said to myself, *My soul! I don't know who this is, but it's been years and years since I have been around this guy!* (I was called "Tommy" until I graduated from high school.)

I said, "Who is this?"

"Tommy, this is your cousin Donald."

"Don Paisley! It's been years, Don. Where are you?"

"I live in the next town, over here at Newark, Delaware," which was just across the state line from Elkton, Maryland, where I pastored.

"Well, Don, what can I do for you?"

"I need your help. Now I understand you are pastoring a church in Elkton, and I need a preacher."

"I'll be glad to help you if I can."

"My wife died this morning, and I wonder if you would help with the arrangements and hold her funeral?"

"Don, I will be glad to. Tell me where you live. I want to come by the house and meet your children."

They were three and a half miles from our church, and I drove to their house. Here was my cousin Donald and his sister Lillian. There were two or three of his children, and several were around a big table. I sat right down at that table and drank a cup of coffee. There were ten of us now—nine others and me. I said, "Don, let me ask you about your wife. Was she a Christian?"

"Oh, she was a wonderful Christian! She read her Bible all the time. She went to church before she got sick. She was a real good Bible believer. There is no question about the fact she's gone to Heaven."

"Don, how about you? Are you saved?"

"No, I never did get saved."

"Lillian, are you saved?"

"No, I am not saved."

"How about you, young man? Are you saved?"

"No, I'm not saved."

"How about you, young lady?"

"No."

"What about you?"

"No."

"How about you?"

"No"..."No"..."No"..."No"—nine "No's."

I said to Don, "Now tomorrow I will preach and talk about your wife being in Heaven. Do you hope to go to Heaven and be with her again?"

"Oh, yes, I'd like to get that settled."

"How about you, Lillian? Would you like to get that settled?"

"I sure would."

"How about you, son?"

"Yes, I would."

"How about you?"

"Yes, I would"—nine "Yeses."

I read Romans 3:23, and I said, "What about you? Do you believe that?"

"Yes."

"What about you?"

Nine times we went down that one verse. Then I went to Romans 6:23, " 'The wages of sin is death. . . .' Now, you realize that, if you die, you will have to go to Hell?"

"Yes, sir."

"You have to go to Hell?"

"Yes, sir."

"Where would you go?"

"I'd have to go to Hell."

"How about you?"

"I'd have to go to Hell."

Nine of them going to Hell.

Then we went to Romans 5:8, " 'But God commendeth his love toward us, in that, while we were yet sinners, Christ died for us.' Now, did Christ die for you?"

"Yes, He did."

"Did Christ die for you, Lillian?"

"Yes."

"How about you? Did He die for you? Do you believe He died for you?"

He died for all nine of them!

Then we came to, "For whosoever shall call upon the name of the Lord shall be saved" (Rom. 10:13). When I read that, they all said they believed it; and they believed it would work for them—nine times.

So I said, "Well, we will pray together if it's all right. I'll pray, and then I'll help all of you pray." I prayed first. Then I prayed with Don, and he got saved. Then I prayed with Lillian, and she got saved. Then I prayed with the next one, and that one got saved. I prayed all the way around, and all nine of them got saved!

The next Sunday morning, when I gave the invitation, they all came right down to the front and made a profession; and all got baptized.

But that is the exception. Usually it is just one on one, and usually while that one is alone. I don't have anything against mass evangelism and great services like we had here yesterday; but it is still one on one. We have to do it when they are alone.

Then I want you to see this:

VIII. JESUS OVERCAME NATURAL BARRIERS

There was a barrier of sin. Here He is—the holy, sinless, perfect, righteous Son of God; and here she is—immoral adulteress, wicked, vile scum of the earth. Sinner and holy Son of God—what a barrier!

Then there was the barrier of race—He a Jew, she a Samaritan.

Then there was the barrier of sex—He a male, and she a female; and nobody ever talked to the opposite sex in public in that area in that day.

Then there was the barrier of religion—she worshiped at Sychar; He worshiped at Jerusalem.

Sometimes I get to feeling like, *Man, you can't get that fellow saved because he's a Catholic*, or, *You can't get that person saved over there because he has this problem.* . . . We let these little barriers stand up in front of us and shake us to the place where our faith is weak. We do not believe the Bible any longer. We shy away and don't enter into that conversation.

I think Jesus is giving us an example here. The reason He did it like He did was so we can understand that we can overcome four major barriers! We are making excuses when we could get over those walls really easily if we had the filling of the Holy Spirit. We could move right in there in boldness, confidence and assurance and win some of the most impossible cases in the world to the Lord Jesus Christ.

Then:

IX. JESUS CAPTURED HER CURIOSITY

He said in verses 10 through 13, "Would you really like to have some unusual and unique water? I don't have a bucket like you do, and I can't get any of this water out of this well like you can. But I have some water that would bubble up from inside and would bubble into everlasting life." She got curious about that! That sounded exciting!

I think He is giving us a lesson here in trying to talk a little about the beauties, the blessings, the joys of Heaven so that people might get excited and interested in what's waiting for them. If we can whet their appetite a bit, if we talk to them about how happy people can be after they get Heaven settled, I believe they'll want to get saved, just like she did. Jesus created curiosity and interest.

Then I see another thing I want to mention:

X. JESUS DIDN'T SCOLD HER OR REPROACH HER

He didn't give her a sermon on adultery. She was guilty, but He didn't blaze away at it. He didn't talk to her about the problems of divorce; she had already been through it five times now. He didn't bring up the possibility of VD or anything like that; He just pointed her to God, saying, "Lady, God is a Spirit, and they that worship Him must worship Him in Spirit and in truth."

I am not saying He didn't talk about her sin, but He eased into it. First—"Lady, would you give Me a drink of water?"

She answered, "Why, You're a Jew!"

"Yes, I know, but if you knew about the water that I have. . . ."

"But look! You don't have any bucket. How are You going to get water? The well is deep."

"The water that I am talking about is different."

Then second, He said, "Hold it. Before we talk any more, maybe it is better if you go get your husband." Oh! There He dealt with her sin problem. He didn't avoid that, but neither did He jump on her and give her a hard time about adultery and divorce and other matters. He led her to the Lord. He spoke about the only thing that would meet her need. He began to talk about everlasting life and salvation.

Suddenly she said, "I know! I know! I am waiting and hoping that the Messiah will come! We're waiting on Him; and when He comes, everything is going to be great!"

Then He opened the whole thing up by revealing Himself to her. Right then and there it was all settled.

While thinking about this yesterday, I said to the Lord, "Lord, I want to give myself over afresh and brand new, and I want to ask You, Lord, to let me be Spirit-filled; and I am going to dedicate myself to winning somebody to Christ just like You got this woman saved. Lord, I don't know who it is, where they are, what I will say. But, Lord, I am available. Would You please help me? Lord, I will try my best to get somebody this week. Please help me!" I felt like He would, and I accepted the challenge.

We had a number of people saved in the service last night. Then a fellow came up to me and said, "I've got to talk to you, Preacher. My name is Luke Jones. This is my wife, Sue. Could we go somewhere and talk?"

We went back in my office. Luke said, "I was a Mormon, but a fellow out of your bus directors' school led me to Christ. I told him I had already been baptized. Because I didn't get baptized like I ought to, it caused doubt to come. I resisted the Lord there, and I resisted Him again. Now I have a problem about whether I am still saved or not."

We talked for a few moments. Then he realized exactly who he was and where he was. He was born again and saved, but was disobedient. He came out with real assurance that he was really saved. He began to beam.

I looked at his wife and said, "Mrs. Jones, are you saved?"

"No...but...but...but, Preacher, I sure would like to be." There mine was! Just a little while before I had asked the Lord to use me if He would. I didn't try hard nor work at it. I just became a yielded vessel, and the Lord seemed to set one up there. I had to have some initiative. I had to bring up the question, but He put things together.

I am convinced that the Lord would like to do that day after day after day for every one of His children. He wants people saved! He wants to use us! The Bible teaches that when we receive the Spirit of the Lord into our lives and then yield ourselves so we have the filling of the Holy

Spirit, then we begin to have a boldness and an assurance like Peter and John had. Then the Lord gives us wisdom and discernment and insight, and He puts us into the right place at the right time, and we win souls all over the place! These Conferences help us to understand how to be filled with the Holy Spirit and how to win others to Christ. And we have our prime Example.

May God help us to be able to win somebody to the Lord.

LEE ROBERSON
1909-

ABOUT THE MAN:

When one considers the far-reaching ministries of the Highland Park Baptist Church and pauses to reflect upon its total outreach, he has cause to believe that it is close to the New Testament pattern.

In the more than forty-one years—from 1942 when Roberson first came to Highland Park until his retirement in April 1983—the ministry expanded to include Camp Joy, reaching some 3,000 children annually; World Wide Faith Missions, contributing to the support of over 350 missionaries; 50 branch churches in the greater Chattanooga area; Union Gospel Mission, which feeds and sleeps an average of 50 transient men daily; a Sunday school bus ministry, which covers 45 bus routes; a deaf ministry; "Gospel Dynamite," a live broadcast held daily, now in its 47th year; a church paper, THE EVANGELIST, which was, at one time, being mailed free twice monthly to over 73,000 readers; and Tennessee Temple University, Temple Baptist Theological Seminary, and Tennessee Temple Academy.

He is an author of many books.

Preaching to thousands, training preachers, supporting the mission cause, Dr. John R. Rice called him the Spurgeon of our generation.

XIV.

Labor Trouble

LEE ROBERSON

"And Jesus went about all the cities and villages, teaching in their synagogues, and preaching the gospel of the kingdom, and healing every sickness and every disease among the people. But when he saw the multitudes, he was moved with compassion on them, because they fainted, and were scattered abroad, as sheep having no shepherd. Then saith he unto his disciples, The harvest truly is plenteous, but the labourers are few; Pray ye therefore the Lord of the harvest, that he will send forth labourers into his harvest."—Matt. 9:35-38.

Labor trouble is an old trouble. One of the first accounts of labor trouble is given in the first book of the Bible. It occurred between the herdsmen of Abram's cattle and the herdsmen of Lot's cattle.

"And there was a strife between the herdmen of Abram's cattle and the herdmen of Lot's cattle: and the Canaanite and the Perizzite dwelled then in the land."—Gen. 13:7.

This trouble was quickly settled by the unselfishness of one man, Abraham. Labor trouble will always and only be settled by the unselfishness of men.

There was labor trouble in Egypt. The Israelites were made to work for the Egyptians. We read:

"And the Egyptians made the children of Israel to serve with rigour: And they made their lives bitter with hard bondage, in mortar, and in brick, and in all manner of service in the field: all their service, wherein they made them serve, was with rigour."—Exod. 1:13,14.

There was labor trouble in Nehemiah's day. When he returned to rebuild the walls of Jerusalem, some of the residents of the country opposed and ridiculed the project. Nehemiah and his people went forward with the work at great cost and effort.

There was labor trouble in Paul's day. He gave this exhortation to the people in Thessalonica:

"For even when we were with you, this we commanded you, that if any would not work, neither should he eat. For we hear that there are some which walk among you disorderly, working not at all, but are busybodies. Now them that are such we command and exhort by our Lord Jesus Christ, that with quietness they work, and eat their own bread."—II Thess. 3:10-12.

James, in his book, recognized labor trouble in his day. In chapter 5 he gives sharp words to the rich and to those who would defraud the laborer of his hire.

There is labor trouble today all over the world. It is here in America; it is in foreign countries. There is great dissatisfaction, both among employers and employees. This will continue throughout this age. Why? Because of sin. Men are selfish, covetous, lazy, envious and thoughtless. There can be only one solution to the labor problem, and that is the Lord Jesus Christ in the hearts of men.

There was also labor trouble in the day of our Lord. This labor trouble was of a very special kind. It is indicated to us in Matthew 9:35-38. Observe four things in this portion of Scripture.

1. Christ's vision. "But when he saw the multitudes. . . ." The eyes of our Lord were always open to see the needs of people.

2. Christ's compassion. "He was moved with compassion on them, because they fainted, and were scattered abroad as sheep having no shepherd." When the eyes of the Master beheld men, His heart was moved to do something for them.

3. Christ's appraisal. He looked upon the multitudes; He was moved with compassion; then He said, "The harvest truly is plenteous, but the labourers are few."

4. Christ's remedy. "Pray ye therefore the Lord of the harvest, that he will send forth labourers into his harvest." It is apparent that one of our great needs is for more prayer for people to labor for the Lord.

I would like to call your attention to three things:

I. THE TASK

Labor trouble implies work. Is there a task for every Christian? Is there a work to be done? Is this task teaching, preaching, singing? Does it belong to just a few, or does it belong to everyone?

The answer is plain. There is a job for every child of God. We are saved to serve, and that service is witnessing and winning souls. Though the Christian may be called upon to do a number of things, the end of every task is the winning of the lost.

Someone tells of the minister who called his leaders together and said that he was going to resign his ministry at the church because he had seen no one saved for a considerable period. They begged him to stay, and pointed out how edified they were by his preaching.

"Edified for what?" he asked. Turning to one leader, he asked him if he had ever led a soul to Christ. The answer was no. The question was put to the next and the next with the same result.

Finally, the minister got all of the members of the meeting to promise that they would also resign with him if within a short period they personally led no one to Christ.

The end of the story is that a revival broke out and many were won within a short period of time.

Every agency and every organization of the church should be directed toward one end—the winning of the lost. Whether we preach, sing, teach, preside or whatever our task may be, it should be for the purpose that men receive the message of Christ and be saved.

Here is the task: Andrew came to Jesus and was saved. The Scriptures tell us that he went out and found his own brother, Simon, and brought him to Jesus. Andrew put his hand to the task at once and did the very thing that God had saved him to do. He found his own brother, Simon, and testified to him and then brought him to Christ.

Here is the task: Four men were concerned about a poor paralytic. They bore him to Jesus, and Jesus saved his soul and healed his body. These four men were applying themselves to the task of bringing others to Christ.

Here it is: Philip was a deacon in the church in Jerusalem. As a deacon, he felt called upon to apply himself to the main task. He went to Samaria and preached the Gospel. Souls were saved, and a mighty work was done. He was called away from this revival to go into the desert, and there he led the Ethiopian eunuch to Christ. He was applying himself to the task as given by the Lord.

Here it is again: Paul and Silas, two missionaries, went to the town of Philippi. They began at once their work of witnessing. It was not long until there were converts: first Lydia, then the jailer and his household, and others.

Have you been applying yourself to the task? Excuses will not avail. God is asking for faithfulness.

We have a *divine task* given to us by our Lord. It was not committed unto angels, but unto the children of God.

We have an *urgent task*. There is no time for delay, for men are passing out into eternity without knowing Christ.

We have a *demanding task*. It calls for the best that every person can give.

We have an *eternal task*. By this, I mean that when we engage in this work, the results will tell for eternity. Buildings may be built, bridges may be constructed, highways may be made, but they will all disappear. But the work of witnessing will abide forever.

Look now to the fields white unto harvest. Is your heart not stirred by the great multitudes without our Saviour? Think of the millions who have never heard of Christ even once. Think of the need among the various nationalities in our nation. Think of a town of 125,000 people with hardly a single representative of fundamental Christianity.

The fields are white unto harvest. May we look upon them. May we pray. May we give. And may we go.

II. THE TROUBLE

Christ said, "We have labor trouble"—"The harvest truly is plenteous, but the labourers are few." This seems strange when we consider the following:

We have labor trouble with God calling men. Yes, the Lord is calling each one of you, even as Jesus called Peter, James, John, Matthew and others. God is calling you, even as He called Samuel and Gideon and Elijah. Perhaps you are saying, "Where is the call?" It is written down in God's Word. To every child of God, the command is given, "Go ye."

We have labor trouble with God paying. Our Heavenly Father pays the best of wages. We are rewarded here and hereafter. Christ said to His disciples, "And every one that hath forsaken houses, or brethren, or sisters, or father, or mother, or wife, or children, or lands, for my name's sake, shall receive an hundredfold, and shall inherit everlasting life" (Matt. 19:29).

Think of the joy that God gives to us as we labor for Him on this earth. Think of the blessings of peace and joy which are ours because of Christ in our hearts. Think of His presence through every hour and every difficulty. What wonderful wages we receive, and yet we will be receiving blessings for eternity.

We have labor trouble with God supplying the strength. No man is asked to serve God in his own strength. The Lord says that He will give power unto us. He promises to supply all of our needs through Christ Jesus. Paul said, "I can do all things through Christ which strengtheneth me." When you are weary, He gives encouragement. When you are weak, He gives power. Isaiah said about it:

"He giveth power to the faint; and to them that have no might he increaseth strength. Even the youths shall faint and be weary, and the young men shall utterly fall: But they that wait upon the Lord shall renew their strength; they shall mount up with wings as eagles; they shall run, and not be weary; and they shall walk, and not faint."—Isa. 40:29-31.

Again, *we have labor troubles with Christ as a co-worker.* "For we are labourers together with God; ye are God's husbandry, ye are God's building" (I Cor. 3:9). What a privilege to labor with the Lord at our side! So often at public work, men are cast into the midst of unfavorable working companions, but not so with those who labor for Christ. He is our Helper.

In spite of all that seems good, we have labor trouble. First, *there is the trouble of quantity.* Jesus said, "The labourers are few." Too few men and women to do the job! Too few who care, who are willing to pay the price for real service. It would seem that with all the people who are volunteering for the mission fields, we would have an overabundance. But this is far from being the case. There is a desperate need for missionaries around the world. There is a dearth of pastors and evangelists in certain parts of the country. The harvest is ready, but there are no laborers.

Not only is there trouble in quantity, but *there is trouble in quality.* Many volunteer to serve, but through laziness, confusion, procrastination and lack of separation, they do not make good workers.

Many have said, "Yes, Lord, I am going to be a witness for Thee," but they are still procrastinating. It may be that timidity is holding some back. Whatever it is, there is a need of quality among the workers for Christ.

Therefore, there is serious labor trouble because of the lack of workers; willing workers who will lay down their lives for Christ.

Again, there is a need for faithful workers who will carry on to the end of the way and be able to say with the Apostle Paul, "I have fought a good fight, I have finished my course, I have kept the faith."

Our labor trouble can be dispelled by three things. First, by *realization of the importance of the task.* A man will volunteer for a life and death job. He will stay with the work when he realizes that it is of tremendous importance.

There is no labor trouble when men join together to rescue another from drowning. There was no labor trouble when hundreds of men and women banded together to rescue the little girl from the old well. Labor troubles will be solved when men realize that it is God who calls and commissions, and that without obedience souls will perish forever.

Again, this work requires *dedication.* There must be a wholehearted consecration of our all unto Christ. Withholding the smallest part of our time or talents will cause a disruption in the work and failure to some part of it. Dedication to the task of getting the Gospel to men will solve the trouble.

Third, there must be *concentration.* If the quality of the work is to be satisfactory, then the Christian workers must say, "This one thing I do."

III. THE TIME

What is the task? Witnessing. What is the trouble? Too few laborers and too poor in quality.

What is the time? It is now. There is no time for delay. Our lives are passing, our energies fail, our opportunities disappear. Sinners are dying. The time for work is now.

It is an interesting story given us in John 4. We read of Christ talking to the woman at the well in Samaria. His disciples went into a nearby place to buy food. Jesus dealt tenderly and yet positively with the sinful woman. She had accepted Him as Saviour and went away to tell others about Him. When the disciples of Jesus returned, they urged Him to eat, but Christ said, "I have meat to eat that ye know not of." The disciples were confused and said, "Hath any man brought him ought to eat?" Christ made answer, "My meat is to do the will of him that sent me, and to finish his work."

And so, our Lord tells us of the time for work. "Say not ye, There are yet four months, and then cometh harvest? Behold, I say unto you, Lift up your eyes, and look on the fields; for they are white already to harvest."

O Christian, now is the time! Your delays are dangerous and inexcusable. The fields are white and ready for harvest. Do not make excuses. Do not blame the hardness of men's hearts. Do not say that you are too busy to take part in this work. Quit being a problem and begin to be a worker.

The story is told of a rich English merchant to whom the Queen gave a commission of importance. He hesitated to undertake it, saying, "Please, your Majesty, if I obey your command, what will become of these affairs of mine?"

The Queen answered, "Leave those things to me. When you are employed in my service, I will take charge of your business."

So it will be with every one of us. If we put the work of our Saviour first, He will take care of our affairs.

To the churches of Asia Minor the Lord said, "I know thy works." To the church at Ephesus the Lord said, "I have somewhat against thee, because thou hast left thy first love." What is the first love of a Christian? It is to tell someone else about Jesus.

Christ is looking at you today and saying, "I know thy works." Many of us need to hang our heads in shame as we come to the consciousness of how the Lord knows us.

The fields are white unto harvest. He commands us to go. It is obey or disobey.

The needs of men are all around us. Do we look upon the multitudes and have compassion as did Jesus?

The common gratitude of a man's heart should compel him to go. Do you love the Lord? Are you grateful for the salvation which is yours? Then go into the harvest fields. Do the work which the Lord has commanded you to do. Christian, God calls you. God needs you. And God wants you. I lay the challenge squarely before you—will you accept the task? Now is the time!

DWIGHT LYMAN MOODY
1837-1899

ABOUT THE MAN:

D. L. Moody may well have been the greatest evangelist of all time.

In a 40-year period, he won a million souls, founded three Christian schools, launched a great Christian publishing business, established a world-renowned Christian conference center, and inspired literally thousands of preachers to win souls and conduct revivals.

A shoe clerk at 17, his ambition was to make $100,000. Converted at 18, he uncovered hidden gospel gold in the hearts of millions for the next half century. He preached to 20,000 a day in Brooklyn and admitted only nonchurch members by ticket!

He met a young songleader in Indianapolis, said bluntly, "You're the man I've been looking for for eight years. Throw up your job and come with me." Ira D. Sankey did just that; thereafter it was "Moody will preach; Sankey will sing."

He traveled across the American continent and through Great Britain in some of the greatest and most successful evangelistic meetings communities have ever known. His tour of the world with Sankey was considered the greatest evangelistic enterprise of the century.

It was Henry Varley who said, "It remains to be seen what God will do with a man who gives himself up wholly to Him." And Moody endeavored to be, under God, that man; and the world did marvel to see how wonderfully God used him.

Two great monuments stand to the indefatigable work and ministry of this gospel warrior—Moody Bible Institute and the famous Moody Church in Chicago.

Moody went to be with the Lord in 1899.

XV.

True Wisdom — Soul Winning

D. L. MOODY

"They that be wise shall shine as the brightness of the firmament; and they that turn many to righteousness as the stars for ever and ever."—Dan. 12:3.

That is the testimony of an old man, one who had the richest and deepest experience of any man living on the face of the earth at the time. He was taken down to Babylon when a young man; some Bible students think he was not more than twenty years of age. If anyone had said, when this young Hebrew was carried away into captivity, that he would outrank all the mighty men of that day—that all the generals who had been victorious in almost every nation at that time were to be eclipsed by this young slave—probably no one would have believed it. Yet for five hundred years no man whose life is recorded in history shone as did this man. He outshone Nebuchadnezzar, Belshazzar, Cyrus, Darius and all the princes and mighty monarchs of his day.

We are not told when he was converted to a knowledge of the true God, but we have good reason to believe that he had been brought under the influence of the Prophet Jeremiah. Evidently some earnest, godly man, and no worldly professor, had made a deep impression upon him. Someone had at any rate taught him how he was to serve God.

Daniel Lived for God in a Different Place

We hear people nowadays talking about the hardness of the field where they labor; they say their position is a very peculiar one. Think of the field in which Daniel had to work. He was not only a slave, but he was held captive by a nation that detested the Hebrews. The language was unknown to him. There he was among idolaters; yet he commenced at once to shine. He took his stand for God from the very first, and so he went on through his whole life. He gave the dew of his youth to God, and he continued faithful right on till his pilgrimage was ended.

Notice that all those who have made a deep impression on the world and have shone most brightly have been men who lived in a dark day.

Look at Joseph; he was sold as a slave into Egypt by the Ishmaelites; yet he took his God with him into captivity, as Daniel afterwards did. And he remained true to the last. He did not give up his faith because he had been taken away from home and placed among idolaters. He stood firm, and God stood by him.

Look at Moses who turned his back upon the gilded palaces of Egypt and identified himself with his despised and downtrodden nation. If a man ever had a hard field, it was Moses; yet he shone brightly, and never proved unfaithful to his God.

Elijah lived in a far darker day than we do. The whole nation was going over to idolatry. Ahab, his queen and all the royal court were throwing their influence against the worship of the true God. Yet Elijah stood firm and shone brightly in that dark and evil day. How his name stands out on the page of history!

Look at John the Baptist. I used to think I would like to live in the days of the prophets; but I have given up that idea. You may be sure that when a prophet appears on the scene, everything is dark, and the professing church of God has gone over to the service of the god of this world. So it was when John the Baptist made his appearance. See how his name shines out today! Eighteen centuries have rolled away, and yet the fame of that wilderness preacher shines brighter than ever. He was looked down upon in his day and generation, but he has outlived all his enemies; his name will be revered and his work remembered as long as the church is on the earth.

Talk about your field being a hard one! See how Paul shone for God as he went out, the first missionary to the heathen, telling them of the God whom he served and who had sent His Son to die a cruel death in order to save the world. Men reviled him and his teachings; they laughed him to scorn when he spoke of the crucified One. But he went on preaching the Gospel of the Son of God. He was regarded as a poor tentmaker by the great and mighty ones of his day; but no one can now tell the name of any of his persecutors or of those who lived at that time, unless their names happen to be associated with his and they were brought into contact with him.

Everybody Likes to Shine

Now the fact is, all men like to shine. We may as well acknowledge it at once.

Go into business circles and see how men struggle to get into the front rank. Everyone wants to outshine his neighbor and to stand at the head of his profession.

Go into the political world and see how there is a struggle going on as to who shall be the greatest.

If you go into a school, you will find that there is a rivalry among the boys and girls. They want to stand at the top of the class. When a boy does reach this position and outranks all the rest, the mother is very proud of it. She will manage to tell all the neighbors how Johnnie has got on, and what a number of prizes he has gained.

Go into the army and you find the same thing—one trying to outstrip the other; everyone is very anxious to shine and rise above his comrades.

Go among the young men in their games and see how anxious the one is to outdo the other.

So we all have that desire in us; we like to shine above our fellows.

Yet there are very few who really shine in the world. Once in awhile one man will outstrip all his competitors. Every four years what a struggle goes on throughout our country as to who shall be the President of the United States, the battle raging for six months or a year. Yet only one man can get the prize. There are a good many struggling to get the place, but many are disappointed, because only one can attain the coveted prize.

But in the kingdom of God the very least and the weakest may shine if they will. Not only can *one* obtain the prize, but *all* may have it if they will.

It does not say in this passage that the statesmen are going to shine as the brightness of the firmament. The statesmen of Babylon are gone; their very names are forgotten.

It does not say that the nobility are going to shine. Earth's nobility are soon forgotten. John Bunyan, the Bedford tinker, has outlived the whole crowd of those who were the nobility in his day. They lived for self, and their memory is blotted out. He lived for God and for souls, and his name is as fragrant as ever it was.

We are not told that the merchants are going to shine. Who can tell the name of any of the millionaires of Daniel's day? They were all buried

in oblivion a few years after their death. Who were the mighty con-
querors of that day? But few can tell. It is true that we hear of
Nebuchadnezzar, but probably we should not have known very much
about him but for his relations to the Prophet Daniel.

How different with this faithful prophet of the Lord! Twenty-five centuries have passed away, and his name shines on and on and on, brighter
and brighter. And it is going to shine while the church of God exists.
"They that be wise shall shine as the brightness of the firmament; and
they that turn many to righteousness as the stars for ever and ever."

How quickly the glory of this world fades away! Over one hundred
years ago the great Napoleon almost made the earth to tremble. How
he blazed and shone as an earthly warrior for a little while! A few years
passed, and a little island held that once proud and mighty conqueror;
he died a poor brokenhearted prisoner. Where is he today? Almost
forgotten. Who in all the world will say that Napoleon lives in their heart's
affections?

Daniel Knew How to Shine Forever

But look at this despised and hated Hebrew prophet. They wanted
to put him into the lions' den because he was too sanctimonious and
too religious. Yet see how green his memory is today! How his name
is loved and honored for his faithfulness to his God.

Many years ago I was in Paris, at the time of the Great Exhibition.
Napoleon the Third was then in his glory. Cheer after cheer would rise
as he drove along the streets of the city. A few short years, and he fell
down from his lofty estate. He died an exile from his country and his
throne, and where is his name today? Very few think about him at all,
and if his name is mentioned it is not with love and esteem.

How empty and short-lived are the glory and the pride of this world!
If we are wise, we will live for God and eternity; we will get outside
of ourselves and will care nothing for the honor and glory of this world.
In Proverbs we read: "He that winneth souls is wise." If any man, woman
or child by a godly life and testimony can win one soul to God, their
life will not have been a failure. They will have outshone all the mighty
men of their day because they will have set a stream in motion that
will flow on and on forever and ever.

God has left us down here to shine. We are not here to buy and sell
and get gain, to accumulate wealth, to acquire worldly position. This

earth, if we are Christians, is not our home; it is up yonder. God has sent us into the world to shine for Him—to light up this dark world. Christ came to be the Light of the world, but men put out that light. They took it to Calvary and blew it out. Before Christ went up on high, He said to His disciples: "Ye are the light of the world. Ye are My witnesses. Go forth and carry the Gospel to the perishing nations of the earth."

So God has called us to shine, just as much as Daniel was sent into Babylon to shine. Let no man say that he cannot shine because he has not so much influence as some others may have. What God wants you to do is to use the influence you have. Daniel probably did not have much influence down in Babylon at first, but God soon gave him more because he was faithful and used what he had.

Remember, a small light will do a great deal when it is in a very dark place. Put one little tallow candle in the middle of a large hall, and it will give a good deal of light.

Away out in the prairie regions, when meetings are held at night in the log schoolhouses, the announcement of the meeting is given out in this way:

"A MEETING WILL BE HELD BY EARLY CANDLELIGHT."

The first man who comes brings a tallowdip with him. It is perhaps all he has; but he brings it and sets it on the desk. It does not light the building much; but it is better than nothing. The next man brings his candle; and the next family bring theirs. By the time the house is full, there is plenty of light.

So if we all shine a little, there will be a good deal of light. That is what God wants us to do. If we cannot all be lighthouses, any one of us can at any rate be a tallow candle.

A little light will sometimes do a great deal. The city of Chicago was set on fire by a cow kicking over a lamp, and a hundred thousand people were burned out of house and home. Do not let Satan get the advantage of you and make you think that because you cannot do any great thing you cannot do anything at all.

Jesus Commands, "Let Your Light Shine"

Then we must remember that we are to *let* our light shine. It does not say, "*Make* your light shine." You do not have to *make* light to shine; all you have to do is to *let* it shine.

I remember hearing of a man at sea who was very seasick. If there is a time when a man feels that he cannot do any work for the Lord it is then—in my opinion.

While this man was sick, he heard that someone had fallen overboard. He was wondering if he could do anything to help save the man. He laid hold of a light and held it up to the porthole. The drowning man was saved.

When this man got over his attack of sickness, he went on deck one day and was talking with the man who was rescued. The saved man gave this testimony:

He said he had gone down the second time and was just going down again for the last time, when he put out his hand. Just then, he said, someone held a light at the porthole, and the light fell on it. A sailor caught him by the hand and pulled him into the lifeboat.

It seemed a small thing to do to hold up the light; yet it saved the man's life.

If you cannot do some great thing, you can hold the light for some poor, perishing drunkard, who may be won to Christ and delivered from destruction. Let us take the torch of salvation and go into the dark homes and hold up Christ to the people as the Saviour of the world. If the perishing masses are to be reached, we must lay our lives right alongside theirs and pray with them and labor for them.

I would not give much for a man's Christianity if he is saved himself and is not willing to try to save others. It seems to me the basest ingratitude if we do not reach out the hand to others who are down in the same pit from which we were delivered. Who is able to reach and help drinking men like those who have themselves been slaves to the intoxicating cup? Will you not go out this very day and seek to rescue these men? If we were all to do what we can, we should soon empty the drinking saloons.

I remember reading of a blind man who was found sitting at the corner of a street in a great city with a lantern beside him. Someone went up to him and asked what he had the lantern there for, seeing that he was blind and the light was the same to him as the darkness. The blind man replied: "I have it so that no one may stumble over me."

Dear friends, let us think of that. Where one man reads the Bible, a hundred read you and me. That is what Paul meant when he said we were to be living epistles of Christ, known and read of all men. I would not give much for all that can be done by sermons, if we do not preach Christ by your lives. If we do not commend the Gospel to people by our holy walk and conversation, we shall not win them to Christ. Some little act of kindness will perhaps do more to influence them than any number of long sermons.

"Let the Lower Lights Be Burning"

A vessel was caught in a storm on Lake Erie, and they were trying to make for the harbor of Cleveland. At the entrance of that port they had what are called the upper lights and the lower lights. Away back on the bluffs were the upper lights burning brightly enough; but when they came near the harbor, they could not see the lights showing the entrance to it.

The pilot said he thought they had better get back on the lake again. The captain said he was sure they would go down if they went back, and he urged the pilot to do what he could to gain the harbor. The pilot said there was very little hope of making the harbor, as he had nothing to guide him as to how he should steer the ship.

They tried all they could to get her in. She rode on the top of the waves and then into the trough of the sea, and at last they found themselves stranded on the beach, where the vessel was dashed to pieces. Someone had neglected the lower lights, and they had gone out.

Let us take warning. God keeps the upper lights burning as brightly as ever, but He has left us down here to keep the lower lights burning. We are to represent Him here, as Christ represents us up yonder. I sometimes think if we had as poor a representative in the courts above as God has down here on earth, we would have a pretty poor chance of Heaven. Let us have our loins girt and our lights brightly burning, so that others may see the way and not walk in darkness.

Speaking of a lighthouse reminds me of what I heard about a man in the state of Minnesota who, some years ago, was caught in a fearful storm. That state is cursed with storms which come sweeping down so suddenly in the wintertime that escape is difficult. The snow will fall, and the wind will beat it into the face of the traveler so that he cannot see two feet ahead. Many a man has been lost on the prairies when he has gotten caught in one of those storms.

This man was caught and was almost on the point of giving up when he saw a little light in a log house. He managed to get there and found a shelter from the fury of the tempest.

He is now a wealthy man. As soon as he was able, he bought the farm and built a beautiful house on the spot where the log building stood. On the top of a tower he put a revolving light, and every night when there comes a storm he lights it up in hope that it may be the means of saving someone else.

That is true gratitude, and that is what God wants us to do. If He has rescued us and brought us up out of the horrible pit, let us be always looking to see if there is not someone else whom we can help to save.

I remember hearing of two men who had charge of a revolving light in a lighthouse on a rockbound and stormy coast. Somehow the machinery went wrong, and the light did not revolve. They were so afraid that those at sea should mistake it for some other light, that they worked all the night through to keep the light moving round.

Let us keep our lights in the proper place so that the world may see that the religion of Christ is not a sham but a reality.

It is said that in the Grecian sports they had the game where the men ran with lights. They lit a torch at the altar and ran a certain distance; sometimes they were on horseback. If a man came in with his light still burning, he received a prize; if his light had gone out, he lost the prize.

How many there are who, in their old age, have lost their light and their joy! They were once burning and shining lights in the family, in the Sunday school and in the church. But something has come in between them and God—the world or self—and their light has gone out.

Reader, if you are one who has had this experience, may God help you to come back to the altar of the Saviour's love and light up your torch anew, so that you can go out into the lanes and alleys and let the light of the Gospel shine in these dark homes.

Win Souls and Live On

As I have already said, if we only lead one soul to Jesus Christ, we may set a stream in motion that will flow on when we are dead and gone.

Away up the mountainside there is a little spring; it seems so small that an ox might drink it up at a draught. By and by it becomes a rivulet; other rivulets run into it. Before long it is a large brook; then it becomes a broad river sweeping onward to the sea. On its banks are cities, towns and villages, where many thousands live. Vegetation flourishes on every side, and commerce is carried down its stately bosom to distant lands.

So if you turn one to Christ, that one may turn a hundred; they may turn a thousand, and so the stream, small at first, goes on broadening and deepening as it rolls toward eternity.

In the book of Revelation we read: "I heard a voice from heaven saying unto me, Write, Blessed are the dead which die in the Lord from henceforth: yea, saith the Spirit, that they may rest from their labours; and their works do follow them."

There are many mentioned in the Scriptures of whom we read that they lived so many years and then they died. The cradle and the grave are brought close together; they lived and they died, and that is all we know about them. So in these days you could write on the tombstone of a great many professing Christians that they were born on such a day and they died on such a day; there is nothing whatever between.

But there is one thing you cannot bury with a good man; his influence still lives. They have not buried Daniel yet; his influence is as great today as it ever was. Do you tell me that Joseph is dead? His influence still lives and will continue to live on and on. You may bury the frail tenement of clay that a good man lives in, but you cannot get rid of his influence and example. Paul was never more powerful than he is today.

Do you tell me that John Howard, who went into so many of the dark prisons in Europe, is dead? Is Henry Martyn or Wilberforce or John Bunyan dead? Go into the southern states, and there you will find millions of men and women who once were slaves. Mention to any of them the name of Wilberforce and see how quickly the eye will light up. He lived for something else besides himself, and his memory will never die out of the hearts of those for whom he lived and labored.

Is Wesley or Whitefield dead? The names of those great evangelists were never more honored than they are now. Is John Knox dead? You can go to any part of Scotland today and feel the power of his influence.

I will tell you who are dead. The enemies of these servants of God— those who persecuted them and told lies about them. But the men themselves have outlived all the lies that were uttered concerning them. Not only that; they will shine in another world. How true are the words of the old Book: "They that be wise shall shine as the brightness of the firmament; and they that turn many to righteousness as the stars for ever and ever."

Let us go on turning as many as we can to righteousness. Let us be dead to the world, to its lies, its pleasures and its ambitions. Let us live for God, continually going forth to win souls for Him.

(From the book, *The Overcoming Life,* published by Moody Press, Chicago.)

XVI.

Excuses for Not Winning Souls

CURTIS HUTSON

The Great Commission is found five times in the New Testament, if you include Acts 1:8, where the Bible says, "But ye shall receive power, after that the Holy Ghost is come upon you: and ye shall be witnesses unto me both in Jerusalem, and in all Judaea, and in Samaria, and unto the uttermost part of the earth."

Mark 16:15 commands, "Go ye into all the world, and preach the gospel to every creature." Yet, as far as we know, no generation since the time of Christ has ever reached every creature with the Gospel.

According to an article I read, if the population of the world could be frozen like it is today so no one else was born and no one else died and we won souls at the same rate we won them last year, it would take 320 years to win the United States of America to Christ and 4,000 years to win the world to Christ! I have also read that 75% of the people in the world have never heard a clear presentation of the Gospel, and 60% have never even heard the name of Jesus! Now that may sound unbelievable; but we would be surprised to know how many people in our own cities, communities and villages have never heard a clear presentation of the Gospel! They may have heard about God or about the Bible, but they have never been given the clear plan of salvation. They don't know how to be saved.

Last year when I was in Atlanta for a speaking engagement, I went across the street from the motel where I was staying to purchase some razor blades. It was early Sunday morning, and I was the only customer in the store, so I took the opportunity to witness to the clerk.

"Before I leave," I said, "let me ask you a question. If you were to die today, do you know you would go to Heaven?"

"No," he said, "I don't know that."

Then I quoted John 3:16 and asked if he had ever heard the verse. When he said, "No," I was so shocked that I almost forgot what I was doing. Very carefully I explained the verse; and the man bowed his head, prayed and trusted Christ as Saviour.

"Thank you," he said. And I could tell by the smile on his face and the gleam in his eye that his gratitude was real.

When we were in Dallas a little more than a year ago for a big regional Sword Conference, I had the opportunity to witness to the maid. Mrs. Hutson and I were in the room when she came in to clean. While she was working, I said, "Let me share with you one of the most beautiful stories I have ever heard. It is the story of why Jesus came to this earth."

With a puzzled look, she said, "Jesus?"

"Yes," I said, "Jesus, God's Son."

"Who was He?" she asked.

Mrs. Hutson looked in disbelief! She had never met anyone who didn't know about Jesus.

As the maid cleaned the room, I shared with her the most wonderful story ever told; and before she left we prayed together, and she trusted Jesus Christ as Saviour!

Now keep in mind that these two experiences happened in Atlanta, Georgia, and Dallas, Texas. If there are people in those cities who have never heard the Gospel, then you can be sure there are people all over America who have no idea what it means to be saved and wouldn't know how to be saved if they wanted to.

There are now over 4 billion people in the world, and more than half of them have never had an opportunity to trust Christ as Saviour. They have never heard the Gospel. And many who think they have heard it have heard a muddy, cloudy version which, in the words of the Bible, is "another gospel" (Gal. 1:6). Any message other than salvation by grace through faith in Christ and His finished work is not the Gospel. Any message that stops short of or goes beyond the substitutionary death of Jesus is "another gospel."

Paul said in I Corinthians 15:1,3,4, "Moreover, brethren, I declare unto you the gospel which I preached unto you, which also ye have received, and wherein ye stand. . . . how that Christ died for our sins according to the scriptures; And that he was buried, and that he rose again the third day according to the scriptures."

The simple fact is, all men are sinners; and as sinners, all owe the sin debt. If we pay what we owe as sinners, we must die, go into Hell, and stay there forever. Two thousand years ago God took all our sins and laid them on Jesus. While Jesus was bearing our sins in His own body, God punished Him in our place to pay the debt we owe. When the payment was complete, finished, paid in full, they placed Him in a tomb; and after three days and nights, God raised Him from the dead and took Him back to Heaven as a declaration of the fact that He was satisfied with the payment Jesus made for our sins. Now those who trust Christ and His sacrificial death at Calvary are saved; they are given everlasting life immediately, and they are going to Heaven just as surely as if they were already there! Because in the Person of Jesus, they have already been received safely into Heaven.

That is the message we are told to give to the world: "Go ye into all the world, and preach the *gospel* to every creature" (Mark 16:15).

Why haven't we reached every creature with this message? The answer is simple: we are not following the Bible plan.

The Great Commission in Matthew 28:19,20 states, "Go ye therefore, and *teach* all nations, *baptizing* them in the name of the Father, and of the Son, and of the Holy Ghost: *Teaching them* to observe all things whatsoever I have commanded you: and, lo, I am with you alway, even unto the end of the world."

Notice that we are to *"go."* There is no substitute for going. And when we go, we are to *teach.* What we are to teach is not given in the Great Commission in Matthew, but it is in Mark. There the Bible says, "Preach the gospel" (16:15). After we teach the Gospel and people trust Christ as Saviour, then we are to *baptize* them. That simply means to get them into a local church. There is no substitute for good Bible-teaching local churches. That is the only way to conserve results. The new convert must have a place where he can learn and grow as a Christian.

After we go, teach and baptize them, then we are to 'teach them to observe all things whatsoever I have commanded you.' Many well-meaning preachers say this means to teach them the Bible, but that is not what the verse says. It says we are to teach them to do whatsoever we were commanded to do; and we are commanded to go, teach and baptize the converts. When we win someone to Christ and get him baptized, then we are to teach him how to win someone to Christ and get him baptized. And he is to teach his convert how to get someone saved and baptized. And on and on the chain goes. This is the principle of multiplication, and that is the only way we will ever evangelize the world!

Every believer should be involved in personal evangelism or soul winning, and that is the problem.

I heard the pastor of one of the largest churches in America say, "I doubt if 5% of the members of my church have ever led a soul to Christ." Then 5% of the membership is doing what the entire church should be doing. How could any business expect to succeed if only 5% of its workers showed up and followed instructions? There is not a school in America that would attempt to have classes tomorrow if only 5% of the students and teachers showed up. The church is the only organization or organism in the world that attempts to fulfill its purpose with such a small percentage of its workers involved.

Why is it that such a large percentage of Christians never witness, never visit and never try to lead a soul to Christ? The only way I can answer the question is to share with you some of the excuses given. I am aware that we will not be able to mention all of them, but we will give some of the more popular ones.

If I could gather into one huge room every Christian in the world who does not win souls to Christ and simply ask, "Why are you not a soul winner?" everyone would have some excuse.

I can hear someone saying:

1. "I'm a New Convert and Am Not Knowledgeable Enough to Win Souls."

The woman at the well in John 4 had just been saved. She had never joined a church and been baptized. She had never attended a Bible conference, a revival meeting, nor had she read any books on how to win friends and influence people. She had never heard a soul-winning lecture. Yet the Bible says in John 4:29 that she went to town and said, "Come, see a man, which told me all things that ever I did: is not this the Christ?"

Notice that she did not use one single Bible verse. She simply said, "Come, see a man, which told me all things that ever I did." Keep in mind that she was exaggerating. The Lord didn't tell her everything she ever did; He only told her that she had been married five times and was living with a man who wasn't her husband. But the dear Lord overlooked her exaggeration, and the Bible says, "And many of the Samaritans of that city believed on him for the saying of the woman, which testified, He told me all that ever I did" (John 4:39).

Not only was a great host saved because of her testimony, but the Bible says in verses 41 and 42, "And many more believed because of his own word; And said unto the woman, Now we believe, not because of thy saying: for we have heard him ourselves, and know that this is indeed the Christ, the Saviour of the world."

Now this Bible example of soul winning is contrary to some modern-day teaching on evangelism.

A preacher wrote, "I understand that when you were pastor of a church in Atlanta, you sent people out to win souls who had been saved only two or three weeks!" I wrote back and reminded him about the woman at the well who had been saved only a few minutes!

According to Matthew 5:14, the Christian is the light of the world. Do we expect a candle to give light when we first light it or after it burns halfway down? The truth is, young converts are usually more effective soul winners than those who have been saved for several years. Why? Because no one has had time to mess up their minds with so-called Bible teaching explaining why you can't do it now. Almost the first desire in every new convert is to see someone else saved.

I pastored the same church for twenty-one years, and hundreds of times I have seen a man get saved and immediately go back and speak to a friend about trusting Christ.

In a service where I spoke last Sunday morning, a young man who had only been saved two weeks brought 12 visitors to church with him, including his mother and father. When the invitation was given, eight of those came forward to trust Christ as Saviour, including his mother and father.

When I was saved as an eleven-year-old boy, my first desire was for my brothers, sisters and cousins to be saved; and how my heart rejoiced when several came forward the same night to trust Christ as Saviour.

Nowhere does the Bible even hint that one must be saved a certain length of time or have a certain amount of knowledge before he sets out to win souls. When Jesus healed the maniac of Gadara in Mark, chapter 5, He said unto him, "Go home to thy friends, and tell them how great things the Lord hath done for thee, and hath had compassion on thee." And the Bible says in Mark 5:20, "He departed, and began to publish in Decapolis how great things Jesus had done for him: and all men did marvel."

Other believers excuse themselves by saying,

2. "I Don't Have the Gift of Soul Winning."

Nowhere does the Bible teach or even intimate that soul winning is a gift. There are spiritual gifts, but soul winning is not listed among them. First Corinthians 12:4 says, "Now there are diversities of gifts, but the same Spirit." Verses 8 to 10 list these gifts: the word of wisdom, the word of knowledge, faith, gifts of healing, working of miracles, prophecy, discerning of spirits, different kinds of tongues (languages), and the interpretation of tongues (languages). Soul winning simply is not listed as a spiritual gift. And Bible teachers and preachers do an injustice to the Scriptures when they even hint that it is.

I heard one Bible teacher say, "Not everyone has the gift of soul winning." That would be like someone's excusing not tithing by saying, "Not everyone has the gift of tithing." Soul winning is not a gift; it is a command, just like tithing and baptism are commands.

When Jesus said in John 15:16, "Ye have not chosen me, but I have chosen you, and ordained you, that ye should go and bring forth fruit, and that your fruit should remain," our Calvinistic friends stop in the middle of this verse and say it means that some are chosen to be saved and others are chosen to be lost. But the choice is not for Heaven or Hell; the choice is for fruit bearing, and fruit bearing is soul winning.

Proverbs 11:30 says, "The fruit of the righteous is a tree of life; and he that winneth souls is wise." Paul said in Romans 1:13, "Now I would not have you ignorant, brethren, that oftentimes I purposed to come unto you, (but was let hitherto,) that I might have some fruit among you also, even as among other Gentiles."

Paul wanted to win souls to Christ in Rome just as he had won other Gentiles to Christ.

We must not confuse the fruit of the Spirit, described in Galatians 5:22,23, with the fruit of a Christian. The fruit of apple trees is apples. The fruit of the peach tree is peaches. The fruit of a pear tree is pears. winning is a command, not a gift; and the only alternative to soul winning is disobedience to a clear command of Scripture.

But I hear some Christian saying, "That is not my excuse. The reason I don't personally witness to people is

3. I Win Souls Through My Local Church."

Some believe that when they give their tithe through the local church they have fulfilled their soul-winning responsibility. Since some of the money goes to missionaries and the missionaries win souls, the tither thinks he has fulfilled his obligation. We suppose some missionaries have been guilty of leading Christians to believe this error. I have heard them say, "If you can't go, send someone else." There is no such teaching in the Bible. It is impossible to win souls by proxy. You cannot pay someone to win souls for you any more than you can pay someone to be baptized in your place or to tithe for you. It is something that every individual must do for himself. The souls won by the missionary are his personal responsibility, but the man who supports the missionary has a responsibility to win souls on the home front.

Soul winning is not an institutional but an individual responsibility. Let me explain. Psalm 126:6 says, "*He* that goeth forth and weepeth, bearing precious seed, shall doubtless come again with rejoicing, bringing *his* sheaves with *him.*" Notice it doesn't say the church that goes forth, etc., but, "*He* that goeth forth. . . ." Verse 5 says, "*They* that sow in tears shall reap in joy." And Daniel 12:3 promises, "*They* that be wise shall shine as the brightness of the firmament; and *they* that turn many to righteousness as the stars for ever and ever."

Anyone who reads these verses can see that soul winning is a personal, individual responsibility. There are five crowns which could possibly be given to the believer at the judgment seat of Christ. One is mentioned in I Thessalonians 2:19: "For what is our hope, or joy, or *crown of rejoicing?* Are not even ye in the presence of our Lord Jesus Christ at his coming?" Every Bible teacher who believes in the judgment seat of Christ agrees that the "crown of rejoicing" is the soul winner's crown; and it will be given to individuals, not institutions.

Now I don't mean the Great Commission is given to an individual. The Great Commission includes baptizing converts, and converts should be baptized by pastors in local churches. We talk about the church winning souls, but souls are won by the local church when the individual members win them. I think we preachers have let our people off the hook by making it easy for them not to win souls.

The Bible says in Ephesians 4:11,12, "And he gave some, apostles; and some, prophets; and some, evangelists; and some, pastors and teachers; For the perfecting of the saints, for the work of the ministry, for the edifying of the body of Christ." It is the pastor's job to perfect the saints for the work of the ministry. "Perfect" means to equip. We are to equip the saints by training, teaching and getting them ready to win souls.

"Saints" refers to *every* believer, from the newest convert to the oldest, and from the youngest child to the gray-headed saint, the educated and the uneducated, the rich and the poor, the introvert and the extrovert. All ought to be busy at the most important work in the world—getting souls saved. And in the words of the Great Commission, this work is to continue "even unto the end of the world" (Matt. 28:20). Personal soul winning is not to stop until "the end of the world."

Not everyone will trust Christ as Saviour, and it is not our job to save people; but it is our responsibility to show them how to be saved.

A missionary in India was questioning whether it was of any use to preach the Gospel to the Hindus. The Duke of Wellington asked, "What are your marching orders?"

"Our marching orders are, 'Go ye into all the world, and preach the gospel to every creature.'"

How they receive us is not our responsibility, but getting the Gospel to them is. Many Christians excuse themselves for not winning souls by saying,

4. "I Am Waiting to Be Led by the Holy Spirit."

I have heard men say, "I don't witness because I don't want to do it in the flesh, and the Holy Spirit has not led me." If we took that same approach about tithing, every church in America would have to close its doors tomorrow for lack of funds. The truth is, tithing is a command; and a person is to tithe whether he feels led or not.

One of my members asked, "Should I tithe if I begrudge it?"

"Absolutely," I said. "That way you commit only the sin of begrudging. But if you don't tithe, you commit the sins of stealing and begrudging.

Too many Christians are sitting around waiting for a mystical feeling while souls are dying and going to Hell. How sad it will be to live and die and never witness to our children, relatives and friends! Many reading these lines have friends in Hell who could have been won to the Saviour. Some have mothers, fathers, sisters, brothers, uncles and aunts who could have been won to Christ had someone only tried.

I have already mentioned that soul winning is a command just like tithing and baptism are commands, and you don't have to have any special feeling or leading to obey God.

When I was a boy, it was my duty to feed the chickens; and my father raised hundreds of them. Suppose before going to work one morning my father gave me an order to feed the chickens, told me how much to give them and the time they should be fed. During the day I got busy playing and neglected my duty. That night when my father returned, he discovered several dead chickens.

Immediately he calls for me and asks, "Curtis, did you feed the chickens?"

Sadly I reply, "No, sir."

"Why didn't you?"

I answer, "I didn't feel led."

"What do you mean, you didn't feel led? Did I tell you to feed the chickens?"

"Yes, sir."

"Did I tell you how much to give them?"

"Yes, sir."

"And when they should be fed?"

"Yes, sir."

"Then what were you waiting for?"

"Well, dad, I was waiting for a feeling!"

Brother, my father would have given me feeling enough to put me in the chicken-feeding business for the rest of my life!

And what will our Heavenly Father say at the judgment seat of Christ when we tell Him we never led a soul to Christ because we were waiting for the feeling? How can we give such a silly excuse in light of the clear command of Scripture!

The greatest soul-winning experiences have come when I went without a feeling. As a matter of fact, there have been very few times I really wanted to go soul winning. On the other hand, it has been my experience, after winning several people to Christ, that I wanted to continue visiting with people and sharing the Gospel.

I read this week where a preacher said, "We want to catch someone on the street, buttonhole him with a tract, give him the Romans Road, get a profession out of him, go back to the office and say, 'I have had two or three saved today.'"

Now I know thousands of preachers, and I preach in sixty or seventy churches a year; but I don't know anyone who *wants* to go out on the street and buttonhole anyone. That is hard work. Those who win souls do it because they know they should, not because they have a certain feeling.

How sad it will be at the judgment seat of Christ when we tell God that we didn't win souls because we didn't feel led!

Someone else says, "I would like to be a soul winner, but

5. I Don't Know How to Win Souls."

Suppose a soldier received orders in a sealed envelope giving detailed instructions as to what he should do and exactly how it was to be done, but rather than open the envelope he laid it aside and went on about his merry business. Months later his superior officer came to visit with him and asked, "Have you obeyed my orders?"

"What orders? I don't know anything about any orders."

"I told you to move camp, to put so many men in charge of one responsibility and so many in charge of another."

"Oh," he said, "I have been given no such instructions."

"Did you receive my letter?" asked the commanding officer.

"Oh, yes, I did receive a letter three or four months ago." In a few minutes he produces the letter and says, "Here it is," and hands it to the superior officer unopened. Do you think he will be excused for his negligence? Absolutely not.

Two thousand years ago God gave us marching orders and gave specific instructions as to how they were to be done. It is all in this Book called the Bible. Will God excuse us at the judgment seat of Christ simply because we have been too lazy to read the orders and learn how to do it? I don't think so. We had better make it our business to learn how to win souls. And the best way to learn is by doing. One learns to ride a bicycle by riding one. He learns to talk by trying to talk. He learns to walk by trying to walk. And the more he tries, the better he learns. It is the same with soul winning. We learn by doing. Take what little knowledge you have and start now. Every time you witness to an individual, you learn more about soul winning.

I don't claim to be an expert, but nearly everything I know about soul winning I have learned by experience. I often use the wedding band as an illustration of baptism. I learned that by trying to explain the importance of baptism to an individual in his home. The illustration I use about an airplane to show a person what it means to trust Christ was first used in a home where I was trying to explain to one what it meant to trust Christ as Saviour. The most effective illustrations I use regarding salvation came from my experiences in personal soul winning.

Preachers would be surprised at how fresh their messages would be if they spent more time in actually doing the work of an evangelist, and those who doubt some of the stories told by soul winners would soon learn that they are true.

Some careful soul says,

6. "I'm Afraid I Will Drive Them Farther Away."

Years ago I had that same impression because I had heard people warn against witnessing lest we drive them farther away.

The truth is, if a man is lost, you cannot drive him farther away. Sinners are dead in trespasses and sin (Eph. 2:1). There is no such thing as being dead, deader and deadest. I can't imagine going to a funeral home and having the funeral director take me into one room and say, "This man is dead"; and then farther down the hall in another room he points to someone else and says, "This one is really dead!" and then across the hall he points to yet another and says, "This one here has an old-fashioned case of death!"

Everyone is either saved or lost, justified or guilty, condemned or not condemned, dead or alive, has everlasting life or the wrath of God is abiding on him.

Two groups of people are described in John 3:36: "He that believeth on the Son hath everlasting life: and he that believeth not the Son shall not see life; but the wrath of God abideth on him." Every person is either trusting Jesus as Saviour or not trusting Him. Those who are trusting Him have everlasting life, and those who are not trusting Him shall not see life, but the wrath of God abides on them. That is as clear and plain as it can possibly be. When we witness to individuals, we do not drive them away. On the contrary—we bring them closer to Christ.

The Bible says in Romans 10:17, "So then faith cometh by hearing, and hearing by the word of God." Every time we share the Scripture with an individual, we are building his faith. The more he hears, the more his faith is increased. If a man is lost, it is impossible to drive him farther away. He is already as far as he can go. His sins have separated between him and God, and he is dead in trespasses and sins.

Some excuse their sinful lack of soul winning by saying,

7. "I Don't Want to Pick Them Green."

There are those who worry about what they call "false professions"

and are afraid they may get someone to trust Christ before God is ready
for him to be saved. We find no such teaching in the Scripture. Jesus
never warned against picking green fruit. That is terminology used by
preachers to excuse their sinful laziness and neglect in not winning souls
to Christ.

In Matthew 9:37 Jesus said, "The harvest truly is plenteous, but the
labourers are few." The problem has never been with the harvest; it
has always been with the laborers. God's shortage is a man-power shortage. That is why Jesus said, "Pray ye therefore the Lord of the harvest,
that he will send forth labourers into his harvest" (Matt. 9:38).

Jesus warned in John 4:35, "Say not ye, There are yet four months,
and then cometh harvest? behold, I say unto you, Lift up your eyes,
and look on the fields; for they are white already to harvest." Some
may worry about so-called green fruit, but the Lord says the fields are
white already to harvest. Nowhere does the Bible even hint that there
is a danger in getting a person to trust Christ too soon. To the contrary,
we are warned in II Corinthians 6:2, "Behold, now is the accepted time;
behold, now is the day of salvation." There is no such thing as getting
a person saved too early.

My beloved predecessor, Dr. John R. Rice, trusted Jesus when he
was only 9 years old. Was he "green fruit"? Absolutely not!

Dr. Bob Jones, Sr., great evangelist and founder of Bob Jones University, trusted Jesus when he was an 11-year-old boy. Was that too
early? Was he "green fruit"? We don't think so.

I rejoice that I trusted Jesus when I was only 11 years old. As I look
back on my life, I now see that I could have trusted Him even earlier
in life.

Thousands upon multiplied thousands have died and gone to Hell
because some well-meaning preacher or Christian was afraid he might
"pick them green," get them saved too early!

Dr. John R. Rice told the story of a Christian worker who found that
in a rather large Sunday school children sometimes went through four
years of the junior department and even through the teenage department and were never won to Christ. This Christian worker earnestly
protested and said, "We must set out to win these children. Every teacher
ought to be able to win those to Christ who come regularly to Sunday
school."

But one worker placidly answered, "You can't rush the Holy Spirit"—

as if all this delay while people were going to Hell unwarned were the fault of the Holy Spirit, as if all the people around us who have never been warned and have never been faced with the Gospel are lost because God does not care enough or because God is too slow!

We sin when we blame God for the lost rather than facing our own responsibility to warn them and show them plainly how to be saved.

Some today are excusing their sinful lack of soul winning by saying,

8. "I Believe in Making Disciples, Not Getting Decisions."

We hear a lot today about discipleship, and we are all for it; but there can be no disciples without decisions. Vine's *Expository Dictionary of New Testament Words* defines a disciple as "a learner." In Matthew 11:28 Jesus said, "Come unto me, all ye that labour and are heavy laden, and I will give you rest." That is a decision. Here a man decided to come to Christ for salvation. But in verse 29 our Lord continues, "Take my yoke upon you, and *learn* of me; for I am meek and lowly in heart: and ye shall find rest unto your souls." No one can learn about Christ until he makes a definite decision to trust Jesus Christ as Saviour. There can be no Christian growth apart from Jesus. The person who is not trusting Jesus as Saviour is dead in trespasses and sins (Eph. 2:1), and dead things do not grow. Growth always presupposes life.

How can any pastor teach and feed believers unless someone leads those individuals to Christ? Decision making always precedes disciple making. Jesus said to Simon Peter, "Feed my lambs," and again, "Feed my sheep," and yet again, "Feed my sheep" (John 21:15-17). Does that mean that Simon should not win souls? Of course not. Did Peter retire to the quiet life of a Bible teacher and leave soul winning, getting decisions, to others? On the contrary. The next time we see him, after the pre-pentecostal prayer meeting, he is preaching with mighty power at Pentecost. Then he saw 3,000 converts in a single day (Acts 2:41)! But Peter's soul winning did not stop here. Throughout the first chapters of the book of Acts, we see him preaching the Gospel to unsaved people and find that multitudes were saved under his ministry.

It is wicked and sinful for any pastor to excuse his lack of soul winning by saying that he believes in making disciples, not in getting decisions. Bible teaching and feeding the sheep are the responsibility of the evangelist and pastor. Ephesians 4:11-13 says, "And he gave some, apostles; and some, prophets; and some, evangelists; and some, pastors and teachers; For the perfecting of the saints, for the work of the ministry, for the edifying of the body of Christ: Till we all come in the unity of the faith, and of the knowledge of the Son of God, unto a perfect man, unto the measure of the stature of the fulness of Christ." Just as Bible teaching and feeding the sheep and maturing believers are the responsibility of both evangelists and pastors, so soul winning is also their responsibility. Paul said to Timothy, "Do the work of an evangelist" (II Tim. 4:5).

The term "sheep" is not used exclusively for those who are saved. Throughout the Bible it is used in connection with a whole mass of people, including the lost. In Isaiah 53:6 we are told, "All we like sheep have gone astray; we have turned every one to his own way; and the Lord hath laid on him the iniquity of us all." Here "sheep" is used to describe the lost. The Bible says concerning Jesus, "But when he saw the multitudes, he was moved with compassion on them, because they fainted, and were scattered abroad, as sheep having no shepherd" (Matt. 9:36). Here Jesus saw lost people "as sheep having no shepherd."

The parable of the lost sheep in Luke 15:3-6 is an illustration of an unsaved person. Concerning the lost sheep Jesus said, "What man of you, having an hundred sheep, if he lose one of them, doth not leave the ninety and nine in the wilderness, and go after that which is lost, until he find it?" In this parable, in its context, our Lord insists that the one lost sheep is of far more importance to the shepherd than the ninety and nine that represent saved people.

If some man then feels he is called of God to be a shepherd of God's flock, let him learn that the poor lost sheep is the one God would have him spend most of his time and energy upon. To Jesus, the lost sheep come first.

We are all for making disciples. And when I was pastor of a church for twenty-one years, we did our best to teach, instruct and feed believers. We wanted the members to be strong, mature Christians. But we must keep in mind that disciple making is not an end in itself but a means to an end. Believers are to grow in Christ, not that they can boast of their spiritual maturity but that they can be more effective soul winners.

I recently read in an article that "pastors now realize that disciple making is New Testament evangelism." That simply is not true. It is one thing to lead souls to Christ; it is another thing to teach and feed the new convert. And building Christians is not evangelism. Evangelism is soul winning. No man has the right to excuse his disobedient life by saying, "I believe in making disciples, not in getting decisions."

Some excuse a disobedient life without soul winning by saying,

9. "Some Are Called to Sow; and Others, to Reap."

In an article on lifestyle evangelism, the author said, "Evangelism is a process involving sowing and reaping." He went on to say, "Some people sow; others reap." Then to prove his point, he quoted I Corinthians 3:6, "I have planted, Apollos watered; but God gave the increase."

Paul had preached at Corinth; later Apollos preached at Corinth, and God gave the increase. But does this mean that Paul won no souls, that he only planted seed, and then later Apollos came, won souls and saw the results? Absolutely not. In Acts 18 we have the story of how Paul came to Corinth and preached. Verse 11 tells us "he continued there a year and six months, teaching the word of God among them." Then we are told in Acts 18:8, "And Crispus, the chief ruler of the synagogue, believed on the Lord with all his house; and *many* of the Corinthians hearing believed, and were baptized."

Paul won multitudes in Corinth. That Apollos came later and won some others to whom Paul had preached does not mean that Paul was only to sow the seed while Apollos reaped. This is not an honest interpretation of that Scripture. First Corinthians 3:6 does not teach that some are to sow and others are to reap. It means that oftentimes when a man preaches in a community some of the results may not appear under his own ministry but later under the ministry of others.

The Bible clearly promises that the sower shall do the reaping. Psalm 126:5: "*They* that sow in tears shall reap in joy." Notice that the one who does the sowing is the same one who does the reaping. And it is dishonest to teach otherwise. Psalm 126:6: "*He* that goeth forth and weepeth, bearing precious seed, shall doubtless come again with rejoicing, bringing *his* sheaves with *him*." The same one who goes weeping, bearing precious seed, is the very one who comes back rejoicing, bringing his sheaves with him.

It may be that he will get some sheaves from seed sown by others and that others may get some sheaves from seeds which he has sown. But the obvious intent of the verse is that the one who sows is also the one who reaps.

The Bible teaches that one's reaping is determined by his sowing. Second Corinthians 9:6 says, "But this I say, He which soweth sparingly shall reap also sparingly; and he which soweth bountifully shall reap also bountifully." The verse does not say, "He that soweth bountifully shall reap sparingly." How much a man reaps is determined by how much he sows.

Matthew 6:26 reminds us, "Behold the fowls of the air: for they sow not, neither do they reap. . . ." God could not have made it plainer than He makes it in these verses. No sowing, no reaping. Little sowing, little reaping. Much sowing, much reaping. And the preacher who claims to be sowing bountifully and never reaps is not being honest with the Scriptures.

Let no man excuse himself saying that it is not his business to win souls but only to sow the seed. That is not the teaching of the Bible nor the practice of New Testament Christians. Every Christian is to be a sower, and every Christian is to be a reaper.

Some lightly brush away the command of God to be fruit-bearing Christians by saying,

10. "We Are Simply to Live the Christian Life Before the Unsaved."

This is what some call "lifestyle evangelism." In the same article, "Lifestyle Evangelism," from which I quoted earlier, the writer said, "Evangelism is allowing the non-Christian to turn the pages of the book of your life and read the fine print." He went on to say, "God wants non-Christians to observe and experience His love, holiness, and righteousness through our caring conduct."

He contrasts this type evangelism with what he called "a confrontational approach." If we understand this kind of teaching, then one is not to confront individuals with the Gospel; he is simply to live a good Christian life before the unsaved and hopefully they will eventually come to know Christ as Saviour after observing his godly life.

It is true that every believer should live as godly and holy as possible. We should do our best to maintain a good testimony in our community. But simply living a good Christian life is not evangelism. To be sure, it gives us more credibility and makes us more effective witnesses; but people are not saved by observation.

The Bible says in Romans 10:13, "For whosoever shall call upon the name of the Lord shall be saved." And then verse 14 asks, "How then shall they call on him in whom they have not believed? and how shall they believe in him of whom they have not *heard*? and how shall they *hear* without a preacher?" This verse makes it plain that God only saves those who *hear* the Gospel.

Again, the Bible says in John 5:24: "Verily, verily, I say unto you, He that *heareth* my word, and believeth on him that sent me, hath everlasting life, and shall not come into condemnation; but is passed from death unto life." The person who never hears the Gospel is never saved.

There is no way to win souls without confronting people with the Gospel. The Bible plainly says, "It pleased God by the foolishness of preaching to save them that believe" (I Cor. 1:21). Notice the verse does not say, "It pleased God by godly living to save them that observed."

And Romans 10:17 says, "Faith cometh by hearing," not "Faith cometh by observation."

When I was only 11 years old, I trusted Christ as my Saviour. I think I lived a good Christian life, but no one ever trusted Christ because I was a good Christian. No one ever came up to me and said, "You're such a good Christian, I'd like to be saved."

I pastored a church with over 8,000 members, and no one ever came up to a one of those 8,000 members and said he wanted to become a Christian because he had been observing his life.

For six years I pastored a small country church and never led a soul to Christ. I loved the Lord and did my best to preach the Bible; but I never personally confronted anyone with the Gospel, presenting the plan of salvation and asking him to trust Christ as Saviour. After attending a Sword of the Lord Conference on Revival and Soul Winning, it was obvious to me that I had been disobedient to the clear command of Scripture. God expected me to win souls. I asked God to forgive me for my negligence; then I set out to win souls to Christ.

The first three people I witnessed to, trusted Christ as Saviour, and they all joined my church the following Sunday morning by baptism. I made up my mind that I was never going to have another week pass without leading souls to Christ. Several nights a week I visited in homes all over Atlanta, Georgia, and we saw that tiny church grow to become the largest in our state. Never a week passed without people being saved and baptized in the public services. A dead church became a thriving, soul-winning church because a pastor saw his sinful neglect and began winning souls and taught his people that the salvation of sinners was the most important thing in the world.

Every Christian ought to be a soul winner. Jesus said in John 15:16: "Ye have not chosen me, but I have chosen you, and ordained you, that ye should go and bring forth fruit, and that your fruit should remain." The fruit of a Christian is other Christians.

The last invitation in the Bible is found in Revelation 22:17: "And the Spirit and the bride say, Come. And let him that heareth say, Come. And let him that is athirst come. And whosoever will, let him take the water of life freely."

If the bride is the church, then every member in the church should be telling men to come to Christ. But the call is even broader: "Let him that heareth say, Come." Everyone who hears about Jesus should invite others to the Saviour.

Let us put aside our excuses for not winning souls and do our best to win as many as possible to Christ.

This generation of saints is going to answer to God for this generation of sinners. What will our answer be?